GAME OF X V.2

GAME OF X V.2
THE LONG ROAD TO XBOX

RUSEL DEMARIA

CRC Press
Taylor & Francis Group
Boca Raton London New York

CRC Press is an imprint of the
Taylor & Francis Group, an **informa** business

CRC Press
Taylor & Francis Group
6000 Broken Sound Parkway NW, Suite 300
Boca Raton, FL 33487-2742

Printed on acid-free paper

International Standard Book Number-13: 978-1-138-35019-9 (Hardback) 978-1-138-35018-2 (Paperback)

Visit the Taylor & Francis Web site at
http://www.taylorandfrancis.com

and the CRC Press Web site at
http://www.crcpress.com

Contents

Foreword

An ancient Chinese proverb says, "The best teachers are excelled by their students."

In this book, I am named as a teacher and mentor of Microsoft's "Technology Evangelists." That fact had been previously established in the public records of more than one anti-trust case against Microsoft. However, reading those records is not fun, whereas reading this book is. ;-)

This book is not about me. My exploits (notably, seducing Mac developers to switch to Windows, and opening up the .NET Runtime and Visual Studio to all programming languages) are undocumented, and are likely to remain so.

Furthermore, I do not claim to have invented any of the strategies and tactics described herein. Who could patent "divide and conquer"? Who was the first to attack the enemy's weaknesses, instead of its strengths? Sun Tzu wrote "The Art of War" over a hundred generations ago. Every strategist since then has cited him (sometimes ascribing new ideas to "Master Sun," to give them greater credibility).

Similarly, it was already well-established, by the time I arrived at Microsoft in 1992, that increasing miniaturization (Moore's Law) made each new generation of computers more powerful and less expensive. Likewise, by 1995, Harvard professor Clayton Christensen's seminal paper on "disruptive technology" was the talk of the industry, showing how waves of technological change disrupted entire industries. Also, the idea was "in the air" from many sources that the pace of technological change was, itself, accelerating. Finally, the concept of "network effects" had been worked out by the early 1990s.

The only contribution to the state of the art that I can claim as my own is twofold: First, I saw that each new wave of technological competition created an experiment, in which we -- Microsoft's Technology Evangelists (TE's) -- could determine the effectiveness of different combinations of evangelism strategies and tactics. Second, I realized that evangelizing technologies *efficiently* must become one of Microsoft's core competencies, due to the acceleration of technological change, and the increasing importance of network effects (especially later, due to the Internet).

It is true, as the book states, that I trained Microsoft's newly-hired TE's on the strategy and tactics of technology evangelism. More importantly, though,

I consulted on the development of their evangelism plans, mentored them on those plans' execution, and de-briefed them on the results afterwards. (Each evangelism campaign lasted a year, give or take, and there were a dozen or so campaigns ongoing at all times.) Each campaign was designed to test a different combination of strategies, tactics, and situations. Within a few years, we had tested and verified the most effective combinations (just in time for Microsoft's TE's to be re-orged into Marketing, throwing my work down the crapper...but that's a different story).

The key take-away of my research was this: speed was everything.

Which brings me back to Alex and DirectX.

Alex and his team were often criticized, as you will read herein, for being overly-aggressive and internally combative. The fact is, however, that they had no time to play nice. Windows 95 was to be followed by Windows NT, and every single engineering trade-off in Windows NT was harmful to gaming. As I write this in 2017, it is 100% clear to me that if DirectX hadn't gotten its hooks into Windows 95, the XBox never would have happened, and Windows would STILL suck for games. So, yes, as you will read, his team did not play nice. They played rough, and they played dirty, because speed was everything...and the payoff was an industry worth billions every year.

Nonetheless...when Alex cites me, in this book, as Wise Old Master of Technology Evangelism, take that with a grain of salt. He cites the Wise Old Master the way many strategists have "cited" Sun Tzu with new ideas, and the way I cited the phony Chinese proverb that started this Forward: to lend credibility to a statement that is obviously true, but which cannot be otherwise supported. It's a rhetorical trick.

I taught him that.

Yet today, I am confident that, from him, I would have much to learn about Technology Evangelism. Because, whether the ancient Chinese ever said it or not, "the best teachers are excelled by their students."

Hoping that you will enjoy reading Rusel's excellent book, I am

Yours,

James L. Plamondon

Phnom Penh, Cambodia

Foreword

It is a strange thing to be asked on more than one occasion in the course of one's life to write a foreword to a book that is, in part, about you. Of course, it's a tremendous honor and very flattering when somebody finds your career activities worthy of documenting … especially while you are still alive. Although I am proud of the many achievements associated with the creation of DirectX, I am not entirely proud of all of the means by which they were accomplished.

We were ruthless at pursuing our vision for real-time gaming on Windows. Microsoft was a very competitive environment full of very intelligent competitive people. We definitely found that we had to raise our game to a very high level to accomplish our objectives. The early DirectX team of Eric Engstrom, Craig Eisler and I were all trained by James Plamondon to be extremely effective at influencing markets and industries. Cameron Myhrvold, who hired all of us, told us our job was to influence Microsoft itself to do the right things to dominate the computing industry. We turned the tools James taught us on our own company.

I supported Rusel DeMaria to the best of my ability in producing as much accurate history as possible even when it didn't always reflect positively on myself. I believe that this is a very important account of events that, among other things, led to Microsoft creating the first successful US game console since the Atari 2600, and the creation of the general purpose GPU architecture as an alternative to CPU based computing. Personally I believe that GPU computing will displace CPU's over the coming years. Rusel has done a phenomenal amount of research and brought to light emails, documents and stories that were taking place all around me that I had forgotten or had no idea were happening at the same time. Reading the book was like reliving the events from many more perspectives than my own.

I would like to take the opportunity Rusel has presented me with to make a few relevant points:

1. I was young and raised by wolves.
2. I feel remorse for crushing people who stood in our way, I was just following orders.

3. I am eternally grateful to Microsoft and the people I worked with and sometimes against, for the incredible lifetime experience I had in that era. I've dedicated the remainder of my working career to trying to pay it forward to a new generation of entrepreneurial kids who deserve the opportunity and patience that my greatest mentors afforded me.
4. I apologize to the folks we treated as "crushies" in this narrative. With old age and introspection I have slowly come to the discovery of better, subtler tools to achieve the same ends with somewhat less bloodshed.

Finally, you're about to read a story that includes some very crazy and aggressive people doing highly unprofessional things to overcome insurmountable odds. I feel compelled to share how it worked out for many of us 25 years later and what lessons I learned, if any, that I would presume to pass on.

Crazy and aggressive really works. In retrospect, probably 95% of it was completely unnecessary but I couldn't tell you exactly which 5% was utterly essential to success. I just know that some was. There were definitely better social tools available to accomplish most of what we did.

Facing and overcoming insurmountable hardship is the only way anybody becomes great. It's hard, it's painful, it demands unreasonable personal sacrifices, and it can come with a significant measure of personal tragedy. There were 20,000 young engineers at Microsoft in those days, twenty five years later nearly all of them either retired rich or went on to phenomenal career achievements on the backs of the incredible and intense experience we all had at Microsoft. The people I knew from that era who went on to become titans of the technology industry would tell you that they wouldn't trade any of those sacrifices for anything. The few, brief moments when the world stops for half a second and you realize that you have accomplished something timeless and significant beyond the span of your years is worth every drop of sweat, blood and tears that got you there. All of the people I know who have experienced such a moment in life, have dedicated the rest of their lives to recapturing that fleeting experience.

If people don't hate you, you're not challenging them enough. People who can't be shaken out of their comfort zone never grow and never accomplish anything extraordinary. A great many talented people waste the potential of their lives in balanced pursuits. They squander the gifts and potential they were born with to avoid discomfort or conflict. Once you've learned what fearless ambition can accomplish, it's impossible to go back to reasonable expectations about anything.

There are very few great things you can accomplish in technology alone today. Founding companies is not a rational pursuit for reasonable people. When entrepreneurs and Venture Capitalists talk about creating "disruptive technologies" they generally selectively avoid addressing how disruption is really accomplished. It takes irrational zealots and relentless fanatics to cause disruption and face the unpopular backlash that comes with disrupting people's livelihoods and world views. Nobody likes being forced to learn new things and adapt to change involuntarily, but it turns out that the people who hated you and opposed your ideas most adamantly when you started are often the ones who remember you most fondly with respect when the dust has settled and revolutionary change has been embraced.

Twenty five years later, I still work over 100 hours a week, I still found companies and despite knowing that I can make more money and live a more "balanced lifestyle," I just don't care. I can't get visions of the future out of my mind and I can't forget that I know firsthand how to render those visions into reality. I can't think of anything I would rather consume my fleeting moments alive pursuing than those rare, flashes of achievement that make all the sacrifices worthwhile.

This book is an amazing achievement by an author dedicated to find the stories, the characters, and events that took Microsoft from DOS to Xbox, warts and all. Once again, I'm honored to be a part of that story.

-The Saint

(Alex St. John)

About this Book

Game of X Vol. 2 *is actually a prequel. It deals with early game efforts at Microsoft like Flight Simulator, Minesweeper, entertainment packs and early acquisitions, but it also is about several additional types of games: the games that Microsoft played against its competitors; the games that people at Microsoft played to get their way and bypass the orthodoxy of the bureaucracy; the games they played against each other in the hallways and in meetings; and finally, the methods of certain members of a certain team, the Developer Relations Group, that took internal and external games to a highly refined level of manipulation.*

One of the themes of the Game of X books *is that one thing leads to another. In this sense, the practices of personal manipulation and bypassing authoritity led directly to the creation and ultimate success of core technologies that, in turn, led directly to Xbox. This book is full of wild, amusing, absurd, and humorous stories, but all of them are ultimately tied to the final outcome of Microsoft becoming a true player in the industry of games.*

AUTHOR'S PREFACE

In its earliest years, Microsoft was not quite sure what it wanted to be when it grew up. With their Microsoft Disk Operating System (MS-DOS), they held the keys to the rapidly emerging personal computer market. While companies like Apple, Commodore, and Atari were creating personal computers, it was the entry of "Big Blue," with the IBM PC coupled with the transformative spreadsheet Lotus 1-2-3, that started the landslide of personal computer adoption – primarily as work machines. And as IBM PC clones began to proliferate, Microsoft was still in control and DOS was king.

Even so, IBM dwarfed Microsoft, a scrappy startup. But Microsoft's Bill Gates and Steve Ballmer were ambitious. They were hardly content to own the operating system alone. They wanted to create a company that expanded into different markets. They created their first spreadsheet, called Multiplan, in 1982, which enjoyed some success on the pre-DOS CP/M systems, but was clobbered by Lotus on DOS systems. They released the first Excel spreadsheet on Macintosh in 1985 and the DOS version in 1987 to synchronize with the Mac version. In 1998 they also released the first version of Office with versions of Excel, Word, and PowerPoint – the first version of a suite of business applications destined to become dominant under Windows several years later, and with more than a billion customers to date.

It was definitely a part of Microsoft's DNA to expand and take over different market segments. Early on, they produced various versions of the BASIC programming language under IBM's brand and have continued to produce programming and system tools. But in those early days, they also experimented with hardware and publishing, in effect trying things on for size. They even dabbled lightly in games, initially by distributing SubLOGIC's Flight Simulator.

This book is about people, internal culture, conflict, strategy, courage, and vision—with a good dose of calculated craziness, devious manipulation, outright skullduggery, and accidental successes. It is a book of stories based on the words of the people who lived them. And finally, it is about the forces within and outside of the company that drove Microsoft, reluctantly, to become a major player in the video game industry. It's about the growth of an industry giant in business software that always found reasons to support a minimal interest in games and ended up risking billions it never planned to spend – on games.

This is Microsoft's long road to Xbox.

Online Appendix

Many original documents, key email threads, and technical details referenced in this book can be found in a special Online Appendix at https://www.crcpress.com/9781138350182. We highly recommend that you explore the various documents in the Appendix.

~0~

Looking Back

Every story has more than one beginning. It's up to the storyteller to decide which beginning to choose. The story of World War II arguably began with the German *blitzkrieg* of Poland, or perhaps it really began with the Treaty of Versailles and the severe economic depression that followed. Some storytellers might go back even further into the history of Europe and of the Jews to find the basis of the events that followed. Still others might start with the saga of an obscure failed artist who somehow becomes one of the most powerful people of the 20th Century.

This book is the prequel to *Game of X Vol 1*. It is about Microsoft, its culture and its slow evolution as a game company. It is about the people who enabled that evolution, both artistically and technically. It is about unlikely events, accidental succcesses, and catastrophic failures. It is also about visionairies and people who asked permission after. It is about big events, and small technological details. It's about "very smart people" who could disagree, sometimes heatedly.

The accounts I have related in this book are true to the best of my knowledge and are based primarily on interviews with people directly involved. Whenever possible, I interviewed people with opposing views, although that was not always possible.

There are sections of this book about the double face of the Developer Relations Group, who on the one hand were fully dedicated to supporting developers for Microsoft's platforms, and on the other hand often used devious and manipulative practices—internally to accomplish their goals, and externally to cause grief to Microsoft's rivals.

This book is about Microsoft and the internal and external drama that led to its adoption of games. There were unlikely heroes who did not wield ostensible power, but who changed the course of history nonetheless. And there are monsters in this story—like IBM and Apple and even Microsoft itself—and often a kind of good and evil dichotomy. But mostly this story is about grey areas where absolute good and evil are debatable and based on individual perspectives, and in some cases, its characters can be seen as both heroes and villains at the same time.

Stepping back to the early 1990s, nobody—and I mean nobody—would have bet that Microsoft would one day become a major developer of video game console systems. At the time, Japanese powerhouses Nintendo and Sega were duking it out over who could sell more millions of consoles and engage the most players with characters like Mario, Link and Sonic the Hedgehog. Microsoft was DOS and early Windows. They were tech, operating systems and a budding supplier of business applications. And in that context, something as completely divergent as games didn't just happen by accident. If you follow a series of events within and outside of Microsoft, along with some tectonic cultural and technological events within the company, it becomes clear that one thing led to another, and to another, and ultimately to Xbox. And so, looking at it through the lens of history, it becomes clear that the Xbox story has several beginnings, depending on how you tell it. The true beginnings of Xbox could be attributed to events that took place in a boardroom in the late 1990s, but in order to understand how and why Microsoft ultimately took the highly improbable step of creating a video game console, it helps to look back at Microsoft's surprisingly long history with games, as well as the culture of Microsoft, its internal and external battles, and the efforts of small, comparatively powerless groups of people, often working under the radar of the massive organism they inhabited.

Game of X: The Prequel, is the beginning of the long road to Xbox.

Part I:

The Long Path to Xbox

MICROSOFT
FLIGHT SIMULATOR
For IBM Personal Computer

MS DOS
MICROSOFT MS-DOS
Microsoft Home
Microsoft Space Simulator
Go to the Edge of the Galaxy—and Beyond

-1-
Microsoft Always Had Games

Games are inevitable. People play games. Even animals play games. Pick up a rock and you can make a game with it. Add a stick and you have more game possibilities. It's just natural for human beings to invent ways to play.

Pretty much as soon as there were computers, there were computer games. Games like Colossal Cave: Adventure and Star Trek, the whole PLATO system, and many others were created on huge mainframe computers, which only large corporations and universities owned. There was no game industry. There were no game companies as we know them today. But there were games.

The first home computers were game machines. Pong was essentially a single-purpose computer, as was the Odyssey. Over time, game machines became more sophisticated, and more general home computers began to appear—the TRS-80, Commodore PET, Altair kits and others. Early home computers weren't great game platforms, but they always had games.

The first home computers to achieve widespread popularity, the Apple II, Commodore's VIC-20 and C-64, and the Atari 400 and 800 systems boasted full color displays. This crop of early home computers allowed users to do real work as well as play games, but games proliferated on them, while productivity was hampered by the limitations of the systems themselves and the slow evolution of technology. For instance, at the beginning, the Apple II and Commodore systems relied upon slow, linear tape drives to load and store data. Floppy drives eventually appeared, but during the early years there was no such thing as a hard drive, and memory was counted in bytes, not kilobytes, megabytes or gigabytes. They also printed text all in caps on lines only 40 characters wide. (I wrote my first book using an Apple II with all caps, 40 character lines, using a black and white TV as a monitor. Talk about headaches.)

One game-changing productivity innovation appeared first on the Apple II—VisiCalc, the first real spreadsheet. It might seem hard to imagine that something as utilitarian as a spreadsheet program could revolutionize the world of computers, but VisiCalc was a wonder in its time. It was a very sophisticated toy in some ways, and a major empowerment to businesses and individuals at the same time.

Then came the giant—Big Blue. IBM was a huge, respected, and very serious company. They didn't make games. They made giant computers, and they were the dominant brand in the mainframe and business world. They were International Business Machines, with emphasis on business.

So when IBM introduced their first home computer, it was a big hairy deal. And when Lotus introduced Lotus 1-2-3, a spreadsheet even more powerful than VisiCalc, the combination rocked the world. And that's where Microsoft first appears in the story, because they provided the operating system for the IBM PC. The Disk Operating System. DOS. The story of how Bill Gates managed to secure the operating system deal with IBM has been told many times and I won't go into detail about it here. But this is where the Microsoft story begins.

The effect of the IBM PC combined with Lotus 1-2-3 can't be overstated. They took the revolution in personal computers and made it legit. They made it business. And they made Microsoft rich, even though they were still small and nowhere near as important as Big Blue.

The First Game

Chronologically, Microsoft's first game was an unlicensed, but mostly faithful to the original version of Will Crowther and Don Woods' Colossal Caves: Adventure text-based game for the TRS-80, published in 1979 and later ported to Apple II and the brand-new IBM PC in 1981. The game was part of a new Consumer Products Division that Microsoft formed in 1979 under Vern Rayburn, one of the earliest Microsoft hires. But the story is even more convoluted, and it starts with an argument between Gordon Letwin and Bill Gates.

Letwin had written a disk operating system, H-DOS, for the Heathkit H8 and also his own version of BASIC. But then a very young Bill Gates showed up at Heath Company and started working to convince them to adopt Microsoft's product. Letwin challenged Gates, pointing out some differences

Three versions of Microsoft Adventure—TRS-80, Apple II, IBM PC.

between their products. One of the key features he brought up was that his version would immediately check syntax if you entered a bad line of code, where Microsoft's product didn't. Stuff like that. Gates is later quoted as saying, "Anyway, he was being very sarcastic about that, telling me how dumb that was."

Heath decided to implement Microsoft BASIC instead of Letwin's version, but in typical Bill Gates fashion, he later hired Letwin, apparently valuing the man's talent more than his tact. And it was Letwin who produced Microsoft's first game. Technically proficient, he found a way to extract the content of the original Colossal Caves: Adventure code from the original FORTRAN, and recreate it with only a few intentional changes, mostly in jokes for programers and some simplication of puzzles. He also solved several technical problems with memory and code access by using a memory expander and random access, at the time very expensive, floppy disk to load and access the games, instead of cassette, which was the most common way of loading games like Scott Adams' series of very popular text adventures.

Microsoft Adventure was never licenced or authorized, but Crowther and Woods never sought any credit or royalties to the game, and so Microsoft was never challenged in their use of the game.

Microsoft Flight Simulator

The game people remember as Microsoft's first official "game" was Flight Simulator. Originally developed by Bruce Artwick and his partner Stu Moment, and released in late in 1979*, it first appeared on the Apple II and was published by their company, SubLOGIC. An improved version was licensed to Microsoft and was released late in 1982. Although Flight Simulator was not technically a game but a simulation of flight, it did include both a crop-dusting mode and a legitimate game called World War I Ace where you could dogfight while flying a Sopwith Camel.

According to at least one source, Microsoft and IBM both tried to get the Flight Simulator license, but Artwick chose Microsoft. The same (unverified) source also states that Microsoft's 18th employee, Vern Raburn, was Artwick's main contact. Although PC version was released as Microsoft Flight Simulator in 1982, it was still developed by SubLOGIC until 1988, which is when Artwick left and founded a new company, BAO (Bruce Artwick Organization), taking Flight Simultator with him.

Flight Simulator was very successful before the Microsoft deal, having sold well on a number of platforms, and the Microsoft version remained consistently profitable for several deccades. By the end of 1999 it had sold more than 21 million copies. Fight Simulator also set a Guinness world record as the longest running video game series (more than 32 years) as of September 2012.

Back in 1982, Microsoft was growing quickly, largely because its lucrative deal with IBM, but they were still in some ways figuring out what they wanted to become, other than the dominant force in the microcomputer industry. So it's not clear how Flight Simulator figured into their plans, which had, in addition to their operating systems, featured forays into hardware peripherals like the Z-80 SoftCard, an upcoming computer of their own called MSX, and their first mouse; applications such as an early version of Word; and even a book publishing division.

Why, then, did Microsoft acquire the Flight Simulator license? I haven't found anyone who can answer that question. Perhaps it was an experiment. Possibly someone just saw it as a successful product on other systems, and decided to acquire it as yet another direction for the fast-expanding company to enter into. What is is clear in retrospect is that publishing Microsoft Flight Simulator was not the start of a grand plan to become a major player in the computer game field.

**According to one source, on Dec. 31, 1979*

The Added Benefit of Flight Sim

Whatever the reason for having Flight Simulator, it ended up serving a purpose that most people would not have guessed. According to Russ Glaeser, a veteran of both BAO and Microsoft's ACES studio formed around Flight Simulator, "one of the interesting things about early flightsim was that it basically just went around DOS. It was written in one hundred percent assembly language. It just hit the hardware directly. And it was such a good test of Intel compatibility that that's what they used it for. That was one of their tests to see if new chips coming out were Intel compatible." In fact, Flight Simulator was such a good predictor of compatibility that it was used in testing all the way until Windows 7.

Jon Solon had moved from Minneapolis to Seattle largely because of his love of hang gliding, but as an early hire at Microsoft, he began in the applications test division. After doing some testing on Project and Word, he had the opportunity to test Flight Simulator 3 by virtue not only of his hang gliding experience, but because he was also a licensed pilot.

Solon and Artwick were partially responsible for turning Flight Simulator into a Windows testing application. He says, "It was rather dramatic in the sense that Bruce Artwick and I had benchmarked the performance of the early Windows, and we basically submitted a memo to Bill Gates and Brad Allchin, Silverberg—all the main Windows folks—and said that Flight Simulator version 5 and Space Simulator version 1 would NOT be Windows products, and here's why." In the memo, they demonstrated the constraits involved in writing to the screen quickly, especially in aerial maneuvers such as banking the aircraft or even moving quickly through the galaxy in Space Simulator. Instead of Windows, he says, "we had to do it in DOS using expanded memory - not extended memory, but expanded."

Solon says with pride that he and his team were responsible for nudging the engineering team to address Window's deficiencies in graphics. They would not be the last ones to point this out, but they may possibly have been the first.

**Part II of this volume focuses heavily on Windows' ability to support games and the story behind the technology that allowed fast-paced games to excel on PCs, despite Windows.)*

The Purchase

On December 12, 1995, Microsoft announced the purchase of BAO, stating "Under the terms of the agreement, Artwick will consult with Microsoft in the design and development of new titles while the majority of BAO's development team will relocate to Microsoft's Redmond campus."

Glaeser was one of the BAO developers who relocated. "We were in the process of working on Flightsim 95 when they announced to us that we were all going to be moving to Seattle. At that time we were located in Champaign, which is 120 miles outside of Chicago. They did the transition in a very strange way. They didn't want to be disruptive, and by not being disruptive, they made it way worse. They basically didn't want to bring the whole team down for 2 weeks while everybody moved, so they just took one or two people and moved them, one at a time, which meant that some part of the team was unavailable for 2 weeks. And that went on for 6 months." This was only the first of several awkward transitions of companies acquired by Microsoft over the years. More examples later...

Eventually, things got sorted out and the ACES division of Microsoft continued to develop and consistently improve Flight Simulator until the studio was closed down in 2012.

Microsoft released one other DOS game in 1982 called Olympic Decathlon (also known as Microsoft Decathlon), which had originally appeared on the TRS-80 in 1980 and the Apple II in 1981. Although there were well over 2000 games available for DOS systems—many of them classics—only Flight Simulator, Olympic Decathlon, and Space Simulator (published in 1994) were from Microsoft.

Time Pilots

In addition to becoming a product manager on Flight Simulator, Jon Solon also spent many years working on Space Simulator. Because space is so vast, there were specific challenges to developing a real simulator for space travel in DOS. One of the compromises they made was to use time in a unique way - essentially as a gas pedal. If you wanted to go long distances, you essntially sped up time to get there in a reasonable period of time, instead of months, years, or light years. Solon got a lot of joy out it, though. Coming to work, he would "boot it up and, using the joystick, fly out of Cape Kennedy and do a quick shot to the Moon, one orbit around the Moon, then come back to Earth and glide back down for a landing, using time as a gas pedal."

During his time on Flight Simulator and Space Simulator, Solon had the opportunity to experience several commercial and military flight simulators and to meet several astronauts - most notably Donald Williams who had flown the Space Shuttle twice and was an F4 pilot during the Vietnam war with 745 carrier landings. Williams was very helpful in many ways, including facilitating several visits to NASA's Johnson Space Center.

Solon also gave presentations about their work, including one at Cornell University where he was hosted by a professor named Carl Maas, a colleague of Carl Sagan. Sagan keynoted the Cornell Flight Simulation Conference, and after the event, over a banquet, some cocktails, and conversation, "Carl and I slipped out the back door and secretly drove to the professor's house where we—my boss Tony Garcia, Leigh Cole and I— we showed Space Simulator to Carl Sagan." They were hoping to get his thoughts on the product.

Sagan was impressed enough to request a repeat showing the next day, where he also invited his wife and son, his father-in-laws, and writing partner, Ann Duryan and her father. "A real thrill for me was rapidly approaching Mars at high speed and then turning the spacecraft 180 degrees to fire the thrusters to slow down so that I could be captured in Mars orbit, and I looked to my right and there sitting on Carl's knee was his young son, Sammy, 3 or 4 years old, with his eyes as big as saucers, and I thought to myself, 'What the hell? I'm showing Carl's boy how to orbit Mars.'"

**Solon kept many momentoes of his time on Microsoft's simulators, including some prized autographs. See last page of the Online Appendix.*

Tomorrow Makers

Former Associated Press science writer Grant Fjermedal started working at Microsoft in the 1980s after writing *The Tomorrow Makers: A Brave New World of Living-Brain Machines*. Originally published by Macmillan in 1986, it was later republished by Microsoft Press in 1988. "I went to MIT, Carnegie Mellon, Stanford AI Labs, think tanks, DEC in the Midwest and in Japan. I wrote this book about computers, artificial intelligence, robotics, and creating our evolutionary successors," says Fjermedal.

One of Fjermedal's readers was young Bill Gates. "I was at a conference at their campus and Gates came up to me and said he'd read the book and liked it. That's how small the company was. I had a nametag on and Gates just wandered up to me."

Through his connection with Gates, Fjermedal started working as a contractor at Microsoft. One of his interests was astronomy, and he had just published a book on astronomy for Putnam. He had another book in mind that would combine actual science along with science fiction, and although Microsoft's publishers liked the idea, they actually had something else in mind for Fjermedal. They said that they had a product in the works called Space Simulator and suggested that he meet with the team and consider writing a book about the new product. He and the team hit it off from the beginning, and while working with them he wrote the book: *Adventures in Space Simulator*. Next, they asked him if he'd be interested in writing help files for the game. He had never written help files before, but he thought it would be fun.

And so Fjermedal began to carve out a unique role within the organization. He wasn't a designer, an artist, or even a manager. Sometimes he was a writer, but he was also a researcher who was more than willing to experiment in a new medium.

"So I end up with an office at Microsoft in Building 10 and started working crazy hours—12-14 hours a day just researching this. And in the meantime, whenever there was a delay in Space Simulator, they said would you be interested in doing something else? And I think one of the first things I did for them was the Windows Entertainment Pack. I'd just get the games, start playing with them, and rather than just doing a help file, I would write these wacky stories, like for Blackjack I wrote about this Dr. Blackjack who traveled, played in all the major card places around the world... across the Atlantic, Monte Carlo. And the people really loved it. It was fun. And when the work got hot and heavy on Space Simulator, I had a custom-made futon that was sleeping bag width rolled up underneath my desk, and I kept a sleeping bag there. I kept cereal there. I was getting quite well known for sleeping in my office."

Wacko UI

At one point, Fjermedal was asked to write help files for Fight Simulator, which was still a DOS game at the time. He set up three computers, one playing the Mac version of Flight Sim, and the two others playing the current and upcoming versions in DOS.

What struck Fjermedal almost immediately was how confusing the user interface was. "Even the Mac commands were pretty wacko." And as for the DOS versions, they were just illogical and cumbersome. So he wrote a 4-page memo that proposed a complete restructuring of the UI that went back to BAO and was adopted.

Gates Sees the Future and It's GUI

Despite these early forays into game publishing, Microsoft didn't see itself as a game publisher, and with DOS looking more and more outdated after the successful introduction of the Apple Macintosh, one of Microsoft's most serious initiatives was to create a new operating system that could move them into the modern age of graphical user interfaces. Bill Gates had seen the writing on the wall as early as the late '70s when he, like Jobs and many others, saw the Xerox PARC GUI, and perhaps again in 1982 at COMDEX, where he saw the early PC graphical interface of Visi On from VisiCorp.

Even as late as 1984, Gates was working closely with Apple, sending top programmers to create versions of Word, MultiPlan, Chart, and File for the Mac debut. DOS was very successful for many years, but the future was GUI, and Gates knew it. Apple's Macintosh without doubt signaled the oncoming obsolescence of DOS, and though they were fierce competitors, Gates and Jobs were sometimes collaborators, sometimes parties to lawsuits over the ensuing years.

But there was a time when they were friendly, as this quote from *http://www.mac-history.net/apple/2011-01-30/microsofts-relationship-with-apple* reveals.

> "With the rise of the Apple II in the late seventies Microsoft became more and more successful – even before the IBM PC was invented. When Apple developed the Macintosh Bill Gates and his team were the most important software partner – despited the fact that Microsoft was also the driving force behind the IBM PC and the PC clones. And Steve Jobs even invited Bill Gates for the preview of the Mac: The high point of the October 1983 Apple sales conference in Hawaii was a skit based on a TV show called The Dating Game. Jobs played emcee, and his three contestants, whom he had convinced to fly to Hawaii, were Bill Gates and two other software executives, Mitch Kapor and Fred Gibbons. As the show's jingly theme song played, the three took their stools."

To make a long story short, when Jobs refused Gates' offer to help Apple license the Mac OS, amid falling Mac sales in 1985, Microsoft responded by launching Windows 1.0, which soured the relationship and resulted in a lawsuit by Apple against Microsoft and Hewlett-Packard, and an ultimate compromise between the companies. Yet Windows, weak as it was at the time, was destined to take over and shake up not only the computer industry, but the game industry, which unlike Microsoft, had been very busy publishing DOS games and wasn't eager to change to a new operating system.

Almost Zorked

Zork was one of the most popular text adventure games in the early 1980s and the product that launched the quintessential text adventure game company, Infocom. In 1980, Joel Berez remembers sending a query about Zork, which was first launched on a PDP-11, to several publishers, including Microsoft. "We got a letter back from Vern Rayburn, who I think was one of the top people at Microsoft then, telling us that they already had the Adventure game, and didn't really think the market would support another text adventure." Berez says that they made a deal with Personal Software to publish Zork on TRS-80 and Apple II, but after a year, the company decided to focus entirely on productivity software, specifically the groundbreaking spreadsheet, VisiCalc. They got back the rights to Zork and Berez, on the verge of graduating from MIT's Sloan business school, conferred with his team and they decided to become publishers of their own products. "In retrospect Rayburn did is a great favor by rejecting Zork."

Years later, at a launch event for a new PC clone, Berez met Bill Gates for the first time. Somehow the conversation turned to the issue of Rayburn's rejection of the game to which Gates responded that he had known about Zork and would have overriden Rayburn's decision, adding "If I had gotten my hands on it, you never would have gotten it back."

In an aside, Berez mentioned that Mitch Kapor, the founder of Lotus, the developers of the breakout spreadsheet product Lotus 1-2-3, was a classmate of his. He adds, "I believe that Mitch spent some time in marketing at Personal Software, which perhaps is where he got the idea to create his own version of the spreadsheet."

-2-
Microsoft Culture

At the time, IBM was utterly dominant in the market, so they were gnomes running between the toes of giants.

-Alex St. John

While it's interesting to note that Microsoft had games, even back in its early days, nobody identified the company with entertainment. Early on, Microsoft was a tech company, and while today it's hard to think of Microsoft as having ever been small and feisty, that's how some old timers describe the company's self-perception in the early 1990s. Even though they were already very successful by any standard, and DOS was *the* PC operating system, there were always competitors poised to gain the upper hand. IBM was promoting the OS2 operating system to compete with DOS. Bill Gates was constantly concerned about Apple and what Steve Jobs would do next. And when Windows was released, he worried about not being able to make it popular in the consumer markets. And so, in order to be competitive and remain so, Gates encouraged a unique company culture. And to further explore Microsoft's history with gaming, it's important to understand that culture and some of the major events that took place within its walls over the next few years.

Clash Culture

You have to be firm in your convictions, sound in your technical basis, and be willing to withstand waves and waves and waves of conflicts.

-Brad Silverberg

Microsoft's hiring policies strongly favored intelligence and technical skills, and as a consequence the people who walked the halls, gathered in lunch rooms, and populated Microsoft's offices tended to be very smart. They were also, for the most part, quite young. John Ludwig, who joined Microsoft in

1988 was one of the older ones at 28. "I was surrounded by 25- and 26-year-olds, and even younger 22- to 24-year-olds."

Gates also favored people who could come up with great ideas and defend them. He wanted people who could create a plan, determine a direction, find an opportunity, and, especially, those who could convince others. "When I was at Microsoft, the whole challenge was to get the right people in the right seats on the bus," says Cameron Myhrvold, a 13-year Microsoft veteran who served in multiple senior executive positions. "A lot of times you'd hire people, and they'd ask, 'So what should I be doing?' I don't know what you should be doing. Your job should be to go out and figure that out, and then come back and tell me. And some people loved that… and then there were people who were like, 'I can't grok that.' They were big company people and they wanted to be a cog in a wheel, and this idea that your first job is to go out and find your job just didn't work for them. But that is how Microsoft was most successful."

As much as Gates saw himself as being in competition with all number of outside rivals, he also encouraged competition between divisions and technology groups, to the point where some veterans report that a person could get ahead by out-yelling their competitor in the hallways. The truth is that Microsoft employees were expected to be at the top of their game. If you were in a meeting with Gates and you weren't completely prepared to answer his questions, you would be in big trouble. If you couldn't defend your project or your position, you lost.

According to Brad Silverberg, who headed the Windows Division from 1990 through 1995. "You have to be firm in your convictions, sound in your technical basis and be willing to withstand waves and waves and waves of conflicts. And what you have to learn about Microsoft is that people are relentless, and even if they lose a battle, they just keep coming after you and after you and after you… The only time you really know the decision sticks is when the product is on the shelf. Until then, it can still be overturned."

Myhrvold tells a story that illustrates how competitive people were at Microsoft. Myhrvold was an executive very high up in the hierarchy at Microsoft, but for a couple of years his key card never worked at the applications group building where Microsoft's internal applications were developed. "I later discovered the fuckers deliberately turned my card key off so I could not enter the applications group building," he says. "I was not in the loop for tightly held information from the applications guys, but they were concerned enough about my exposure with ISVs (Independent Software Vendors) that somebody thought that I should not have access to the building. Which is pretty funny."

Revenge of the Nerds

It's worth remembering that everybody at Microsoft hated high school because they were nerds who were picked on by the popular kids.

-James Plamondon

James Plamondon, who would become one of the behind-the-scenes architects of Microsoft's competitive strategy, saw Microsoft as the ultimate revenge of the nerds story. To him, the rules of high school favored the strong. In a foot race, the fastest runner would win, not the smartest. In boxing, strength and speed were more important than a deep knowledge of calculus. Popularity and glory rarely went to the smart guy.

And so, according to Plamondon, rules "didn't mean shit" to the people at Microsoft because the rules they had grown up with had been imposed upon them by the strong, popular people. At Microsoft, everybody was smart. "It was so incredibly liberating, you can't imagine." At least in the 1990s, Microsoft was a meritocracy, where having the best ideas, being able to persuade people that they were the best, and being able to execute on those ideas were the ways to advance.

Microsoft veteran Jason Robar offers another unique way that people at Microsoft viewed themselves. "Bill had a particular culture that he created. A lot of people described it as a 'binary' culture. Either you are intelligent and capable or you're not. If you're intelligent and capable, you're a one. If you're not, you're a zero. And if you're a one, you really could do anything. You might have been hired to work in the Excel group, but five years later, why couldn't you build rocket ships? Whatever task Bill decides you should be working on, you should succeed at it because you're a one and you were intelligent enough to have joined Microsoft and be a part of that culture."

In a culture of ones vs. zeros, there was definitely a culture of belief. Another veteran, Drew Angeloff, says, "If you took ten engineers and you just extracted them from Microsoft, and you put them in a paper bag and you shook them up and you spit them out and you said, 'Build me software,' and that's their only instruction, they will figure out how to self-organize because they're effectively like a Seal team. Every person has learned how to be independent and function, and they know how to build software, and they know how to build software a specific way, and they're going to self-organize into a team, and they're going to build you something. You don't know what it's going to be, but they're going to build you something, and it's going to be good."

Nerds Against the World

If Microsoft thought it could outsmart you, you got screwed because you just weren't smart enough to keep up. And Microsoft thought that was totally fair.

-James Plamondon

If Microsoft employees were competitive with each other, using their brains and their voices—sometimes loudly—to convince their colleagues, and often to defeat other ideas within the company, they also applied their collective intelligence to enter into new businesses, strengthen the Windows platform, and sometimes to defeat or weaken their competitors.

Jason Robar compares Microsoft in the '90s to Genghis Khan's Golden Horde, or "a giant protoplasmic pseudopod organism looking for new sources of food." He saw Microsoft always looking for new opportunities and businesses they could take over, such as printing or set-top boxes… or, perhaps, video games. Inside Microsoft, there were always groups looking for new opportunities, new technologies, and new ways to make the company grow. Internal groups often competed with each other, coming up with or adopting divergent technologies that were meant to solve the same problem, as was the case with computer graphics or consumer-oriented products. Such competition often led to bitter rivalries and campaigns to gain the upper hand using arts of persuasion and subterfuge. And nobody did persuasion and subterfuge better than the Developer Relations Group.

-3-

The Developer Relations Group

I think in those days we were trying to be a consumer focused company, and then with NT and everything else, we ended up becoming a pretty powerful enterprise company. And people forget that that was an issue for us. I remember reading in the press, it would be Novell or it would be Sun Microsystems, and guys saying, hey, they can never do it. They can never span enterprise and consumer products.

-Cameron Myhrvold

The Developer Relations Group was the brainchild of Cameron Myhrvold and Steve Ballmer, formed ostensibly to encourage developers to develop applications and tools for Microsoft's software and to help them be successful in doing so. Guy Kawasaki, who spearheaded Apple's evangelism program, had become practically a cult figure, and in doing so, he had helped raise Apple's credibility with developers while—intentionally or not—affecting developers' attitudes about Microsoft. So, while it's fair to say that Microsoft was responding to Apple's evangelism success, there was more than just evangelism envy involved.

Bill Gates was obsessively competitive, and the growing success of the Apple Macintosh platform, as well as ongoing lawsuits over the GUI interface and the use of the mouse, had put them squarely in his sights. According to developer relations specialist Alex St. John, "Bill Gates had a fierce competitive frustration with Apple and could be said to be nearly obsessed with crushing his only real consumer OS rival."

**NOTE: This is the first of several chapters devoted to the Developer Relations Group (DRG). When I titled my book Game of X, I considered the double meaning of video games and the games played by certain people at Microsoft, both internally and externally. DRG was one of those organizations within Microsoft with a very game-like mission, and a crew of evangelists who were, in their way, expert game players. And their efforts and philosophy lead in a very clear path toward Xbox in the end.*

In an early response to Apple's success, Microsoft had fired up a developer relations group of sorts in the mid-1980s, run by Scott Treseder. This early group was comprised primarily of ex-salespeople taken from Microsoft's OEM group, but according to Cameron Myhrvold, it wasn't very effective. Myhrvold had observed Treseder's team and had come to realize that his evangelists couldn't really interact effectively with developers because they lacked the technical skills to do so. Their outreach was also unfocused and seemed to lack a clear strategy. Treseder's team ultimately fell apart, but the need for developer relations didn't go away. Developers were the lifeblood of a software or hardware platform, and Apple was winning the battle for their loyalty.

Cameron Myrhvold

Seattle natives, brothers Cameron and Nathan Myrhvold co-founded Dynamical Systems Research Inc., which was developing multitasking solutions for the PC. In 1986 they sold the company to Microsoft for $1.5 million and became Microsoft executives. With only a Bachelor's degree from the University of California at Berkeley, Cam Myhrvold ultimately became a vice president in charge of the Internet Customer Unit, but before that, he helped form and direct the Developer Relations Group, often referred to simply as DRG. His brother Nathan became a senior VP and helped pioneer Microsoft's Internet strategies and founded Microsoft's research division. (More on that later.)

Technical Evangelism

And the thing that was fascinating was that Microsoft's interpretation of DRG was to think, not only are we going to hire charismatic engineers that people like and want to work with, but we're going to figure out how to use our influence with the market to really destroy major competitors.

-Alex St. John

The Macintosh had opened people's eyes. It became clear that DOS was not the only operating system, and that the next dominant operating system for the PC would be up for grabs, with several companies positioned to develop it. Microsoft's strategists, including Bill Gates and Steve Ballmer, knew that owning the operating system was the key to success, and if DOS was becoming obsolete, they would have to be the ones to create its successor. Once they created the operating system, the most important way to make it dominant was to have it run applications that people wanted, and for that they needed software developers, both internally and externally. As Cameron Myhrvold observes, "'Nobody in the world ever buys an operating system; they buy an application. And if the application they buy happens to require your operating system, then boy, you just made a sale."

Eric Engstrom, who was one of Myhrvold's early evangelists still remembers what he was told on day one: "It's my first day there, and he said, 'We are competing for a scarce resource. There are only so many desktops with computers on them. Period. So if somebody is putting a computer application on a desktop that's not running Windows, I want to know why. And I want somebody out there talking to the people who make that feature, and winning them over. If we have to pay them a little bit of money, if we have to put a new feature in Windows, if we have to give them better marketing access so their consumers…' It was literally total market share. Just about getting every single customer."

Apple's promotion of the Macintosh placed the word "evangelism" square onto the map of people's consciousness. A word that once had religious connotations became associated with Steve Jobs' mission to promote the Macintosh and its approach to personal computing. While many people who were involved with computers in the early 1990s had heard of Guy Kawasaki and his work as Apple's evangelist, far fewer people have ever heard of Cameron Myhrvold or James Plamondon, Craig Eisler or Eric Engstrom. Alex St. John became notorious in some circles in retrospect, but he was never the public figure that Kawasaki became. However, fame and notoriety are not always synonymous with accomplishment. At Microsoft, the evangelists took on many roles, some of which scrupulously avoided the limelight… while others sought to make titanic waves.

As a strategic thinker, Myrhvold's vision of evangelism diverged from Apple's in some significant ways, the first of which was that he would only hire technical people instead of the sales-oriented people that Apple employed. "I was going to hire people who understood the technology and could talk the talk with developers, because we didn't have the scale to go out and touch multiple points inside of a software vendor."

Using his "technical evangelists," but with limited resources, Myrhvold decided to narrow his targets. "So it's like, if you can touch one point within a software vendor, and you're trying to get them to make this change and write for our operating system, who are you going to talk to? Are you going to talk to the CEO? Are you going to talk to the investors? Are you going to talk to the VP of marketing? Are you going to talk to a sales guy? And I decided it was the engineering guy."

Myhrvold also targeted his evangelists by technical domains instead of by geographical regions like Apple. For instance, if they were going after developers of medical software, they hired someone with both medical and programming background to evangelize with those developers.

Clearly DRG was not created to evangelize DOS, which already dominated the existing market. DRG was created for what came next, and with the introduction of Microsoft's next-generation operating system, the role of evangelists to promote the new platform would be critical.* The Mac, with its graphical user interface (GUI), had disrupted people's perceptions and expectations, and for the first time, DOS was looking like a backward technology. Microsoft's response was Windows.** Windows 1.0 was first announced in 1983 and was released on November 20, 1985.

**DRG initially evangelized IBM's OS/2, and had to go back to their ISVs (Independent Software Vendors) and convince them to drop OS/2 for Windows.*

***Windows was originally code-named Interface Manager, but (fortunately) the name Windows was ultimately chosen instead.*

-4-
Windows Gets Gamed

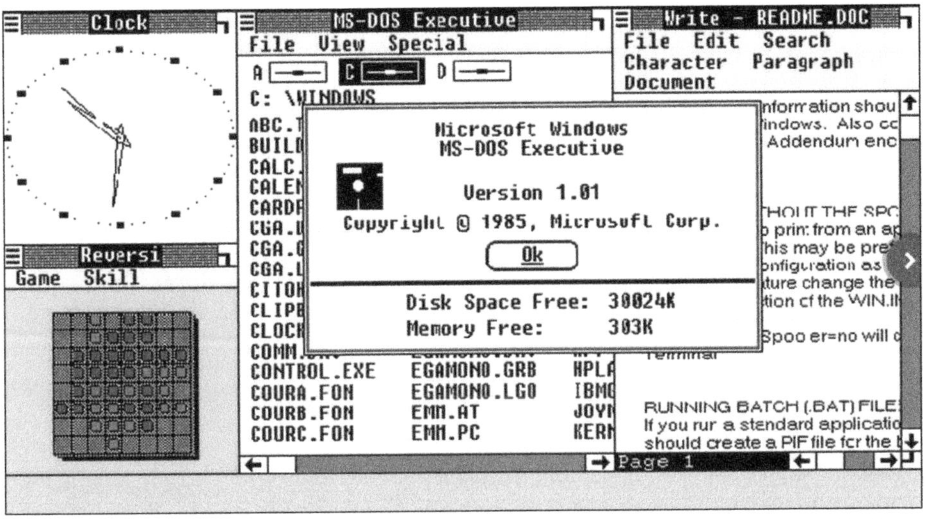

Screen from the original version of Microsoft Windows, released November 20, 1985.

Windows 1.0 (originally "Interface Manager) was released on November 20, 1985 and included several applications, including MS-DOS file management, Paint, Windows Writer, Notepad, Calculator, a calendar, card file, clock, and the game Reversi. Windows was a radical departure from DOS, upon which it was built, but although it was inspired by the Macintosh operating system, it was not it was not so much a groundbreaking innovation as a work in progress that would take years to gel. Because it was built as a 16-bit multitasking shell on top of MS-DOS, it didn't come close to matching the smooth performance and graphical look of the Macintosh, which had its operating system built into the hardware. But it was a start—the first step in the creation of an industry dominating platform.

To promote the new system, Steve Ballmer actually recorded a video ad for Windows 1.0 that was very much like a used-car salesman pitch, complete with high-pitched screaming voice and throwing money around. Here's a transcription of the last part of it:

"That's right. All these features plus Reversi, all for just… (smarmy voice and facial expression) how much did you guess? Five hundred? (holds up wad of cash in left hand). A thousand? (more cash in right hand—then throws both wads into the air) Even more? No! It's just ninety-nine dollars. That's right. JUST NINETY-NINE DOLLARS! It's an incredible value, but it's true. It's Windows from Microsoft. Order today at P.O Box 2 8 6 D O S. (reads off the address)."

The screen shows:

P.O. Box 286-DOS
Redmond, Wash.
(206) 882-8448
Ballmer ends with "Except in Nebraska…"

Cameron Myhrvold puts it succinctly, "Windows 1 was pretty hard. It was a tile-based operating system. It didn't run very well," However, despite its rocky start, Windows did have some high-profile developers, such as Page-Maker developer Aldus and Reuters in New York, who did a whole trading workstation based on it.

Microsoft's Final DOS Game

After publishing Microsoft Flight Simulator and Microsoft Decathlon (sometimes called Olympic Decathlon), Microsoft published its third and final DOS game, Space Simulator, in 1994 on the eve of a major milestone in Windows history—Windows 95. Grant Fjermedal also remembers his manager, John Solon, moving from working on Flight Simulator to Space Simulator. "At that point we could see the Windows interface coming. Basically Space Simulator was the last DOS game Microsoft ever published, and John, much to his credit, hand-tooled an interface that really mimicked Windows

95. He had all of the proper menu structures. It was kind of a clunky forbearer of Windows 95, but in DOS."

Meanwhile, working with Solon, Fjermedal completed not only his *Adventures in Space Simulator* book for Microsoft Press, but also a 100-page user manual to accompany the product, which required working very closely with the developers.

Fjermedal tells a story that would cause any game designer to laugh—or wince. One of Fjermedal's goals for Space Simulator was that it should be accessible to everyone. "I wanted someone to be able to sit down and just be able to use it." One of the developers, Charles Guy, was just the opposite. "Charles was a mathematician and a theorist—a hell of a good programmer—and he had come up with a command set of menus that mimicked his own internal thinking. And he could logically explain why everything was there, but god help anyone else. And I remember just being exasperated with him, and in one meeting I'm going, 'Charles. This is a beautiful game you're developing. You want to open the door wide. We want everyone to be able to use it.' And he goes, 'Well, I'm not sure I want everyone to use it.' It was like he was essentially saying, 'I want there to be an intellectual threshold here.'"

Just for Fun

Certainly we put games in for fun. We thought of Windows as more than just an OS, more than a bag of device drivers. We thought of it like an application, and wanted people to have fun and have something to do with it right out of the box.

And no doubt, once we're including games, they might as well help teach people stuff, too, like new UI techniques. Better than some dumb tutorial.

-Brad Silverberg

Even though Microsoft actually published only a few games for DOS between 1982 and 1994, games were often present behind the scenes at Microsoft, even if they were only the off-hours hobbies of developers. And so, when Windows 1.0 was released, it was easy to find a game to include, which is how Reversi was the first in a long tradition of little time wasters to be part of each Windows release.

One of the all-time favorite games on Windows was Solitaire, which debuted in Windows 3.0, but got its unlikely beginnings several years earlier in the Excel spreadsheet division.

Wes Cherry was an intern at Microsoft who, along with several members of the Microsoft Office team, had been playing around with poker AI programs. Among the other people involved were Hans Spiller, David Norris, Tom Saxon, and Ed Fries. "We were writing little poker AIs as just something fun to do on the side," says Fries, "and we had a little front end so we could watch them play. And we needed cards."

Cherry copied card images from a DOS game and created cards.dll, which made it possible for any program to access the card images. In an interview he said, "We had an interface so the dealer could deal hands to any set of player programs and then the AI in the individual players would bet and we'd see who wrote the best player. Of course we needed a DLL to draw the cards and so one evening I wrote the 50 lines of code or so and called it cards.dll. We were programmers, not artists, so initially we did screen grabs of a DOS solitaire game's cards and used those bitmaps."

Cherry later created the Solitaire game for Windows with improved card graphics provided by Macintosh interface artist (and ultimately creative director at Apple), Susan Kare. (In an interview, Cherry said that his girlfriend did most of the final art, which contradicts the more popular story about Susan Kare. On the other hand, through much of the interview, Cherry's answers were noticeably tongue-in-cheek.)

http://b3ta.com/interview/solitaire/

http://blogs.msdn.com/b/adam_nathan/archive/2006/12/04/thoughts-from-the-author-of-cards-dll.aspx

Bogus Software

Poker wasn't the only game to come out of the Excel division. Other programmers were also making games on the side, in part just for fun and in part to become more familiar with programming for Windows. Probably mostly the former, though.

Spiller and Norris decided that, because they were all working on games on the side, partly at Microsoft and partly at home, they didn't want to call them

Microsoft games, so they came up with a name for all of their extracurricular efforts: Bogus Software. The name took hold, and all the developers who were creating games for fun used it. Spiller even says that engineer Todd Laney also put the name into his diagnostic tools.

Fish

Ed Fries had created something on the side, as well. It started with a character-based aquarium screen saver, which he updated to a real graphical version for Windows called Fish. It, too, became Bogus Software. Then Tom Saxon created a Macintosh version and added a fish editor, which allowed people to create their own fish. Fries says, "We had put out a version that had an address on it for people to send the fish—just send fish—and instead of sending fish they started sending money. So we were getting these checks." Fries and Saxon decided to set up a little shareware company and market the animated screensaver, which may have been the first of its kind.

For some reason, whenever Fries traveled and was away from Microsoft for several days, people would play pranks on him, such as closing off his office with wallboard and making it look like it never existed. During the Fish days, they covered his entire floor with Dixie cups and used cups filled with colored water to depict a fish. You can see them at work here: *https://www.youtube.com/watch?v=19Jf09-3QCE*

To distinguish their shareware product from the internal Bogus Software, they named their company Tom and Ed's Bogus Software. "I ran the little shareware fish screensaver business for quite a while and sold Fish all over the world," says Fries. "The way it worked was, you got the screensaver for free, but if you wanted to make your own fish, you had to pay to unlock the editor."

In one of our conversations, Fries told me that he was getting ready to move and that he still had boxes of letters from people all over the world, "which I probably should have thrown away a long time ago, but I have all these boxes full of Fish letters."

A Weekend Project

Robert Donner had released a couple of games through Virgin Interactive—Risk and Clue for the Apple II—before joining Microsoft in 1989. Although his previous creative work in games helped him get the job, he found a position in the Office division, joining the Word team just before the first version released. Working within the Word codebase, however, didn't give him too much direct experience with the new Windows OS. He said, "Writing in Word you're at this layer, and you're separated from the OS, so I wanted to write a real game."

One of Donner's friends had written a game for IBM's OS-2 Presentation Manager and offered him the code. So one weekend Donner took his friend's code, rewrote it, and came up with a simple game. He called it Minesweeper.

After placing his weekend project on the internal shared servers, he began to get some feedback. Initially, the goal of the game was simply to find a path from one corner of the game area to the diagonally opposite corner without getting blown up. But one friend commented that he wanted the goal of finding all of the mines. Another colleague came and showed him how he could beat the game. "I watched him play, and he was really lightning fast with it, and I said, 'How did you do that?' Thinking, are there rules here? I knew how to play the game, but he was obviously much better." Another weekend later, Donnor had added some minor features. Still, Donnor admits ruefully that he's not very good at the game. "My wife is much better... everybody I know is better."

At times, Donnor experimented with different features. "I think the very first version I had there were coins involved for something because of Super

Mario and coins and stuff like that involved collecting coins. I decided it was too complicated. There's no point in this thing." Another idea he tried out was changing the mouse cursor into a shoe, and when the player stepped on a mine, "dripping a little bit of blood." But he decided to censor himself, thinking, "This is not the way I want it to go."

One of the major decisions Donnor made was to exclude any keyboard interface. "People were still confused about how to use the mouse," he said. "And I said I can do the keyboard interface, but I actually want people to click." So Donnor considered how to use the left and right mouse buttons (and even the third mouse button for those who had them) to control all operations in the game.

Within Microsoft, people were discovering Minesweeper and having fun with it. Even Bill Gates famously got involved. Donner recounts the story: "We got mail from Bill Gates at the time saying, 'I got 4 seconds on beginner mode. Is that good? If you want to see it and verify it, it's sitting on Mike Holman's machine over here.' He left it sitting there. It was a pretty good score at the time," says Donner, "but I'm sure there was a little bit of luck involved." Bruce Ryan did go and verify the score, but Donner had mixed feelings. "I wanted to apologize to Bill for wasting his time writing a program he spent a lot of time on. The question I really wanted to ask him was why is he playing games on somebody else's machine?"

http://www.businessinsider.com/bill-gates-was-a-microsoft-minesweeper-addict-2015-8

Eventually, Minesweeper got bundled with Windows. Donnor notes that, in part it was because the program was small and took up no resources once it was loaded. "It was consistent; it was pretty bug free." Not that there weren't bug reports, it's just that there weren't any bugs. "I kept getting bug reports from people. No. Send me a screen shot. No. You just don't know how to play the game." But on the lighter side, Donner laughs when he recalls how Minesweeper replaced Reversi. "That was a nice thing to see happen, especially since it kicked out Chris Peter's Reversi, mainly because he was my boss's boss's boss at the time."

At one point, Donner added a cheat to the game. By typing "XYZZY" on the keyboard, a small dot would appear over the top left-hand corner that would change from white to black if you hovered the mouse over a mine.

This cheat was actually in effect until Windows 7, when a change in the code made it so that you couldn't put anything outside of your program's window. Because Minesweeper's cheat dot was drawn on the Windows screen, not within the Minesweeper window, it no longer worked.

The Microsoft Entertainment Packs

Meanwhile, there were a lot of games floating around with nowhere to go. Hans Spiller wrote, "One day a marketing type approached me about my games. He said that Microsoft was interested in marketing a recreational package for that Christmas. There would be no development support at all, but anything we wanted to do could go in, presuming it met the legal and testing standards." The "marketing type" also approached the Bogus developers, and so those who were interested—which was most of them—started polishing their games (Spiller adds,"We wound up doing quite a bit of illicit development work before shipping"), and these became the first of several Windows Entertainment Packs. Spiller says that his Space Invaders clone was instantly rejected by the lawyers, but that his Spacewar/Asteroids clone was only rejected at the last minute.

Robert Donner says that his boss, Bruce Ryan, was most likely the "marketing type" who approached Spiller, Fries and the others. "Bruce put together these programs and collected them and they started getting distributed more widely around Microsoft," said Donner.

The first Microsoft Entertainment Pack included card games Cruel and Golf, Minesweeper, Mike Blaylock's Pegged, Norris' mahjong tile matching game Taipei, a licensed version of Tetris, Tic Tactics, and a screensaver called Idlewild by Brad Christian.

Tetris almost didn't end up in the Entertainment Pack. Licensing issues threatened to blow up the deal at the last minute, and so the marketing team made up stickers that said "Now includes Tetris for Windows!" just in case. The deal was finalized at more or less the last minute and so thousands of stickers had to be manually affixed to the outgoing game boxes.

There were three subsequent entertainment packs, which introduced, among others, very popular games like FreeCell, Pipe Dream, and WordZap. Some of the games originally seen in the entertainment packs were later bundled into various versions of Windows. Of course, Solitaire, FreeCell, and Minesweeper were perennial favorites.

Later Microsoft released a Best of Microsoft Entertainment Pack collection including Chip's Challenge, Dr. Black Jack, FreeCell, Golf, JezzBall, Pipe Dream, Rodent's Revenge, SkiFree, Taipei, TetraVex, Tetris, TriPeaks, and Tut's Tomb. They also released a collection for Game Boy Color that included Tut's Tomb, TriPeaks, FreeCell, TicTactics, Minesweeper, Life Genesis, and SkiFree.

Also in 1993, Microsoft ported several classic Atari arcade games—Tempest, Battlezone, Asteroids, Centipede, and Missile Command—to Windows and called it Microsoft Arcade.

Both the entertainment packs and Microsoft Arcade were very successful, so when people think that Microsoft wasn't interested in games, it is clear that they saw entertainment as not only worthwhile, but also at least a small profit center—small when compared with their enterprise software.

First Console?

William Volk is a long-time veteran of the game industry. He was one of the earliest developers to work with CD-ROM, and while at Activision he was involved in the development of the first CD-ROM game, The Manhole. He remembers a conversation he had with Bill Gates at a party following the first CD-ROM Interactive Conference in 1985. He and Gates talked about graphics resolutions the advantages that Microsoft had over Macintosh because of their ability to create good graphics using low resolution 320 x 200 pixel resolutions. The Mac was trying to drive multimedia titles using 640 x 480 resolutions, and the CPUs at that time weren't capable yet of handling the graphical load very well. Gates understood that this was an advantage, and he also knew that games were worthwhile, telling Volk, "You know Flight Simulator has always sold well for us. We actually care about that. We care about games."

In 1984, Philips began developing CD-i (Compact Disk Interactive), an interactive multimedia CD player, that was announced in 1986, but not released until 1991. According to Volk, the main reason for the long delay was that Microsoft came out with their desktop video standard for PCs–DVI (Digital Video Interactive)–at the next CD-ROM Conference, the same year that Philips announced CD-i, which caused them to panic and spend years developing the first major digital video standard, MPEG-1. The full story of CD-i is too involved to include in this book, but the short version is that it was ultimately considered a failure.

Microsoft also wanted to get in on the action, and they partnered with Tandy, which owned Radio Shack and Memorex at the time. The Tandy VIS (Video Information System) was launched in 1992, and it was a direct competitor to CD-i and Commodore's CDTV systems. Microsoft provided the software, a version of Windows 3.1 called "Modular Windows," which was intended to be an embedded operating system for various devices.

The VIS was arguably even less successful than CD-i. It was sold exclusively at Radio Shack, and earned the nickname from employees as "Virtually Impossible to Sell." It is estimated that it sold only 11,000 units before being discontinued. The Windows 3.1 version of Modular Windows was also discontinued, but Microsoft remained comitted to the concept of Windows powering devices other than PCs, and later implimentations include Windows CE and the Xbox Operating System.

~5~

Windows: Path to Dominance

Windows continued to improve with each new release and to gain traction. Windows 286 and Windows 386 were increasingly successful and by 1988, Microsoft had become the world's largest PC software company based on sales. Although adoption of the Windows platform had increased, it wasn't universal, and so Microsoft promoted bundling the installation software for Windows in applications like PageMaker, which helped disseminate the OS into more and more offices and homes.

Finally, with Windows 3.0 and 3.1, Windows began to hit its real stride, and Microsoft even showed a rare sense of humor when they added Solitaire, Hearts and Minesweeper to the basic configuration and released an ad that stated, "Now you can use the incredible power of Windows 3.0 to goof off." (There had been some similar humor in the ads for the entertainment packs, such as, "No more boring coffee breaks" and "You'll never get out of the office," but the Windows 3.0 ad was a very rare acknowledgment of games by the more serious OS and business software group.)

Windows 3.1 also shipped with Watson, a tool to help developers with debugging, and the evangelists of the Developer Relations Group were there to help developers learn to use the new tool. According to Myhrvold, "Watson added much better support from tools vendors. And that was also a major focus. We had a guy in my group named Bob Taniguchi who worked with all the tools vendors, and that was super important."

So part of the DRG's mission was being accomplished. The Windows platform was beginning to gain traction, and Microsoft's technical evangelists were working hard to encourage developers to write Windows applications.

While hiring technical evangelists was one important way in which Microsoft's developer evangelism differed from Apple's, perhaps even more significantly, the DRG mission was always about making Microsoft's platforms stronger and its competitors weaker. Everything they did was to further those two missions, and they found ways to do both at the same time. To do so, Myhrvold required people with very special qualities.

The Battle Plan

Jesus Christ. Gotta hire this guy. I mean, he's written the battle plan.

-Cameron Myhrvold

One of the most influential and outspoken, but rarely celebrated, Microsoft evangelists originally came from the Apple camp. James Plamondon had spent much of his youth in the wilderness of the redwood forests of Del Norte, California, just south of the Oregon border. His conservative Republican parents had moved out of Southern California, according to Plamondon, because they "were concerned that there was way too much sex and drugs going on in the local school, and so they wanted to get us out of that evil big city environment and back to nature." Plamondon quickly points out the irony of that move because, with the timber industry and commercial fishing both collapsing in the north woods, "all that was left was growing dope."

Because he had contracted polio as a child, Plamondon's father was unable to join his college mates in the Korean War. Out of frustration, he became obsessed with military campaigns. "He had been following those wars with maps on the walls and listening to the radio reports... just following them as closely as he could." Plamondon and his brothers were included in their father's growing interest in military strategy, but it was their father's other interest that most fascinated the Plamondon boys —computers. In 1977, Plamondon's father brought a TRS-80 computer into the home, and even more than war history, the computer became young James' obsession.

James Plamondon ultimately went to college and earned a degree in computer science with a focus on artificial intelligence. He was fascinated by the potential of using artificial intelligence in games. "And so I got this bachelor of computer science degree that was focused on artificial intelligence, and then—duh—after I did all that, I then did my market research, talking to various game companies, and they said, 'You know there is absolutely no demand for what you're offering. That's just great and everything, but the reason it sucks is because we don't care.'"

There was no plan B. It was time to shift gears. Fortunately Plamondon had gotten an early "phone book" edition of *Inside Mac* before the Macintosh was even released. He taught himself Mac programming, even though there weren't any Macs to program—yet. When the Mac did come out, "I convinced my girlfriend at the time—who later became my wife—to buy a Macintosh so that she could start up her own print design business, which she actually did fairly well at for a while." And, of course, Plamondon used his girlfriend's Mac to hone his skills.

Soon Plamondon found work at Reference Software, a company started by semi-retired professor, Bruce Wampler, to market the world's first spell-checker and thesaurus. After at one time selling his software to WordStar, Wampler was able to buy it back again when Word Perfect came to dominate the word processor market and WordStar began selling off its assets.

Plamondon worked for Wampler for about a year, while they sold the spell-checker/thesaurus software as an add-on for other products, but eventually he came to realize that the job was a dead end. "I'm the only other guy there. It's him and me. What? Am I going to get promoted?"

The Apple Guy

Plamondon took other jobs, specifically choosing them for what they could teach him about programming. He had seen the promise of the graphical interface, and believed that it would reshape the world. On the other hand, there was DOS. "Mac was the vehicle of the graphic user interface, and was therefore morally superior to DOS. (spit) DOS (spit). You have to spit after saying DOS. Otherwise the taste of it might remain in your mouth and poison you later. I once wrote that DOS was proof that there was evil in the world."

Completely convinced that the Mac was the future of computers, Plamondon began writing Mac programming articles.

Plamondon decided that he wanted to find jobs that would help him refine his Mac programming skills, and Silicon Valley was the place to find those jobs. So he moved. He got a job at a company that wrote statistics software, and it was there that he had a revelation that propelled him forward. "One of the guys, who was the senior programmer there, would write the same list management code over and over and over, so that he could rename the functions, so that when he was debugging he would know which list he was debugging because of the function names. Which meant that whenever there was a problem in his list management code, he'd have to change it N times, because there were N different versions of this code scattered around. He had different code for each different list. It was insane. So that led me to think there had to be a better way." Which is how Plamondon discovered object oriented programming.

He found a job where he could learn more about this new kind of programming at a company called Power Up Software, which provided him with the opportunity to work with the first widely used object oriented application, MacApp. While he was working at Power Up Software, Plamondon organized an object oriented programming Framework group, which met at Apple's headquarters. "I was already a mover and shaker in the Framework world," he says, which led to an offer from Microsoft to write a book about their Microsoft Foundation classes. However, he was "stony cold broke" at the time, and had to turn down the offer, knowing that he wouldn't see any money from the book for months, at best.

In the market for another job, Plamondon interviewed at Apple and at Taligent—a cooperative venture between Apple and IBM to build a new operating system. Plamondon described Taligent as "a real sheep lying down with the lions kind of thing" because Apple and IBM had been enemies, at least until Microsoft became their common rival.

Plamondon considered working at Taligent, even though he was sure the venture would fail. "They tried to write an object oriented operating system using C++, and C++ just wasn't up to the task… It was like you were using a screwdriver to solve a hammer problem. And they just weren't likely to succeed." Still, he considered it, seeing it as an opportunity to learn valuable skills, getting out before it crashed and burned, thereby avoiding the "odor of failure" that would attach to those involved.

While he was musing the pros and cons of a job at Taligent, another opportunity presented itself. He was invited to interview for an evangelist job, not at Apple, but at the much-hated Microsoft. Why would he even consider the offer?

Cognitive Load

"It all comes down to cognitive load. With a graphic user interface, everything you need to know is embedded in the user interface. It may be four menus deep, which is bad user interface design. It may be a really shitty window… a bad dialog box or something, but it's all right there. You don't have to remember, and you don't even have to remember how to get to it, if the interface is sufficiently explorable, so that you can discover how to use it. The ideal graphic user interface program has no manual because it is so self-explanatory. And I just loved that to pieces, because if you thought computing was a powerful and a good tool—those two things together: powerful and good, liberating creativity, which everybody of my generation, and probably yours, believed was true—then you wanted to empower as high a percentage of the population to use computers as possible. And the command line interface was a barrier to that because you had to fucking remember everything. It's not discoverable. You have to memorize everything. Every secretary on the planet had this little Word Perfect cheat sheet on the top of the first drawer to her left. Right? Something where she could pull it out and check, 'How do I do this again?' It made everybody feel stupid. And it was the same with DOS commands… So my goal in my early stage of computerdom, was to drive this whole graphic user interface notion better because it was a way of democratizing computer usage—empowering computer users."

-James Plamondon

Switching Teams

Why abandon Apple? Simple. According to Plamondon, Apple had abandoned him, and all the other small developers.

Plamondon's personal goal—his mission—was to "empower users with computing power… to bring the power of computing to the masses." As he saw it, Apple had lost track of their identity. In the early days of the Macintosh computer, it was "the computer for the rest of us," but by the late '80s, they had changed. In Plamondon's words, "They were now the Mercedes of computers." They catered to the elite customers while people who used DOS and Windows were driving Fords and Chevys.

"Well, first of all, that's antithetical to what they set out to do. It's the exact opposite of what they were saying originally, and what I signed on for, and everybody else I knew who was writing Mac programs. Secondly, it was selling their developers down the river because if a third-party developer targets a platform that he thinks is a Chevy, it's because a Chevy sells a shitload of copies, and therefore he has a big platform to sell into. But if suddenly he's now selling into the Mercedes market, his installed base has just shrunk like crazy. His opportunity to sell copies has just collapsed. Therefore he must jack up his prices beyond all reason. And so the ability to make a living as a developer of third-party Mac applications collapsed in the late 80s, early 90s because Apple took this change of focus from the computer for the rest of us to we're the elite computer. Really pissed me off. They just stabled all their developers—my friends."

Moreover, Plamondon asserts that Apple did not truly appreciate its independent developers. He cites a story of one senior vice president at Apple calling all Mac developers parasites. Plamondon also tells a story about Steve Jobs and the Next machine (see next page).

Microsoft "Technical" Evangelist

Plamondon decided, what the heck, why not interview for Microsoft's technical evangelist role? To him, the important quality that differentiated Microsoft's evangelism from Apple's was the same distinction that Myrhvold had made— it was technical. It was a role that fit him perfectly. Combining his love of code, his love of sharing information, and his amateur military studies, he came in prepared. In fact, Cameron Myhrvold hired him on the spot. "He's a guy who walked into my office with a mission. I mean he walked in to the interview knowing exactly what he wanted to do. Those are sometimes the easiest interviews. It's like, 'Oh. Wow. OK. How would that work? Tell me about it.' And by the end of the interview, you're like, 'Jesus Christ. Gotta hire this guy.' I mean, he's written the battle plan."

At first, Plamondon remained in the Bay Area, now working for Microsoft at what they somewhat facetiously called the "Bay Area Embassy." This was just before the release of Windows version 3.1.1. "The Bay Area viewed Microsoft as being the evil, dark enemy up in Seattle," says Plamondon.

The Next Machine

"Steve Jobs, when he introduced the Next machine, he had an event called the Next Day; because it was after a presentation to financial analysts and stuff in New York. On the next day he came to Silicon Valley and pitched to software developers, and I was one of the developers he was pitching to in the audience. And everybody loved the Next operating system and the interface builder and all these wonderful object-oriented libraries. It was using Objective C, which was one of the early dynamic languages. You could do it in Objective C. You couldn't in C++. And everybody was just, 'Oh, this is such an exciting thing. I'm dying to do this.' And then he said, 'Oh, and by the way, all of your software will be delivered on this optical drive that we'll send to every customer once every three months.' And somebody raised their hand and said, 'What? What? Did you just say that I can't distribute software myself? That I have to distribute my software through you?' And Steve Jobs said, 'Nononononono. You're thinking of this wrong. We're not taking away from you the freedom to distribute your own software. We're enabling you to not have to worry about software distribution at all. And we'll only take a 30% cut.' And we all stood up and walked out of the room. Almost literally. At that point, we all looked at each other and said, 'Oh, after you.' 'No, after you.' 'Oh no, no. After you.' And nobody wrote for the Next machine because nobody was willing to hand over all their distribution to Steve Jobs and Next. What's funny is.... He always wanted to get a piece of the developers' action. He always felt, and Apple has always felt, that application developers were parasites, and that there had to be a way to get a piece of their action. And they finally figured it out with the App Store. With the App Store, they're skimming the cream off the top. It doesn't matter whether you sell one copy or a million copies. It's like the patent business. Patent attorneys get their money up front, before you've made a dime selling your invention. It's the same way with the App Store. They're making their percent on everything that sells, whether it sells one copy or a million copies."

-James Plamondon

Network Effect

According to Plamondon, one of Apple's chief failures was their failure to understand the "network effect," which he describes as "positive network externalities and the relationships between applications and platforms and tools." According to the Financial Times, "A network effect (also known as network externality) exists when a product's value to the user increases as the number of users of the product grows."

Understanding the network effect is critical to promoting platforms, and if you're in the platform business, you want to encourage as many applications as possible to use your platform. Having more applications increases the value of the platform to the user. And, according to Plamondon, you want to do all you can to help these applications to be successful, not out of altruism, but because it makes your platform stronger, and the stronger your platform becomes, the weaker rival platforms are by comparison.

Part of helping developers succeed is to develop tools internally, or to encourage and support others to develop tools. While tools are important to facilitate application development, they are a loss leader. "If you try to profit from the tools, you're raising the cost of targeting your platform."

Plamondon asserts that Apple never understood the network effect or the platform business. He even cites how Google's Android mobile operating system has so quickly encroached on Apple's seemingly dominant IOS business. Back in the late 1980s and early 1990s, Apple lost market share, at least in part, because they didn't treat their Mac OS as a platform the way Microsoft did Windows.

At Microsoft, Plamondon found people who understood the network effect and the importance of empowering developers to make applications for your operating system, starting with Cameron Myhrvold. And Myhrvold also gives major props to Bill Gates and Steve Ballmer, commenting, "They completely believed, just in their bones, that that was true. When I would talk with other people who had my role in other companies, they'd have to go through these massive justification exercises. I never had to do that. These guys just knew."

Myhrvold describes Apple as "the counter culture and the prima donna of the UI," and although they were effective, he points out their critical weakness. They thought like a hardware vendor. "If you think like a hardware vendor, you look at a pie and you think, how is the pie going to be divided between hardware and software? And that is what causes you to then deliberately think about how to make software cheaper because it's a zero sum game, and that you're going to sell more hardware." The problem is, once again, the network effect. Apple wanted to sell hardware, and they believed that cheaper software was the way to do that, but they didn't seem to appreciate the importance of their independent developers the way Microsoft did, nor did they seem to understand how to use the developers as pawns in the operating system game of chess. Because they were trying to sell hardware, and Microsoft wasn't.

Even though they were a developer, too, Microsoft understood that the more people developing for their platform—in this case, the Windows operating system—the more indispensable that platform became. Plamondon saw at Microsoft an opportunity to support developers and to proselytize his idea of computers for the masses. In his mind, Apple had become the bad guys, and Microsoft—at least the people in the DRG—were the good guys fighting the good fight.

Microsoft Office

In part, developers hated Microsoft in the early days of Windows because of their policy of consolidating Office applications into bundles, which made it harder for independent developers to compete. Of course bundling was purely a marketing decision. Describing the initial bundle of Word, Excel and PowerPoint, Plamondon observes, "They had different menu structures, and they had different core code. They had almost nothing in common. It was as if they were from separate companies." Clearly a kluge, the bundle was a good deal due to Microsoft's aggressive pricing. During the years following the launch of Office 1, Microsoft added Outlook to the basic package, and in some configurations, Access.

Office also became more consistent, with menu structures and commands being shared among the different applications, but that consistency did not come easily. At the time, different product divisions at Microsoft operated almost like small, independent businesses, what Plamondon called a *keiretsu*, a Japanese word describing a set of companies with interlocking business relationships and shareholdings.

Plamondon explains, "It was a Japanese *keiretsu* that basically just provided capital and a thin layer of high-level management to a bunch of individual companies that were product lines. And so the powerful people in the company were the PUMs, the Product Unit Managers. <*He pronounces it 'pum'.*> And if you were the Excel PUM, you did whatever the fuck you wanted to with Excel, as long as you could keep driving its numbers up. You were the king of Excel. And if you were the PUM of Word, you were the king of Word. You did whatever was necessary to sell more copies of Word. And if it fucked Excel, that was too damned bad for Excel. And there was a thin layer of tax that was imposed on this. For example, I think it was the Word guys came up with OLE (Object Linking and Embedding) because they wanted to be able to bring in Excel objects—particularly Excel, but from other things as well—and manage them from within Word. And the Excel guys didn't want to put Word objects into Excel's spreadsheets, so they didn't care. But the Word guys cared a lot, so they created this OLE and component object model infrastructure to make that happen. And it was kluged up. It was a grotesque kluge, OLE 1.0, but they fixed the technology in OLE 2.0 by creating COM, the Component Object Model."

Plamondon's job description—the public version—was to bring Mac developers to Windows, and because he was known as a "Mac guy," he had a certain advantage. "For at least a couple of years I was able to say, 'I'm not saying X because I work for Microsoft. I work for Microsoft because X is true. X is cool. X is a pretty compelling technology. And you should consider using X because it's awesome. And I'm not just saying that because I work for Microsoft. I work for Microsoft because they're producing cool technology.' But after a while, after you've been working for Microsoft for a couple of years, even if that's true, it's not credible anymore."

COM: The Common Object Model

About the Common Object Model, DRG operative Alex St. John explains what it is, what it was meant to do, why developers hated it, and why it was necessary: "Common Object Model. It's a technology Microsoft cooked up to enable API's to change and evolve overtime while remaining backwards compatible. For example DirectX could evolve frequently as it did without breaking earlier applications that used it because of COM. Non-COM based API's are just frozen in time for years in-order to preserve stability of all of the software that uses them. COM was clever but also very cumbersome for developers to adopt.

"It started out rough and got better fast. It's major sin was that we felt that we had to support COM which was a big push at msft back then and made API's much more complicated. OpenGL being an open-standard API couldn't be "COMified" and be OpenGL. So there was certainly a lot of developer rejection of COM. We hated doing it. The other big issue with developers was the execute buffer API. You couldn't just draw a triangle in early D3D, you had to fill out a really complex data structure called an execute buffer. The reason for it at the time was that 3D consumer hardware acceleration was very limited and using execute buffers helped them get acceleration. Without using them, a lot of hardware didn't actually accelerate anything. The operating system couldn't automate filling out an execute buffer for a game without losing performance because only the game knew how many polygons it intended to draw. It was a pain and confusing for the developers. Being pragmatic our guys said, why do the work to add an API that goes slower?

"It was stuff like that that worked itself out with time. In that example OpenGL had a draw triangle API that would simply have run slow and then the developers would have complained about that. It was the nature of developer relations."

The Good Guys

Guy Kawasaki had a degree in psychology and later obtained an MBA. He wasn't a programmer. He didn't code, and he didn't talk code. Microsoft's evangelists were all—every one of them—technical people who could sit down with developers and discuss their technical problems and needs meaningfully.

Plamondon describes the contrast, saying "Aristotle wrote a book called 'On Rhetoric,' and everything he wrote about rhetoric, about persuading audiences, is absolutely as true today as it was then. The only thing that he missed is the concept of identification—that you need to get your audience to identify with you, to think that you are one of them—because the only people he could imagine speaking to were fellow Greeks. Who'd want to convince a barbarian of anything? They're barbarians. You don't want their support.

"So this notion that you get people to identify with you, he didn't get. And it's really critical to what we did. We always made sure that when we were

Plamondon on MortWare

"My favorite example is a company called MortWare... MortWare: the Software for Morticians. And if you look up on YouTube, I think you'll find a video in which I talk about why the Developer Relations Group was able to kick the rest of the world's ass. It was because we empowered some young kid. His parents ran a mortician's thing, and he really wasn't into the mortician thing, but he really liked computers. He could get started with Visual Basic and write an application that would enable his parents' funeral parlor to run better. That would satisfy his desire to improve the operations, and to be empowered. All the things we wanted. He could do that without a computer science degree… without anything like that. To try to do that on UNIX, he would have to be a UNIX guru. He'd have to have at least four years of school. You know the tools were obscure. They're all command line stuff that you have to have a PhD to figure out how to read the manual, let alone how to use the software. We took that guy by the hand and brought him into programming in little baby steps and made it really easy so that he could help his family's undertaking business."

going to talk to doctors—technologists in the medical field—we'd send a doctor, somebody who was a medical professional who we'd hired because he was also keen on computers. And Microsoft in the '90s was able to hire those guys. So… empowerment. It's all down to empowerment. So we at Microsoft believed that we were the good guys empowering the masses. Apple was selling this elite computer to the elite artsy fartsy people who we hated in high school anyway, and we were *kamikaze nerds*, fighting on behalf of secretaries everywhere, to make their lives easier, to make it so that our grandmothers could use computers, to bring computing power to the masses, a role that Apple had originally taken… and had abdicated."

Being the good guys wasn't necessarily a matter of fighting evil. Their main rivals at the time—IBM and Apple—were not necessarily the real threats to Microsoft's dominance of the personal computer space. IBM had long ago lost interest in the personal computer space, and Apple was on the decline. The ongoing challenge was to bring new people to the market, as Plamondon put it, "creating a solution for a problem that people had never been able to solve before." New solutions included bringing computers into retail stores, doctors' offices, auto shops… and even mortuaries. Their goal—Gates' goal—was *a computer on every desk and every home, running Microsoft software.*

The Strategists

The DRG, as Myhrvold saw it, was a bit more complex than Apple's version, and when he first met James Plamondon, he recognized that here was a man with a plan. Plamondon already understood why Apple was failing to live up to their early promise, and he also saw that Microsoft had the potential to usher in an age of computer empowerment, and to accomplish that goal, he had a take no prisoners attitude. This was a campaign, much like those war maps he had studied with his father as a child. And there were rules of engagement, and if you followed those rules, you would prevail.

"Cameron Myhrvold is a brilliant guy," says Plamondon, "and he understood network effects extremely well. And so he understood what it was that the group needed to get done. And his degree was in rhetoric… not kidding. So he was a professional persuader. He understood what needed to be done, and wasn't exactly sure how to do it, that was clear. By this I mean no criticism. Nobody else did either. And I decided, since no one knew what to do—I didn't know what to do, either—that I'd try something and see if it worked. And what I decided to apply to it was military strategy and tactics, because at least there was a well-established body of strategy and tactics there. And I happened to have always been interested in it. It's not like I went to West Point or anything, but I was a dilettante in these things, had read *The Art of War* and various other books of military strategy."

So while the evangelists of the Developer Relations Group were busily reaching out to developers and helping them solve problems and genuinely rooting for them to succeed (for admittedly selfish reasons), internally, Plamondon was developing a battle plan—not for any particular battle, but for each and every battle still to come.

-6-

The Other Face of the DRG

"Microsoft has been accused of a bunch of things, and when it came down to something like our work with Microsoft application competitors, we're clean as a whistle. We never ever did anything remotely unethical to advantage the applications group. Now when it comes to platform vendors. Oh, absolutely. Absolutely, my friend. My job was to put other operating systems out of business, from my perspective. So if we could do that through application support, if we could do that through tying them up technically, if we could do that by having them chase red herrings, absolutely. Did that all day long."

-Cameron Myhrvold

With the addition of people like James Plamondon and Alex St. John, the DRG became a potent force both internally at Microsoft and externally in the world of developers and competing software. More to the point of this book, they also established attitudes and tactics that would be inherited by the people who originally fought for Xbox. *One thing leads to another...*

The DRG was a two-headed beast. On the one hand, they fully supported independent software vendors (ISVs)—developers. On the other hand, they engaged in a focused campaign to make sure Microsoft was the winner in every arena in which they competed. The basis of this thought is expressed by Cameron Myhrvold while talking about a meeting they had with a guy from Claris, which was Apple's business applications spinoff.

How Not to Make Money

Don Eilers represented Claris, Apple's software spinoff company. Myrhvold describes him as a very nice guy. Ellers came to Seattle to meet with Myhrvold and Steve Ballmer about the possibility of Claris developing applications for Windows. Early in the conversation, Ellers proudly observed that the retail price of the average Macintosh application was half the price of a Windows app.

After the meeting, Myhrvold remembers Ballmer's reaction. "Steve is hooting and hollering. 'Can you believe it? Can you believe those idiots? They can't deliver volume or price point. How are they going to help people make money?'" In other words, selling apps at half the price might appear to be a competitive advantage, but with lower sales volume, Claris was not supporting its developers, and without successful developers, the platform on which they depended—the Macintosh—would not prosper. Ultimately, they would lose as their developers went where the money was.

Myrhvold goes on to explain that, in order to win the software war, there were only two things you needed to do:

1. "You need to make the other guy's platform priority 2. It doesn't have to be priority 10; just priority 2. Because in a resource constrained world, priority 1 is going to get the resources and on the margin, priority 2 is going to starve."

2. "You have to make your platform the best way to make money. And if your platform is the best way to make money, people can hate you, but they're still going to write for your operating system."

Myrhvold also points out that Microsoft was continually creating more technology for developers to adopt. "There's nothing I hated more in life than a release of Windows that didn't have a major ISV (Independent Software Vendor) agenda. Because I don't want these guys to have idle cycles. I don't want them to think about, 'Oh, what else should we do with our engineering group?' I want to absorb all the oxygen in the room with them working on Windows related technology."

Plamondon's Art of War

If you're curious about the foundation of DRG's competitive philosophy, what follows is a complete transcription of what James Plamondon taught at Microsoft in regular seminars to new groups of DRG evangelists. The original document was used in the U.S. Department of Justice Anti-Trust trials against Microsoft, which began in the late '90s, and is in the public record. Please read only if you are truly interested in the foundations of Microsoft's competitive strategy.

Effective Evangelism

Evangelism is War

Our mission is to establish Microsoft's platforms as the de facto standards throughout the computer industry. Our enemies are the vendors of the platforms that compete with ours: Netscape, Sun, IBM, Oracle, Lotus, etc. The field of battle is the software industry. Success is measured in shipping applications. Every line of code that is written to our standards is a small victory; every line of code that is written to any other standard, is a small defeat. Total victory, for DRG, is the universal adoption of our standards by developers, as this is an important step towards total victory for Microsoft: 'A computer on every desk and in every home, running Microsoft Software.'

Our weapons are psychological, economic, political—not military. No one is forced to adopt our standards at the barrel of a gun. We can only convince, not compel. Those who adopt our standards do so as a rational decision to serve their own ends, whatever those may be. It is our job to ensure that those choosing an operating system are presented with an overwhelming abundance of evidence and reasoned argument in favor of our standards—so overwhelming that the choice of our standards seems obvious, or (ideally) that the developer is not even aware that a decision was faced, and a choice made.

We do this by understanding the barriers that might otherwise prevent the developer from adopting our standards, and removing them; by understanding the inducements that might facilitate the developer's adoption of our standards, and providing them; by understanding the arguments of our competition, and countering them.

Our Mission

The Charter of Microsoft's Developer Relations Group is clear:

Drive the success of Microsoft's platforms by creating a critical mass of third-party software applications and business solutions.

This mission statement contains both the goal which we are striving to achieve (the success of Microsoft's platforms) as well as the means by which we are to achieve it (by creating a critical mass of third-party applications and business solutions).

Definition of Evangelism at Microsoft

"Evangelism is the art and science of getting developers to ship products that support Microsoft's platforms."

Below are the slides that were used in Plamondon's presentations:

Effective Evangelism

Evangelism is WAR!

- Mission
  - o Establish Microsoft's platforms as de facto standards
- Enemies
  - o Other platform vendors
- Battlefield
  - o ISV Mindshare
- Progress
  - o Shipping ISV applications

Role of ISVs

- ISVs are just pawns in the struggle
  - o But have you ever tried to win a chess game without any pawns?
- We need the support of ISVs to win
- We must earn the support of ISVs by
  - o Shipping technologies worthy of support
  - o Helping ISVs implement and market their support for our technologies
- We work hard to help our ISVs succeed!

So, We're Just Here to Help Developers, Right?

We're Here to Help Microsoft©!

- Microsoft©Pays our wages
- Microsoft©provides our stock options
- Microsoft©pays our expenses
- We're Here to Help Microsoft©
  - By helping those developers
  - …That can best help Microsoft©
  - …Achieve Microsoft©'s objectives
- Did anyone miss the point here?

Enlightened Self-Interest

- We help ISVs to help ourselves
- But we really do help them
- We fight for our ISV's
  - APIs, hooks, tool support
  - Design Reviews
  - Strategies, timelines, etc.
  - …because we need their support for our own ends

Too Many to Help

- Can't help 'em all
- We help those who can help us.
- If they can't or won't help us
  - Screw 'em!
  - Help their competitors instead.

Art of War

"To win one hundred battles is not perfection; to subdue the enemy without fighting is perfection."

Sun-Tzu: The Art of War, written in China by Sun Wu in roughly 400 B.C.

- "Thus, the best military strategy is to attack the enemy's plans.
- Next best is to disrupt his alliances.
- Next best is to crush his army.
- The worst policy is to attack his fortified cities. Attack cities only when there is no alternative.

Attack the Enemy's Plans

- Do not attack directly
  - No debates, no white papers, no lawsuits
- Do the unexpected; attack his assumptions

Attack the Enemy's Fortified Cities

- Big ISVs that compete with Microsoft
  - Lotus, Novell, Oracle, ...
- They hate us
  - And there's nothing we can do about it
- Don't throw yourself against their walls
- Help their competitors instead
  - Let them attack the cities for us
  - They'll be grateful for our help (for a little while...)

All is Not Fair

- We are under close scrutiny
  - Any unethical acts WILL BE uncovered
- Besides—we're the good guys!
- Simple rule to live by: Never Lie
  - Tell the truth, and nothing but the truth
  - Be selective in which truths you emphasize
  - Let the competition fill in the gaps

Key's to Plamondon's "Effective Evangelism"

Plamondon's approach hinged on several key concepts:

1. The goal was for Microsoft's platforms to dominate the market using third-party developers.
2. Nobody is forced to do anything. Persuasion and psychology were the weapons of choice.
3. Supporting ISVs (Independent Software Vendors) is critical to the platform's success...
4. ...but ultimately, their loyalty and effort is in support of Microsoft.
5. If someone is too strong to attack directly, or unwilling to help Microsoft, help their competitors.
6. The best strategy is the most subtle: 1. Attack the enemy's plans. 2. Disrupt the enemy's alliances. 3. Destroy the enemy's army. 4. The worst approach is to attack the enemy's strength (fortified cities).
7. The authorities are watching, so keep it ethical and honest, but selectively honest.

To the point of selective honesty, Plamondon says, "Something I always said when giving this part of the presentation: 'In a court case, the presecution tells those truths that support the prosecution's case; and the defense tells the truths that support the defense's case. Neither side tells "the whole truth," but between them the whole truth comes out. Similarly, DRG tells those truths that support Microsoft's case, and which condemn our competition's case. We cannot be reasonably expected to make our competition's case for them. That'st their job. And the ISV is on the jury, choosing which platform API to support.'"

DRG Strategy in Action

"Tactical evangelism is getting ISVs to do what you want."

-James Plamondon

Plamondon and others may have seen themselves as the "good guys," but Microsoft could hardly claim to be an altruistic organization. If they did something good for you, it was to further their own interests. And if you failed to appreciate their largesse, they had ways of making you regret it. ISVs were pawns in their game… very necessary to win the platform war, but, like pawns in chess, they were used strategically and easily sacrificed if necessary.

Plamondon puts this idea in context: "ISVs—independent software vendors—are pawns in the struggle between platform vendors. They are today's allies… tomorrow, who knows? Tomorrow, you know, it could have been that Netscape was a little applications company that we thought was great and we worked with, and then suddenly they came up with this competing platform. The bastards! You never know which way they're going to go."

Infiltrating the Enemy Camp

At Microsoft, Plamondon had become the "anti-Apple" guy, and he found numerous ways to attack his former ally. To many of his Mac friends, he was a heretic, but… "I was such a hell of a nice guy that they'd go, 'You know, that damned Plamondon, you know, he's working for the Evil Empire, he's seducing people to the Dark Side, but, you know, he's such a hell of a swell guy…. I hate Microsoft, but he's OK.'"

So Plamondon had no problem promoting Windows right under Apple's nose. He even had rules that governed his approach to Mac-oriented conferences. If the conference was controlled by the platform developer—what Plamondon calls an enemy conference—"You go to the enemy sessions, see what they're saying, talk to people, be nice. Just be super nice. You never say anything rude; never, never, never stand up at the microphone at an enemy conference and say, 'Excuse me, you're full of shit," you know.'" In contrast, his strategy with independent developer conferences was to "subvert them."

Plamondon, friendly and generous to a fault, in separate cases managed to get two ongoing developer groups to end operations simply by getting them to include Windows in their programs. Although it might have been beneficial to their members to learn about Windows, allowing it into previously Mac-only conferences and groups ultimately pissed off the Mac faithful, as well as Apple, which withdrew support. In time, the leaders of both groups found the situation too frustrating and called it quits. In Plamondon's world these were two fewer channels that Apple could use to reach its developers. In other words, mission accomplished.

Windows Seminars

Plamondon also held special Windows seminars for Mac developers during Apple's yearly MacWorld Expo and their WWDC (World Wide Developers Conference). He made sure to get plenty of Mac programmers to present, including a well-known author, Don Bachs (who later joined Microsoft), and another author, Dan Weston.

Although he was successful in getting people to attend the seminars, overcoming their dislike (to put it mildly) of Microsoft was another problem altogether. He credits Don Bachs with the idea of having each attendee stand up, announce their name and company, and then say why they hated one of the following: Microsoft, Windows, or Bill Gates. "It gave everybody an opportunity to not only vent their displeasure, and kind of affirm that 'we're all Mac guys here and we all hate Microsoft, Windows and Bill Gates. But you know what? The reality of the marketplace is that we've got to support Windows. And now I suddenly realize that I'm not alone.'" They would see other people from notable companies, people whose articles they had read. And suddenly, they realized that there was no shame in developing for Windows as well as Mac. And always, Plamondon was careful not to bash the Mac, but only to emphasize the benefits of programming for Windows.

Before entering the seminar, each attendee was also required to take a short survey with questions like "How long have you been doing Windows programming?" "When do you expect to write your first Windows program?" Basic questions… and there were also questions like, "File management. Which platform has better file management?" "Which platform is more object oriented?" and, "Which platform has more motherhood and apple pie?" and whatever. And they filled out the same survey when they left. As a reward, they received a white t-shirt with black lettering that said, "Windows 95 sucks less," which was a direct rip-off of an Apple t-shirt that said, "System 7.5 sucks less." The Apple shirt, however, was white lettering over black, and with better typography and better quality cotton. "I did all that intentionally because it was the anti-shirt. Exactly the opposite of what Apple had done. Because I was making the argument that that was what Windows is. Windows is sort of the anti-Mac operating system in a variety of ways."*

Cameron Myhrvold remembers the "Windows sucks less" t-shirts well because he had to go to Brad Silverberg, who was running the Windows group at the time, and tell him what they were up to. "It was definitely, like oh my god, do I want to have this conversation?" Fortunately, Silverberg understood the purpose and Ok'd it. (Some years later, Alex St. John would take Plamondon's "anti-marketing" concept to the extreme and apply it effectively to gain developer support for DirectX, which ties the story directly back to our game narrative.)

Plamondon also got quotes from people who had attended the seminars, which he inserted into various magazines. The message was, "We love the Mac. We just love Windows, too. And so should you."

Plamondon was not the only one working to strengthen the Windows platform. Myhrvold recounts the efforts of Brian Moran, an evangelist working with UNIX developers. Moran wanted to start what he called a "special program," and Myhrvold was quick to tell him there was no budget for it. But Moran wasn't looking for money. His plan was to bundle up all the resources that Microsoft already gave away free to developers and, call-

**Plamondon says, "The developers who created the 'System 7.5 Sucks Less' t-shirts were shut down by Apple's marketing apparatus. "Think different," my ass. My shirt went on to win a "best T-Shirt of the Year" award (I don't remember from who)."*

ing it a "special program," he would get commitments from the UNIX ISVs in order to enter the program. It cost nothing, but appeared to give value to the developers.

Creating Opportunities

"The guys who competed with Microsoft applications group the most were guys who were kind of recalcitrant in wanting to adopt Windows. It does make sense, but of course that's what ultimately killed them because guys who didn't make that transition quickly and well, with good products, lost tremendous share."

–Cameron Myhrvold

Evangelists were often opportunistic, capitalizing on mistakes, changes of circumstances, or other moments of weakness. For instance, evangelist Todd Needham was going after a company called InterGraph, a company that, in Myhrvold's words, "famously hated NT." So Needham found an engineer at the company who was willing to do a skunkworks project in secret. "So Todd supported the hell out of him, and then, when the market was changing and Intergraph's sales were going down because of issues around UNIX and the growth of the NT workstation, he was able to help this guy unveil this fully formed NT port. So they did what Microsoft did back in those days, and that was you did whatever it took."

The Big Carrot

"You can't ignore that whatever Microsoft says is going to be the standard because they're so big, so influential, and have so much control of the platform, that if Microsoft says this is the way of the future, you have got to listen."

-Alex St. John

"It was just about carrots and sticks, right? You get this, or I'll hit you with this. And that was how I would see the '90s."

-Eric Engstrom

Microsoft's power ultimately became such that whatever technology they introduced, it was likely to become the standard, and the DRG used that perception to accomplish their goals. They shied away from coercion and worked mostly through inclusion or exclusion. For instance, they might typically invite companies to be part of an early adopter program for a new technology they were introducing. In describing a typical program, Plamondon says, "The early adopter program consists of us giving you a lot of information about the API, all the betas and the developer kits, and all the things you need, inviting you to a number of meetings with our engineers so that you can tell us in person what isn't working and walk them through the code to show them what isn't working—so direct developer-to-developer contact." As part of the program, the developer is asked to deliver a beta of their applications that support the new technology according to Microsoft specifications and to commit to having people demonstrate their product at Microsoft events. In exchange, Microsoft offered co-marketing support.

According to Plamondon, the early adopter program agreement was "just an agreement between two people in two different companies." Of course, they preferred to get someone at a director level to sign the agreement. However, there were no penalties for failing to live up to the agreement terms. It was entirely non-punitive. All that would happen is that if you didn't deliver what you promised, you wouldn't be invited to the next early adopter program, and presumably, your competitors would be invited.

"It's a carrot so big, it's a stick," says Plamondon. "We could take that same carrot and give it to your competitor instead, so that he could beat you over the head with it."

In cases where a company was dismissive or not interested in what they were selling, the evangelists would be very polite and thank them for their time, and then find their biggest competitor and take the offer directly to them. And when Microsoft backed the competitor, it had an impact big enough that the original company would think twice before turning Microsoft away again.

Plamondon liked to describe this in terms of the famous NFL player Reggie White, who was reputed to hit so hard that players would simply hit the ground when they heard his footsteps coming, rather than endure the pain of being hit by him. However, Microsoft didn't actually deliver a direct hit. They let a company's competitors do it for them.

Borland

Borland was another competitor that ended up in Microsoft's sites. Philippe Kahn was not a fan of Microsoft. It is useful to note that Borland was once the third largest software company in the world, behind Microsoft and Ashton-Tate, and Kahn was highly competitive. He wanted Borland to be number one. On the other hand, that made him a target.

Cameron Myhrvold remembers how Kahn responded to his evangelists when they would visit. "We'd go down there and talk to them, and then Philippe Khan would call Bill directly and say, 'I never want these assholes back.' He would say these completely outrageous things. Bill calls me to his office. 'I got this call with Philippe and he says, 'Every time you're down there, all you tell him is get out of the tools business.'"

The irony of this interaction is that it occurred almost immediately after Myrhvold and evangelist Bob Tanaguchi were down at Borland's Scotts Valley, CA offices offering to include a Borland compiler as part of a software

Doing or Withholding Favors

Plamondon offers another example of how the Big Carrot worked.

"At the time, Microsoft had tremendous power because people wanted to know what the latest and greatest was from Microsoft. And if your company knew what the latest and greatest was, or even more, what the new stuff would be in six months… if you had a head start on the information, and your competitor didn't, then you had an advantage that your competitor did not have, and therefore Microsoft had the advantage of being able to share this information with Competitor A—that is, product A—or with Product A's competitor. And I encouraged our guys to use that power to achieve Microsoft's objectives.

"So for example, there was a company that created Mac software, and I went way out of my way to help them produce a Windows version. I paid for consultants. I did a bunch of stuff to help them produce their Windows version. And then afterwards, I went to them and said, 'I would like a quote from you please that says something along the lines of, 'We produced this Windows version of our product, and now its sales are X compared with our Mac sales, which are Y, and we wouldn't have had that boost in sales if we hadn't produced a Windows version.' Whatever X and Y were, whatever the facts of the matter were, I just wanted them to say that. And they said, 'I'm sorry. We can't give you that quote because it might hurt our relationship with Apple.' And I said, 'Thank you very much. I appreciate your time.' And then sent around an email that said, 'Under no circumstances should anyone from Microsoft help this company do anything until they hear back from me. And they won't hear back from me for a minimum of six months.' So these guys are on the shit list. Don't lift a finger to help them. And if they are in a position to possibly be helped or possibly not, be sure they're not. Go out of your way to shit on them whenever possible.

"So three, four months pass, and they've been calling me, and I've heard contacts from other places in the company that they're trying to get hold of people at Microsoft, and so on. And after three or four months pass, I go ahead and take their call, and they go, 'Gosh. What happened? Suddenly, we aren't getting the help we used to be getting, and we became dependent on that help, and it's actually putting the company at risk, and what the hell happened?' And I said, 'Oh. Weren't you aware that denying me that quote would harm your relationship with Microsoft? Did you think that Apple was the only company with whom you had a relationship?' 'Oh. Gosh. We hadn't thought of it that way.' I said, 'Do you think of it that way now?' They said, 'Yes. Would you like that quote now?' 'Oh, I'd love to get that quote now. Thank you very much. I appreciate your volunteering that.'

There's this notion of reciprocity. If I do you a favor, I expect you to do a favor in return, and if you don't, there's no punishment. There's just not going to be any more favors. I'm going to remember that investing in you is not profitable to me, and I'll choose to invest in someone else instead. Because whoever you are, you have a competitor, and that competitor may return my favors."

-James Plamondon

developers kit (SDK) for a release of Windows NT. They didn't meet directly with Kahn, but with Brad Silverberg and Paul Gross, so it's possible that Kahn never knew about the offer. Back at Microsoft, however, the offer to bundle Borland's compiler, although a minor offense, it did not sit well with Gates. Steve Ballmer sort of condoned their actions while stating that he didn't condone it. He said, 'I did not condone it, but I understand the motivation of trying to get these guys off the dime,' and as he often did, Gates fumed for a few minutes and then calmed down. In any case, Borland never responded to the offer.

And Silverberg? Yes, it was that Brad Silverberg, who was poached from Borland several years later to run the Windows division. It was no coincidence, however, as Myrhvold recalls. "It was one of the things that Steve Ballmer would ask me from time to time. Who do you think are the smartest guys that you call on? And Brad was pretty much top of the list."

Silverberg was not the only Borland employee to be induced to leave Borland, however. In a 1997 lawsuit, Borland claimed that Microsoft had hired away 34 key employees over the previous 30 months, offering huge signing bonuses, generous stock options, and even real estate.

Meanwhile, DRG's Craig Eisler and Eric Engstrom, began creating Foundation classes that would compete with Borland's DOS and Windows APIs. They then went to all of Borland's smaller, less successful competitors—companies like Symantec and Watcom, who were competitors of Microsoft's as well—and offered their support. Engstrom remembers telling them,"Hey. You don't have the scale and the infrastructure to compete with Borland for these big APIs. We'll give you ours for free. We'll share. You can adopt ours. Go ahead." They also issued joint press releases and further support in the form of marketing dollars. Fellow evangelist Alex St. John put it colorfully. "They used the smaller competitors to surround and peck them to death." St. John continues by observing, "And so, evangelism was not only being helpful and amazingly generous and positive to little companies that were struggling, like Symantec and Watcom, it was simultaneously a very effective strategy of bringing down a competitor without getting any blood on your hands."

Herding Buffaloes (Netscape)

"One of the stories I've heard about how Indians used to hunt buffalo in the Wild West, was not to go chase one with a spear. It was to surround them and then chase the whole herd off a cliff. And Microsoft sort of had that attitude about the market."

-Alex St. John

In addition to empowering a rival's competitors, the DRG employed tactics that were designed to help their major competitors do something stupid. As St. John describes it, "One of the things that James (Plamondon) used to teach us, which was incredibly true, was that to destroy a major competitor requires two things. One, that you have to have amazing execution to take them out and two, they have to fuck up. You can't take out a kingpin—a leader in a market—without them first making a mistake, so one of the biggest elements of DRG strategy was pressuring competitors to make a mistake. A lot of what Microsoft did and said was, again, whooping… making a lot of scary noises to cause people to panic and run in the direction of the cliff."

Skipping ahead a few years, Netscape was Microsoft's prime target in the early browser wars. According to St. John, "Netscape was a fascinating example of a company that owned it. Clearly owned it. Dominated it. There was no good reason that Microsoft should have been successful at running them off the cliff." And yet, somehow, Netscape did run right over the proverbial cliff. How?

Cameron Myhrvold remembers being invited to a meeting with Netscape that his brother Nathan had set up. He wasn't able to attend, but reports that at that meeting the Netscape representatives were told that if they didn't do as Microsoft demanded, they would not get any support from Microsoft. (Cameron) Myrhvold was furious. "That would run entirely contrary to what I would have done, and of course it was my job, so he's saying that you won't get the information from Cam's group that you need to build a great browser, and that's absolute bullshit. That never would happen. I would not let some guy like Dan Rosen tell me what to do, and if I'm going to give that same level of support to Borland and Lotus and Word Perfect and every other competitor that Microsoft had, I certainly was going to do that for Netscape. And if I'd been at the meeting,

I would have said that." This approach was the opposite of the DRG way of dealing with things.

The DRG strategy started with examining Netscape's strengths and weaknesses. They had the best browser and the market cornered, but one weakness was their price point. According to Myhrvold, they charged their corporate customers, mostly telcos, $13 a copy while the telcos were providing their service at anywhere from $19.95 to $29.95 a month. With their expenses, it was a low margin affair, and according to Myhrvold, that $13 per copy was "more than their profit per subscriber for the first year." On the other hand, the early versions of Internet Explorer were inferior, so how could they gain any market share against Netscape and make any money?

At the time, Myhrvold had been put in charge of a sales group focused on interactive TV, a pet project of Craig Mundie, and ultimately an expensive disaster. So in a meeting with Bill Gates and other senior executives, he said, "We should get the hell out of this. It makes no sense. The only partner we have left for interactive TV has no interactive TV license—NTT in Japan. This is a science experiment, and it's costing the company tens of millions of dollars a year. Meanwhile, there's this thing called the Internet, and we should be all over supporting ISPs, because every client is a computer."

Mundie "blew a gasket," but Gates agreed and refocused Microsoft's efforts toward going after ISPs. Meanwhile, Myhrvold was thinking about strategies. He could try to sell early versions of Internet Explorer for less than $13 and undercut Netscape. But what was the right price point? He considered selling it for a dollar. "If the other guy can get twelve dollars, thirteen dollars, I can get a buck a copy.' And then a month later, 'Well, maybe I can get 50 cents a copy.' You know, ultimately I couldn't give the god damned thing away for free." Even giving away the browser, even reaching out directly to the top 500 ISPs in the world, "we came up empty handed."

Not until IE 3 (released on August 13, 1997) did they begin to glimpse some success. Under a new product manager—Ben Slivka—they got one great account—Time Warner—"and that was the beginning of the end because people realized, why am I sending all of this money to Netscape every year, and I've got this free option?"

Even though Microsoft was beginning to establish IE as a potential competitor, Netscape was still the dominant browser and could likely remain so if it played its cards right. But as the DRG continued to put pressure on and to convert more accounts, the people at Netscape began to feel the pressure. According to Myhrvold, "There's a whole bunch of mistakes that Netscape made, and in fact, with most of Microsoft's competitors in the past, what you kind of tend to do is you get up close behind them with your lights on and they drive off the road. People freak out." In the end, the combination of a free browser of increasing quality and a few mistakes by Netscape, and in time Internet Explorer took over the market, but the road to success was not only about price points and making mistakes.*

Although IE had gained considerable market share by late 1997, Netscape was still dominant. In order to overtake Netscape, Microsoft was forced to bundle IE with Windows 95 and later with Windows 98. In addition, they made some hardline deals with hardware manufacturers that gave IE clear advantages over their competitors. Owning the operating system was their ace in the hole, but their practices ultimately got them into trouble with the U.S. Department of Justice. There were also other anti-Netscape projects in the works, but all that comes later.

The story of Netscape was not the only example of a dominant company being herded off the cliff. Myhrvold also relates the story of Word Perfect, which was the dominant word processor at the time Microsoft was trying to establish Word, and Word Perfect felt the pressure and began committing a series of strategic errors, prompting Gates to say, "Oh my god. It's stunning. We could not have scripted a better augur into the earth strategy for Word Perfect than what they've executed over the last 24 months."

**According to Plamondon, "One of the reasons IE3 succeeded in the market was because it had a great Mac version. It had a great Mac version because it was written by the ClarisWorks development team. They had left Claris* en masse *after Apple refused to let them use OLE 2.0 to integrate their constituent apps, insisting that they use OpenDoc instead. I had worked closely with the ClarisWorks team for over a year, giving them a ton of support, to ensure that their OLE 2.0 version worked flawlessly. Apple was furious at ClarisWorks' "traitorous" behavior. They told the team: "We own you. YOu will do as we say." But instead, the team called my up at the end of an offiste meeting, and said that "we have all decided to join Microsoft." I called the VP of HR, who had a heart attack. This was around the time of Borland's competitive hiring lawsuit. She said we couldn't hire the team en masse...but we interviewed them individually, skimmed the cream, and formed the IE3 team from them. Netscape's Mac version sucked. IE3's didn't. That, plus being free, was a compelling advantage."*

-7-
The Disruptor

"If you're going to look up evangelist in the dictionary, of course they're going to give you an ecclesiastical definition, but if they gave you a tech definition, they should have a picture of Alex there."

-Cameron Myhrvold

"We were kamikaze nerds, damn it. We'd throw ourselves on the grenade. We'd do whatever it took to win."

-James Plamondon

The person who probably jumped the most grenades in Microsoft history had to be Alex St. John, a man who embodied genius, audacity, tenacity and foolishness almost in equal measure, along with a prodigious talent for disruption. With Craig Eisler and Eric Engstrom, he waged a war inside of Microsoft that changed the course of the company and, in some very real ways, made it possible for Xbox to happen.

One thing leads to another…

St. John grew up in Alaska in an extremely rustic setting. He got his first exposure to computers and programming hanging around the University of Alaska's library. While his father was on campus working on his PhD, St. John was "playing games on a 300 baud teletype and burning through reams of printer paper playing Super Star Trek, while the graduate students struggled to get their early chess programs to work by loading boxes of punch cards into the punch card reader."

Eventually, St. John's family moved into a log cabin that came complete with electricity, which he observes "greatly facilitated the use of a computer." He received a Commodore VIC-20 for Christmas when he was 14 and immediately began copying game code from tech magazines. His first original game was what he calls a 1981 version of Diablo, with a single-pixel protagonist, "randomly generated dungeons of lines, asterisk treasures and scary single red pixel monsters." Living without television through the long Alaskan winters left little to do but read and program.

First Taste of Civilization—Rejected

When he was 16, St. John's father moved to Amherst, MA, taking his son with him, but St. John, even as a teenager, was furiously independent and headstrong. "I got dropped into a public school, hated it, dropped out, and hitchhiked back to Alaska where I lived in the woods for a year." Despite his lack of formal education, St. John was able to test his way into an electrical engineering/computer science program at the University of Alaska, but after getting married at 19, he dropped out of college to satisfy his new wife's desire to be closer to her family in Boston.

Going to Hell

The first thing on St. John's agenda after arriving in Boston was to find a job, but he had issues. He describes his personal self-assessment and world view after entering what he calls "civilization" as, 'I'm undereducated, therefore I must be stupid. I have to compensate for that somehow."

At St. John's first job interview with Linotype Hell Graphics, one of the interviewers asked him what programming languages he knew, to which he answered that he knew 14 programming languages, listing them out one by one. The incredulous interviewer then pulled out a 200-page book, slid it across the desk and asked, "Well then, how long do you think it would take you to learn PostScript?" After thumbing quickly through the book, he answered, "Well, it's a dictionary based language like Forth… a week." The interviewers were, to put it mildly, skeptical. "I remember they looked at each other and they laughed, like isn't this kid funny, but I'm glad he thinks that. 'Sure kid. Knock yourself out. Show us what you know in a week.'"

When St. John returned a week later and announced, "I know it," the manager he met with regarded his statement with the expected skepticism, but agreed to give him a job working under their resident PostScript expert who had been trained at Adobe and had been using PostScript for years. The idea was that St. John could not possibly know PostScript, but that he might be capable of learning from their expert.

Who's the Expert?

Working under the "expert" didn't go according to script—PostScript or any other script. It turns out that the "expert" had some deficiencies. "He was constantly struggling with PostScript, and he'd call me over to show me a problem, and I'd go, 'Oh, you've just got to do that,' and fix it." After a couple of weeks, St. John began to struggle with that familiar world view of inferiority that he carried around. How was it that he already knew how to work with PostScript better than a guy who's really "seasoned and experienced"?

As it became clear that St. John knew what he was doing, he was placed in a customer support role for a PostScript RIP (raster image processor) clone that had been licensed from a company called Hyphen and then developed around an Apollo UNIX workstation by a team of engineers in Kiel, Germany. The problem with supporting customers of this million dollar product was that, in St. John's words, "It was a piece of shit… just worked like crap."

St. John tried to work with the German engineers, even pointing out the major bugs in their code, but they refused to recognize any shortcomings in the software. In a German accent, he quotes them: "The product is not designed to operate outside those specifications. Tell the customers they are not using it as required. It is not supposed to support that." He might as well go back to the customers and tell them, "The Germans say fuck you, but thanks for the millions of bucks…"

Making it Work

Of course, this translated into job insecurity. He was thinking "Oh my god. It's broken. I can't make it work. If I tell the customers I can't fix it… I can't do anything about it… I'll be fired. They'll find out that I must not be smart enough to solve these kinds of problems because I don't know how to deal with this."

St. John's solution was to take the broken jobs his customers sent in and spend his nights recoding them. "I would modify the code in the job to work around the bugs in the RIP manually and then hand the job back to the customer, rendered, just to make it work."

One of several problems to this approach was that it meant little to no sleep. To keep his job, St. John was working day and night. The other problem was that he was the only one getting results. The other support people were getting destroyed. And so his manager came and said to him, "Hey Alex, we're sending you to New York. They're impressed as hell. Everybody demands you at this point. They want you to drive to New York to train all the other support people to do what you do." At which point St. John was forced to admit that there was no way he could train people to do what he did. "Rick, I'm fixing the fucking postscript jobs," he said. "These poor people can't code at all. There's nothing I can do."

The Harlequin Gambit

At this point, desperate for a solution, he told his manager, "You know, there's another group in the company that's using the PostScript RIP from a British company called Harlequin." Then he added, 'It's a piece of shit, too, but maybe they can fix the bugs."

"So I call up this little English company that also had a shit RIP and got in contact with Jeremy Kenyon, who was running that product, and I said, 'Look. I've got this many of these RIPs out here. How much do you sell them for?' And he says, 'Fifteen hundred bucks each.' Nothing. I could give them away. So I said, 'Listen, if you can run these jobs that I'm going to send you and send me RIPs that run them, I'll buy them from you at fifteen hundred bucks a pop.' And he agreed. And so I'd get a broken job, I'd send it to Harlequin, they would fix a version of their RIP according to my specifications, that ran the job the way it's supposed to, and send it to me. I would replace the German RIP on the Apollo workstations with a Harlequin RIP, and the jobs would magically work."

"It was a secret. Nobody but my manager and I knew I was doing this. By the time I got to Microsoft, I was doing this on purpose. But this was the first time for me, and I was completely ignorant, which is why it's so funny. I was terrified every day that I was going to get found out and fired." Although this was the first time, it was definitely not last time that St. John would come up with a brilliant, but definitely not kosher, solution to a problem.

A Talent for Disruption

The relationship with Harlequin was working so well that soon they had St. John writing the product specifications for them. One of the ideas he came up with was something he called a "parallel throughput pipeline," which he modeled in a spreadsheet. The engineers at Harlequin followed St. John's instructions and produced the parallel processing software he had designed. St. John then began inserting it into the broken systems. And something happened… "Not only was I replacing the Hyphen RIPs secretly and everything was working magically now, but the performance went through the roof—something like ten times the productivity with this new architecture I was slipping in there. And suddenly these things were selling like crazy." St. John's little program, which Linotype considered a low-end product, was out-performing the million dollar systems and beginning to drive them out of business.

St. John had no idea what he was doing, nor did he yet realize what talent for disruption he possessed, but his little "low-end" parallel RIP processor completely disrupted the PostScript printing world. "I hadn't been there that long… maybe six, seven months, and my manager was handling all this and kind of shielding me from it, so I only imagined the conversations that took place. 'Listen, you guys. I gotta tell ya. I got a freak of nature kid here who is just building the shit and replacing it and he designed this product, and we've been replacing your German shit with something over here, and that's why it all works. And the kid doesn't know what he is.'"

And within a few months, everybody in his entire office was laid off, except for him and his manager. "I remember rollerblading around the empty cubes in my office, just stupid-go-lucky, while my manager must have been sweating bullets in his chair, going 'Oh my god. I'd be out of here like everybody else—this late in my career—if this fucking kid hadn't saved my ass.'"

Job Offers

The president of Linotype, with several executives, flew in to meet with Alex and offer him a job in Germany. "I'm trying to remember the phrase, but it was basically like, to work for the Germans so that they could teach me the ways of building great products. The same Germans I hated. Just hated. And so the proposition was, 'We're going to pay all your expenses to move to Germany and work for these guys to help develop…' It was portrayed to me like a 'you're going to learn from them' kind of thing.' At the same time, I'd embarrassed the crap out of them. I made them look so bad, so whatever politics was going on, I definitely made a mess. So they were trying to persuade me to move, and I resigned. I said, 'No. I'm outta here. Goodbye.'"

Harlequin

Shortly after quitting Linotype, St. John landed a job with SciTech, who wanted to send him to Israel, but Harlequin's founder and CEO contacted him and made him an offer that he couldn't refuse. He would move to Cambridge, England and run their PostScript RIP development. And he didn't know it yet, but while he was at it, he would help destroy Adobe's high-end RIP business. "El cheapo off-the-shelf Macs and PCs were blowing away their sixty and hundred thousand dollar proprietary hardware RIPs. So Harlequin did enormous damage to Adobe's own high-end business before Microsoft recruited me. The funny thing, looking back, at the time it was all a great adventure and I didn't know what was going on, but Microsoft… They definitely realized what I was, and then it was probably about that time that I realized, oh wait a minute, I've got some secret sauce here."

St. John recalls that his time at Harlequin was both enlightening and amazingly fun. His desk was in the entry hallway of Barrington Hall, a great manor house set in the countryside where "you'd be sitting there coding and there'd be deer and bunnies running around in the fields." Among the leisure time activities were playing croquet, juggling flaming torches, laser tag, and underground larping—having mock battles "beating the crap out of each other and running around in the dark" with latex weapons in the Chiselhurst Caves, which ran for miles and were "dangerous as all shit." He quips that "it's completely illegal to have that much fun in the United States."

But with all the fun, St. John gained enormous respect for the British engineers and their math skills, while gaining a good deal of notoriety as a contributor to periodicals like Color Publishing and Seybold Magazine. "The products had become famous in the RIP community, so I would write for these tech magazines, like I do now, on printing and publishing technology and color science and screening because I was an expert on all that stuff."

Microsoft

St. John left Harlequin in 1992 and went to work for ECRM, a high end laser image setter company in Boston. He had applied for a job at Adobe, but was told that he was overqualified for any jobs they had in Boston. His consulting work was paying well, but he was getting bored. Then, in late 1992, he somewhat reluctantly gave in to a recruiter from Microsoft and agreed to an interview in Redmond, against his wife's wishes; she wanted to stay on the East Coast.

He knew that Windows sucked as a publishing platform. On the other hand, he admired Microsoft, which he viewed as "the scrappy upstart challenging the evil corporate monopoly, IBM..." So he agreed to come for "a free all-expense-paid vacation to Redmond."

"I arrived in Redmond in December dressed in shorts and a t-shirt for an interview I had little interest in and knew nothing about. They put me through the famous Microsoft interview grinder of that era: eleven interviews in rapid succession each with a blend of different technical, logical and personality challenges."

Ken Fowles, who would become one of St. John's best friends at the company, asked what the ideal remote control would be. St. John suggested something with one button and maybe a thumb rocker switch. Cameron Myhrvold asked some questions about PostScript, and Brian Moran (while using a Bowie knife to pick his nails, although later Moran claims that it was probably a Spyderco), asked some technical questions about debugging protected mode and DOS interrupts.

All the while, St. John had no idea what job he was being interviewed for, and his confusion was actually reasonable, because the people who were interviewing him didn't know, either. "First and foremost, you were taught to look for talent and ability, and then figure out where we fit the guy into the company," said Cameron Myhrvold. And with St. John, he said, "There are people who understand things, and there are people who are able to explain them. And so one of the things in looking for evangelists is you needed guys who were articulate. You needed guys who were compelling. You needed guys who were good storytellers. And he absolutely could do that. All I had to do was start peppering him with questions about Harlequin and their business and Adobe and PostScript, and it became very quickly obvious that this guy had a remarkable handle on the technology, but probably even more impressive was how articulate he was in explaining it."

St. John left the interviews with a job offer and a proposed title—Senior Manager—but no idea what he would be managing—and stock options, which he discounted in the belief that Microsoft's rapid growth had slowed. Because his wife didn't want to move, he was still thinking of saying no.

That evening, he got a call from Ken Fowles, who invited him to come to Microsoft's Christmas party, which took place at the Seattle Convention Center, and to bring the family. "There were huge lines of people checking in. First people checked in at security, then they checked their coats, then they checked their children and were issued beepers coded to bands put on their kids who were subsequently ushered away by clowns to a huge circus they had set up in one of the halls."

Microsoft had taken over the entire convention center, and the party was on a scale unlike anything St. John had ever witnessed. He was told that there were probably 15,000 people in attendance, half of whom were millionaires from their Microsoft stock. "I confess to being pretty awestruck," he wrote later. "I didn't care what they wanted me to do, I just wanted to be part of it… and Ken Fowles had just given me my first lesson on what a Microsoft evangelist was supposed to do."

So St. John convinced his wife to try it for a couple of years and joined Microsoft to become, he eventually discovered, a publishing technology evangelist for the Developer Relations Group.

"Windows is Inferior"

St. John's talent for disruption did not abandon him at Microsoft. In fact, it flourished, and it only took three months on the job to make an appearance. It all began when his boss, Brad Struss, whom St. John described as a tall, soft-spoken kid with seemingly infinite patience, handed him the phone one day. On the other end of the line was a reporter from the very influential periodical *InfoWorld*. Everybody read *InfoWorld* in those days, including Bill Gates, but nobody had briefed St. John on talking to reporters. Struss told him that a reporter wanted to talk to a Microsoft executive about Windows as a publishing platform. "I didn't know at the time that one of my jobs was playing 'Microsoft Executive' as needed. Many evangelists had Microsoft business cards printed with a variety of titles they could deploy as needed in their various endeavors. I had no experience dealing with hostile media before so when I took the call I simply answered the reporter's questions honestly. The next day when I showed up to work I was greeted by Brad wearing his trademark ashen 'What have you done to me?' expression."

St. John opened his email that morning to a guaranteed career death sentence at Microsoft—an angry missive from Bill Gates himself, ccing every senior Microsoft executive, including Brad Silverberg, Paul Maritz, Cameron Myhrvold, his own managers and the head of Microsoft PR. As St. John remembers it, Gates wrote, "Where do you get off telling the press that Windows is an inferior publishing platform? You don't know what you're talking about and you shouldn't be communicating with anybody in the media about it. Windows is a superior platform to Apple at publishing and you were hired to get that message out." Gates had also attached the front page *InfoWorld* article entitled, "Microsoft Executive Acknowledges Windows is Inferior Publishing Platform."

Despondent, St. John decided to take a walk outside in the beautiful, park-like setting that was the Microsoft campus. He wasn't seeing the beauty. All he was seeing was disaster. What was he going to tell his family? He had just signed a lease. What would he do about that? Would they have to return to the East Coast?

After a time, his thoughts and emotions began to change. "I think it took me a good hour of walking to work past denial, and deep into despair such that by the time it was starting to get dark and I felt compelled to return to my office if for no other reason than to pack my desk. Rage had begun to set in. F**K IT! If I'm fired anyway I might as well respond to Bill G's email!"

Here's what he wrote (unedited):

From: Alexstjo@Microsoft.com

To: Bill Gates and everybody else on this F**KING thread...

Bill I'm really sorry if I let you down, I really screwed up, I had no idea how to handle that situation and I said some really stupid things. I absolutely understand if this is my last day at the company. Obviously even if I felt that our publishing technology was obviously inferior to Apples I shouldn't have acknowledged it outside the company.

That said, you don't really believe that Windows is competitive with Apple do you? I don't know who you've been listening to but I absolutely know what I'm talking about and Windows is a complete disaster as a publishing platform compared to Apple and absolutely everybody in the industry you hired me to represent knows it. You don't have a single "publishing" expert here at the company; every single person I have met related to publishing in the technology teams is little more than a 300dpi HP laser printer expert. My credibility with that community wouldn't stand a snowballs chance in hell with that community if you expect me to take the position that Windows is great when everybody but apparently you KNOW otherwise.

St. John then proceeded to list all the specific problems Windows publishing had in comparison with Apple's.

This email prompted a response, but not necessarily the response that St. John had anticipated. He still fully expected to get fired, but in a way he didn't care anymore. He was relieved. Why pull his punches if he was going to be gone anyway? His relief was short-lived, however. Gates had fired off another email, this time saying, "This new guy we hired to be our Publishing Evangelist tells me you people have been lying to me all these years about how great our publishing technology, which has been responsible for our abysmal performance against Apple in this space all along. I'd like to know how the issues he's raised are being addressed by your teams going forward."

The reaction was swift and furious. "Imagine if you will the collective ire of dozens of senior Microsoft Executives with thousands of years of industry experience and credibility and huge teams of the most elite, highest IQ engineers Microsoft's rigorous recruiting standards could hire getting called 'stupid' and/or 'liars' in front of Bill Gates and having Bill apparently agree. I got POUNDED."

Brad Silverberg, who would soon become one of St. John's senior benefactors, had a decidedly strong reaction to the situation. According to Cameron Myhrvold, "Brad called me up and he's like, 'Cam, who the fuck is this guy?' And I was like, 'Here's his background. He hasn't been here this long. I think he really knows his stuff.' So he says, 'Well I've got to meet him. Get him over in my office.'" When they met, according to St. John a wild-eyed Silverberg said, "'If you ever speak to the press or Bill Gates again about my product without first discussing it with me, so help me…' or something to that effect."

Not for the last time, however, St. John's management team and DRG colleagues rallied to his defense. He continued regular email correspondence with Gates and over a period of several months of shouting matches and recriminations, he proved, again and again, that he knew what he was talking about. As he put it, "I had somehow clawed my way from the bottom of the pile to the top."

Vanquishing the Experts

Along the way from the bottom to the top, St. John went head-to-head with some of Microsoft's top printing experts, including Dennis Adler and David Snipp.

St. John expresses nothing but admiration for Adler. "I think of Adler as being in some sense the Microsoft employee archetype. Incredibly smart, incredibly confident, incredibly determined, and absolutely no bullshit. In terms of somebody that got shit done, he was that way." St. John's admiration wasn't reciprocated at first when he completely disrupted the publishing group's schedules and caused him personal embarrassment. So Adler, along with Eric Bidstrup, pushed back, but, as St. John explains, that was what he was expected to do as his domain was being challenged. "Microsoft arrogance aside," observes St. John, "in that environment I think you had to be that arrogant to survive. So I forgave people for the arrogance because they got beaten on from every direction. So if you weren't tough, you couldn't make it. He was a tough guy."

Adler was tough, but practical. This was another trait that St. John recognized and admired. "If you had the winning argument, they would adapt. They'd usually do it very efficiently. They do the most minimal thing they had to. If you won an argument rationally and logically, then they would do the most logical, rational, minimal thing they could do to accommodate your correct point of view. You could say that I came in, surprised them, threw over their apple cart, would not be stopped. Would not be shut up. No amount of pressure on me to shut the hell up, no amount of 'we're too busy. We don't have time. We don't have resources.' I got past all of that with them, and ultimately, they went and did the Adobe deal. They involved me in all of the planning and reviews, and they overhauled all of that print stuff with a very tight schedule."

Besides Adler, there was David Snipp—THE printing guru at Microsoft at the time—the one that everybody deferred to. And he was also in St. John's way.

"I had to destroy his credibility to get anything done. And he was a nice guy." Snipp was an undeniable HP 300dpi laser printer expert, but that was about it, and he was no match for St. John. Like many of the senior people at Microsoft, Snipp did not appreciate being challenged by this brash young man, and so he called a meeting intended to solidify his leadership in the printing division once and for all. St. John recalls that it was a huge meeting with people from both the Windows NT and Windows teams as well as all the significant people from the printing side.

"I decided I was going to go into that meeting and break him. Just break his credibility in front of everybody. What happened was that he was talking about PostScript, and he was going on… this PostScript and that PostScript, and I said, 'You're talking about PostScript level 1.'

"And he goes, 'Yeah.'

"And I go, 'You know the standard for PostScript is Level 2, and it changed in 1987.'

"And he kind of blinked and said, 'What?'

"I go, 'All modern PostScript printers that are being manufactured are PostScript Level 2. The PostScript drivers that you are supporting and developing for Windows 95 and NT are based on 1987 PostScript standards. Have you even read the PostScript Level 2 book?'

"And he said, 'What?'

"And I pulled out this massive red book, and I threw it across the table at him, in front of him and said, 'This is the fucking PostScript Level 2. This is the standard from 1987, from Adobe, for PostScript. You had this entire company building obsolete printing architecture. Apple's fucking PostScript drivers are based on this, and you don't even know it exists?'

"And I just laid into him in front of everybody, and people's eyes went wide. And I just ranted at him in frustration, going, 'Dude. You go pick up the fucking manual. Here's what it is. This is what it's about. The drivers are 32 bit… duh duh duh.' I just raved at him. And after that he was done. People quickly concluded, 'That guy doesn't even fucking know what he's talking about compared to St. John. Whatever Alex says is gospel, and you fucking don't argue with Alex, or he'll destroy you in front of everybody.'"

Soon after that confrontation, Snipp left Microsoft, and although St. John says he feels bad about what he did to the man—"he was a nice guy"—he still believes he had to do what he did. "The nice thing is that Bidstrup and Adler, they just got on board and adapted. So, unlike Snipp, who couldn't learn, they didn't need to be killed because they got with it. Snipp was set in his ways, and that wasn't going to change, and unless his reputation for being the expert got broken, nothing was going to change."

St. John intimidated, bullied and out argued everyone until it became clear that he had won the Windows publishing battle. As he later recalls it, "I wreaked havoc inside Microsoft 'influencing' the product groups to re-design the Windows 95 and Windows NT graphics and print architectures. I brought Adobe in to strike a deal with Brad Silverberg to write the PostScript driver for Windows 95 in exchange for Adobe application support for Windows 95. I recruited senior product managers from Aldus to run the Windows NT print group. We cloned Adobe's Type 1 font technology to kill Adobe's ATM product (ruthless), licensed Kodak's color calibration technology, persuaded every major desktop publishing application developer to port to Windows 95 and booked Bill Gates to keynote the annual Seybold conference. By 1994, the impact of the work had been so sweeping that I was quite possibly the first Microsoft evangelist to succeed himself out of a job. Windows 95 would have every major desktop publishing and media authoring product available for it by 1995. Apple would lose its dominance in media authoring."

On the other hand, he adds, "In retrospect I never recall a day arriving when it occurred to me that I was not going to get fired the next morning and moderated my 'F**K-You I'm out of here!' attitude appropriately. It seemed to be working for me… Brad on the other hand seemed to age rapidly during the time he was my manager for reasons I could only imagine…"

Although St. John began a goat and emerged a hero, this was just the prelude to his career at Microsoft, and the best—and the worst—was yet to come.

Yelling With a Smile

"The key to winning a Microsoft technology debate was a mixture of being right, being confident and articulate, and being aggressive enough to force the issue but not angry enough to cause people to shut-down. You had to get that balance right."

-Alex St. John

Alex St. John was learning on the job. In his put-down of David Snipp, he admits that he yelled because "I was trying to burn him out of his home… so to speak." So even though it wasn't truly personal, it must have seemed that way to Snipp. Over time, St. John refined his approach. "When you get 'mad' in front of people it suggests a lack of confidence and loss of control. When you yell 'With a smile' it's scarier because you're in control, you're confident and you're obviously enjoying yourself. This style of debate has the property of being charismatic and appealing to people. It allows them to change their positions because they WANT to be on your side of the argument, and you've made it clear that you aren't really mad at them while you are arguing with them. It leaves the door open to resolution of the disagreement."

According to St. John, this is an important "nuance" that printed accounts often miss, pointing out that it was a fairly common type of argumentative style used by the Microsoft's executive leadership, including Gates, Ballmer and Myhrvold. "You hear all these stories about how they yelled at people and in print it looks very bad... the missing nuance is that very often they did this with a smile that suggested that this was just a debate among friends and that by challenging you they were inviting you to change their minds. That missing nuance is important to really understanding why these people were actually effective leaders and NOT simply bullies."

"Of course you know I love being described as 'vanquishing' anything... Who doesn't? But I'd like to think that a big part of my influence came from winning respect... sometimes by employing a certain measure of fear along with expertise and certainly by making myself impossible to ignore. You didn't get the opportunity to earn important people's respect at Microsoft if you didn't cut through the noise in their day to become the issue they had to deal with next."

On his relationship with Bill Gates, St. John observes, "While everybody was beating on Gates' door for influence, I had no idea I had a lot of influence with him at that age. I just took it for granted that Bill listened carefully to what I told him. I was loud and brazen and wouldn't shut up, and he seemed to pay a lot of attention to that in retrospect. But at that age, I didn't think anything of it. I yelled at everybody."

Insightful Yelling

Of course, Gates was also known for his outbursts, and almost everyone I interviewed had witnessed at least one of them. And everyone has nothing but praise for the man. Business development specialist Chris Phillips recalls his experiences with Gates: "I've been screamed at by Bill, and been sworn at and told that I was an idiot, and blah, blah, blah, and all those things are true. He'd get pissed and be that way… when you had Bill engaged, even when he was yelling at you, you were like, 'Wow. That's insightful.' If you could put aside your emotions and actually the bullshit that he was screaming about, you could get to where, 'I hear his point.' Especially I learned that in legal stuff, because he was a great legal mind. But all those things are true about him. A complex man. But when it came to strategy and seeing markets and stuff, Steve and he are pretty uncanny in that regard. Very few people I've met over the years can operate like that."

Games Evangelist

"James Plamondon: 'What do you want to do?'

Alex St. John: 'What I want to do is games.'

James Plamondon: 'Why don't you go fuckin' do games? You don't have to be Mr. Publishing. The worst they can do is fire you, and you're already up for that, so why don't you just go do games?'

Alex St. John: 'Do you think I could go do games?'

James Plamondon: 'Why don't you go do games?'"

After his success on the publishing side, his manager offered him a new job, as the MAPI evangelist. MAPI was the Messaging Application Programming Interface, which was part of Microsoft's mail messaging. "I couldn't have been less excited about it." The idea was that St. John would work on MAPI until after the Windows 95 launch, at which point the powers that be would figure out what to do with him next.

Meanwhile, Rick Segal was looking for a games evangelist. Once Windows 95 launched, there would be a huge need for evangelists because, basically, Windows 95 was going to break a lot of existing DOS games. Previous versions of Windows had actually been built directly over DOS, but Windows 95 was not. There was something called the DOS emulation box, but, according to St. John, DOS emulation would break probably 95 percent of currently working DOS games, which would, of course completely destroy the DOS games market, and with it, basically the whole concept of games for PCs if Windows couldn't take up the slack. St. John describes the position essentially as going to the game companies and saying, "Go test your games on our new DOS extender, or you're just going to get obliterated."

St. John applied for the job, as did Craig Eisler. Eisler was already the tools evangelist, and certainly qualified. Eisler was working on, in St. John's words, "killing Borland," and he was the author/creator of Watcom's 32-bit DOS extender, which was a tool that all games used at the time in order to run in 32-bit mode in DOS. "So he in some sense was already a game industry celebrity because he made the technology that everybody used to extend DOS, and was well known for that."

On the other hand, St. John had proved himself unstoppable and persuasive in his Microsoft debut, and he had some knowledge of 3D graphics, which everybody knew was going to be very important. Eisler was already doing a great job as the tools evangelist, and St. John was clearly wasted working on MAPI. Also, "I think Rick also favored me because I was crazier than Craig, and he liked that…"

According to St. John, what flipped it in his favor in the end began with the announcement that Intel was developing its own multimedia architecture, including a whole family of sound and 3D multimedia APIs called Native Signal Processing (NSP). They asked Microsoft to send a speaker to their event, which caught VP Paul Maritz by surprise, again according to St. John, who states that Maritz needed somebody to go to the event and represent Microsoft. The mission, however, was really to find out what Intel was up to. Rick Segal tapped St. John for the job, telling him, "I've got to send somebody on a mission to stand on stage at this Intel event in two days and say some stuff that sounds supportive without looking foolish, and I need to find out what Intel is doing."

So St. John's real job was to study Intel's product and write a strategic analysis for Maritz, which he did, saying in effect that Intel was attempting to usurp control of Windows media architecture with software emulation. In his assessment, he said that Intel was "trying to completely kill the market for hardware and hardware drivers that offload processing from an Intel CPU. It will all be on the CPU. Everything was software emulated and cumbersome. And I recommended that the counter strategy to that would be for Microsoft to provide much more robust driver support for proprietary hardware acceleration, thereby fostering a market for competitive proprietary hardware that outperforms Intel's solution…" In essence, "If you want to prevent Intel from being able to replace all of your shitty multimedia features with software emulation, which is possible because they are so crappy and primitive, the way to do it is make them sophisticated, create lots of hardware vendors that depend on it, and then Intel will have a hard time replacing it with shitty software emulation."

(Under pressure from Microsoft, Intel ultimately abandoned its NSP initiative, which in turn ultimately became part of the famous antitrust suit against Microsoft, with assertions that Microsoft used its considerable influence unfairly to force Intel to back down. Microsoft's lawyers, meanwhile, asserted that Intel abandoned NSP because it was an inferior solution. (*http://www.businessweek.com/microsoft/updates/up81110a.htm*)

St. John credits his actions around NSP with getting the job. He also describes his rival as "a machine and a human calculator and a genius," then he laughs and states, "but his charismatic skills are a little more limited." But Eisler was not just a rival, he was a friend. Along with Eric Engstrom, the three regularly got together in the mornings to lift weights and shoot the breeze. In the aftermath, Eisler's relationship with St. John became somewhat chilly, but only for a while.

DOS is Doomed

The job St. John had competed to win wasn't an easy one. He had to go tell the game companies that they needed to test their games against the "DOS box" to see if they would be compatible with Windows 95. Of course, he really wanted to get them to make Windows games, but he knew how utterly crappy Windows was for games, so that wasn't really a viable option. And besides, he was from Microsoft. "I'm here to help you," just didn't seem to have the desired impact. In Alex' words, what they heard was, "And yeah, we're just going to destroy your little DOS world that you were able to live in while evil corporate blue giants took over the enterprise space. You were able to cozen down here in DOS and ignore us all. I'm here to tell you that I'm just destroying your world, and I want your support for that."

At a meeting at Mindscape, people began doing Darth Vader impressions and heavy breathing while he spoke. This reception became common enough that he adapted to it. "I'd come in with a smile and my business card and I'd say, 'Hello, I'm from Microsoft. I'm here to help you,' and get a laugh out of that, which became a necessary ice breaker. But I mean, I was the herald of doom for these guys. (no pun intended)."

The Unsung Hero of DOS Games

Meanwhile, at Microsoft, there was an effort underway to fix incompatible DOS games. It was basically the work of one man. "One of the fascinating things about Microsoft at that time is there were people there who were giants. I've never met their like since. Their intellectual capabilities surpassed anything I've met in recent times. I know they're out there still, but Microsoft had an amazing concentration of them. Chen was a little like an Asian Craig Eisler in that he had this sort of infinite capacity and patience for minutia."

The man St. John describes is Raymond Chen, who was given an insane mission. "So what Raymond Chen would have to do was, I'd bring these games in… I had boxes and boxes of them. Sometimes all the game developer could do was hand me a box and say good luck. We can't do anything about it. It's done. And Raymond Chen would have to write patches for each of these games in assembly language in order to get them to run in the DOS Box. There were thousands of them, and they were enormously complex, and it was very low level stuff, and he did this. One of the fascinating things—one of the things that won a lot favor in the game industry for Microsoft was the contact between myself and Raymond Chen and these early developers when they saw what this guy did to make their games work. Because he literally did heroics. Just mind staggering. You just go, that's… not only is it insane to do, nobody rational would ever undertake something incredibly tedious."

Another fan of Chen's was Origin Systems' director of technology, Zach Simpson. During that same period of time, Simpson had come to Microsoft to spend a month, along with Tony Braden and Frank Savage, working on Windows interfaces for just about everything, from joysticks to sound and graphics. He talked about how Chen fixed Ultimas 7 and 8.

"Ultima 7 was a DOS game. So was Ultima 8. Ultima used a horrific hack called Big Real Mode where you kicked the processor into this kind of strange mode that nobody used, and it was incompatible with the EMS managers, so it was a real nightmare of people calling in, trying to disable their EMS managers to get it to work. In Ultima 8 we used a 286 DOS extender that we hacked to be a 32-bit DOS extender, and that was a little more compatible with EMS and other DOS management at the time. Ultima 7 and 8 were before Chicago (Windows 95), and Microsoft paid a guy to go through the entire catalog of popular games in the world and make sure each one would run in DOS compatibility mode under Chicago, which is like the most horrific job I think anyone's ever foisted on somebody. And so that poor bastard got Ultima 7 to work, and we brought him flowers to tell him we appreciated his work. He was like a hero, and so you could still play Ultima 7 and 8 under Windows 95."

QuickTime

"Microsoft was just paranoid about QuickTime, and multimedia in general, because it was clearly the way computers were going, and Microsoft just wasn't able to dislodge QuickTime as the de facto standard."

-James Plamondon

Bill Gates always had something to worry about, and Apple was always high on his list. QuickTime was a good example of what concerned Gates. It was a multimedia technology that played videos on the Macintosh, and it did so better than any other video player at the time. In part because of Quicktime, but also because the Mac was a native windowed GUI operating system built into the hardware, Apple was dominating the emerging multimedia space. Microsoft's Windows was not as friendly to multimedia. Windows was built entirely in software that ran on top of the same hardware architecture that had originally run DOS. In the world of multimedia in the mid-90s, Microsoft was playing catch-up—and never quite getting there.

Of course, Microsoft was trying to make the best of the situation, including an attempt to play "let's make a deal." James Plamondon recalls a letter sent by Microsoft's president, Mike Maples to Apple with an offer. Maples' offer was that Microsoft would cede video technology to Apple, agreeing to make QuickTime the video standard in Windows (which would have cost Microsoft *beaucoup* bucks) in exchange for Apple abandoning its OpenDoc in favor of Microsoft's Object Linking and Embedding (OLE) technology. According to Plamondon, it was a case of "We'll give up our innovation if you give up your innovation," and it might not even have been legal. Apple did not take the deal.

There was even a video solution called Tiger that Craig Mundie was leading. According to Jason Robar, Tiger was a plan to serve up videos to people in their homes. One part of the plan involved creating a video server farm. Another aspect of the plan involved having NT Server in everybody's household, residing under their TV. But, as Robar puts it, "You're going to buy a nice $1500-$2000 computer to put underneath your TV, and everyone's going to do that because doesn't everyone have an extra $1500 to spend on TV?" Robar further observes that the people behind this idea were "guys who had already had huge stock options pay out." In fact, the head of the project was an audiophile whose speakers cost $20,000 each. "So his viewpoint of the consumer is very skewed." It was a visionary plan, but way ahead of its time, and of course it was never implemented, despite being in planning and development for several years.

To people like St. John and Plamondon, it was clear that attacking QuickTime directly was like, in *Art of War* terms, attacking a "fortified city". To attack the fortified city was sheer folly. "That's where the enemy had successfully predicted your attack and concentrated his forces to defend against it," said Plamondon. "However, strengthening the city's defenses necessarily meant weakening them elsewhere. The trick, then, to is get the enemy to fortify their defenses in Location A, and then attack in Location B."

So the question was, where do you attack if you want to win the battle? Not many people at Microsoft would have come up with a very viable solution, let alone one that seemed, at first glance, to be utterly loony, but when Rick Segal asked Alex St. John what he thought they should do about Quicktime, his answer was "Go after games."

According to St. John, Segal was in charge of "fucking up Apple's multimedia strategy", and he had a team of media evangelists whose primary purpose was to destroy Apple's perceived multimedia leadership. So when St. John suggested that they focus on games, where Apple was not focused or successful, Segal, who had no problem supporting crazy initiatives, said, 'Go for it.'" St. John gives credit to Segal saying, "He's the one who wound us up and turned us loose. He's the one that lit the fuse with us."

Following his conversation with Segal, St. John teamed up with his morning weightlifting buddies, Craig Eisler and Eric Engstrom, who, according to St. John, "had nearly finished crippling Borland in the Windows tools business and were also looking at new opportunities," and began to conspire to change the world—again.

St. John and the Calculated Approach

St. John puts the two faces of the DRG in perspective. "Again, when I talk about DRG and tell the funny stories about it, because those are fun for everybody to read, underlying it was a very, very calculated approach to using a small handful of people with a particular world view to have enormous influence on a market. When you think about the classic picture of a lever, DRG was one of the most leveraged forces that Microsoft ever contrived to influence markets. Historically, that's so important to understand about it, because people who never lived or experienced that, or who were outside of Microsoft, it's a constant mystery why platform companies like Microsoft are hugely successful. 'They're lucky.' 'I don't get it.' 'It's unfair.' Or, 'I think they're cheating somehow, but I can't figure out how.' And I know one aspect of it. You know. Just competing. Just fighting hard. Working the press and working the developers and platforms to make sure that you come out on top. To put it bluntly, we were monstrously good at it. And in that context, this was not a group whose job it was to design platforms. It was our job to sell the crap that Microsoft was making, and I call it crap because a lot of it was. And that's one of the reasons that's so interesting about the DirectX story, is that James taught us that our job is to get mindshare. Our job is to get people adopting and tangled in Microsoft APIs.

"When I looked back, I said wow. I was so young and dumb, I had no idea what I was a part of, or fully appreciating the scale of it. I was just in there going, 'Yeah. This is great. Whatever. I'm going to win.'

Nathan Myrhvold: the Semantic Level

With DOS about to disappear, what was the strategy going forward? Microsoft Research founder Nathan Myhrvold talks about the challenges for the game development community.

"There is always an issue in battling for attention; do you go for the next little version of the incremental thing, or do you go for something that's bigger? And there's no answer to that. There are cases where people try to create the grandiose system that doesn't actually work yet, and then there's also plenty of cases where they make the other mistake by going with what seems to be tried and true and immediate, and that misses the bigger picture. One of the issues, for example, with games, is that game companies and game developers in a certain era were the last of the hackers who wanted to do everything themselves. And it was a strategy that was completely destined to fail, but it was very strongly felt by them. And what I mean by destined to fail is, as you get more and more capable graphics chips, and as you start targeting different platforms, you need to raise the semantic level at which you program with the system. But the earliest games were written in assembly language by people trying to get every tiny gram of performance, not that performance is measured in grams, but you know what I mean. They were trying to do absolutely everything possible, so they had an attitude about what was the right thing to do. And all of the different approaches, whether it was OpenGL or DirectX or other things, were all different approaches to try to raise the semantic level of the interface to graphics. Because prior to that, all of the graphics stuff had been done by games very, very directly."

PART II:

TALKING TO THE METAL

-8-
The Importance of Graphics

"DirectX was a strange example of a strategy that succeeded in several ways at once when it was expected to fail on more levels than it did."

-Alex St. John

Since the dawn of personal computers there has been consistent growth in speed, memory (RAM and ROM), data storage, and graphics. The quest for better graphics dovetailed with the development of more and more powerful CPUs, specialized graphics chips and cards, and high-resolution monitors. During the 1980s, graphics on personal computers evolved relatively rapidly from the 4-color CGA (Color Graphics Adapter) standard in 1981 to the 16-color EGA (Enhanced Color Adapter) in 1984 to the 256 color VGA (Video Graphics Array) in 1987. These standards were succeeded by Super VGA and, finally, XGA, which could display at resolutions up to 1024 by 768. Following XGA, maximum resolutions continued to increase at a steady pace.

Computer graphics were never easy to produce in the early days of computing. Graphics pioneers had to work directly at the machine level or in assembly language to produce results. They worked not only with limited color pallets, but with extreme memory limitations. And yet, observing the evolution of graphics in computer games alone shows a steady improvement from the crude graphics of games in the 1970s, such as those seen on the Atari 2600, to vastly more detailed graphics in the 1980s, culminating with the 8-bit Nintendo Entertainment System. In the 1990s, 16-bit systems like Sega Genesis and Super NES were brighter, faster, and more detailed than anything before, and during the 1990s, games showed continual graphical improvement, not only on consoles such as PlayStation, Nintendo 64, and Sega's final console, the Dreamcast, but also on PCs. But achieving fast, efficient and competitive graphics on PCs did not come easily.

When it was released, Windows was an abominable platform for multimedia, and games especially, and while DOS was no picnic to work with, Windows was a sluggish quagmire by comparison. DOS programmers worked directly "to the metal," meaning that their games communicated directly to the CPU and graphics processors without any intermediary programs. As a consequence, although it was challenging to program games in DOS, it was possible with good software engineering to coax the maximum performance out of the hardware. Windows required various layers of programming of its own to manage the graphics and multiprocessing it required. Simply put, this meant that early Windows put a lot of layers of interference between the game programmers and the metal. Where these layers did not appreciably interfere with the operations of office types of programs, they were death to any game that required fast graphics and fast responses.

As graphics resolutions increased, opening the door for more detailed and realistic images, the next great innovation in graphics involved adding a third dimension. The concept of 3D graphics was not new in the 1990s. Programmers had figured out how to approximate 3D graphics with wireframes, such as in the 1980 Atari game Battlezone, and with perspective, as in the famous game Zaxxon, which faked the appearance of three dimensions. However, 3D graphics as we know it today, which is seen all through games, animation, and composited live-action films, evolved in steps.

Early workstations, like the ones from Silicon Graphics Inc. (SGI) were among the first to produce high quality 3D computer images and animations, but these workstations cost minimally hundreds of thousands of dollars and weren't meant for consumer use. 3D on home computers was feasible, however, but it would require new hardware and software solutions to become practical and affordable. Again, Windows was not ideally suited for handling 3D graphics, especially in games, but it was a priority at Microsoft that some solution be found. The path to fast graphics and 3D on the desktop spawned several competing visions at Microsoft. There was no single, unified initiative.

OpenGL

OpenGL was the main standard in the mid-1990s for 3D computer graphics. It had been developed by researchers and engineers at Silicon Graphics Inc., without doubt the most advanced 3D experts in the world at the time. It was developed from SGI's high-end workstation API, IRIS GL, but it was released as an open standard in 1992 by its developers, Mark Segal and Kurt Akeley.

OpenGL represented a consistent standard that would work with consumer machines. Where IRIS GL required certain hardware components to use all of its feature—components only found on SGI's high-end workstations—OpenGL allowed developers full functionality by using software solutions where the hardware was not present. Many people, including some at Microsoft, believed that supporting OpenGL was the best option for the industry and for Microsoft, but there were others who saw potential flaws with OpenGL, and they looked for new solutions—Microsoft solutions.

One of the flaws of OpenGL 1.0 was that, even though it was intended to work with lower-end systems, it did not work very well. Many developers, including id Software's 3D guru John Carmack, rejected OpenGL at first. Inside Microsoft, one of their talented and outspoken engineers, Chris Hecker, also rejected it at first, later changing his opinion. He wrote on his blog, "The conventional wisdom used to be that OpenGL was inherently slow—too slow for games—and that Microsoft had to design their own API." Hecker claims that nobody understood the technical issues at the time except for high-level workstation engineers who were not focused on 3D games. Like Hecker, Carmack eventually switched his stance and came to back OpenGL a few years later, escalating an ongoing battle against Microsoft's internal solution. However, back in 1994, Alex St. John had already begun searching for someone who could help him create a 3D API for Microsoft that could rival OpenGL.

WinG

In initially rejecting OpenGL, Hecker decided to create his own 2D drawing API, which he called WinG (pronounced "Win Gee"). Simply put, WinG was designed to help address performance problems with the Windows GDI allow development of faster games for Windows, which, because its graphics architecture had been designed for office applications, was simply not able to handle the demands of animation and interactive applications such as games.

Hecker wrote an explanation of how WinG worked in an article for Gamasutra in 1997. You can read it, complete with technical details at this address: *http://www.gamasutra.com/view/feature/3199/a_whirlwind_tour_of_wing.php*

As Hecker explains in his article, there were two ways to update screen data, through bit level transfer (blt) or page flipping (loading an entire screen in the background and then "flipping" it to replace the existing screen image). Windows did not yet support page flipping, so Hecker found a way to break the major bottleneck in the system by combining the functions of write-only HBITMAPs, which is where the graphic bits are stored, and Device Independent Bitmaps (DIBs), which can be accessed directly by applications, unfortunately resulting in bit transfers many times slower than DOS BitBlt. By creating a hybrid of the two, an object which he called WinGBitmap, Hecker was able to work around the limitations of Windows and achieve DOS level speed.

The WinG DOOM Demo

Hecker managed to produce a Windows 3.1 DOOM demo using WinG that turned heads at Microsoft and gained him a lot of notoriety. The demo video showed the ultra-popular 3D game DOOM running at an astounding 60 frames per second. After seeing the demo, Rick Segal turned to Alex St. John and said, "Alex, this thing's got people really excited. Can you turn it into a gaming technology?" And St. John said, "I betcha I can do something with that."

According to St. John, Hecker was brilliant, but there was a fundamental problem working with him. "He was very young, and he liked fucking around, and so he was having fun getting the fame and the attention for it, but there was a huge amount of really tedious work left to do to finish it... He didn't want to do it. He didn't have the attention span for it."

St. John, meanwhile, was evangelizing WinG, and he managed to get several game companies to use the technology. He'd tell them, "Hey, Hey, we've got this great new API. It's gonna make your games work great in Windows 3.1 that couldn't work before." There were about two dozen games scheduled for Christmas of 1994, all of which would need to have a completed version of WinG by September if they were going to be released in October, before the all-important Christmas season. There were some big names, too, including Disney's upcoming title, The Lion King.

According to St. John, Hecker simply flaked out. He wasn't working on it. Telling Rick Segal, "I've got a serious problem here. It's going to be a fucking train wreck if it's not finished on time," St John also spoke with Craig Eisler who Segal agreed to put on the project with Hecker. "Eisler is a giant," says St. John. "I've never seen an engineer who can do what Eisler could do. He's astounding. And what's amazing is that he was ever in evangelism at all, because of his programming talent. What a waste having a guy like that talk to anybody."

Eisler, along with Todd Laney, managed to get the project done on time, although according to St. John, Hecker was "bucking and screaming the whole way. He was very bitter about the treatment he got." *(I did reach out to Hecker, but he wasn't interested in talking about the old days.)*

Ultimately, 24 Windows 3.1 games launched for Christmas '94 using WinG. The most memorable of them was Disney's Lion King… memorable, but not in a good way as we will see.

Porting DOOM

While WinG was being finished, Alex St. John was thinking about DOOM. The problem with Hecker's video is that it only showed graphics, no gameplay, no networking. In other words, it was a graphics demo, not a full DOOM port. The logical next step was to complete the job by porting the entire game while continuing the development of WinG, which at the time showed considerable promise as a solution to the problem of bringing games to Windows—including the catalog of popular DOS games that would otherwise not work on the new platform.

Eisler, Engstrom and St. John were already planning to develop a set of APIs that would deal with computer data throughput, graphics, sound, devices (such as mice and joysticks), and connectivity. What better way to uncover the roadblocks and challenges of gaming in Windows than to take a fast-paced game like DOOM and find a way to make it work?

St. John had originally helped Hecker get the source code for DOOM from John Carmack at id, but as he closely watched over the porting effort, he saw all the problems they were encountering, "making me an authority on what was broken." St. John decided that porting DOOM to Windows should be an official project, so he made a deal with Carmack that Microsoft would do the work if id would publish the Windows version—providing that the port met his requirements.

St. John didn't have any engineering resources, so he approached Gabe Newell, who was working on set-top box UI at the Advanced Technology Group and asked if he could spare somebody.

Radio Silence

Newell (who later would co-found Valve Software) came up with an engineer and St. John put him to work porting the game. "The guy went radio silent. Weeks would go by and I would just hear nothing. Couldn't reach him. So finally I go by his office. The window was blacked out and you'd bang on the door, and it would be dark and he'd be sitting over his computer, like sweating… perspiring, and it would be too hot in his office and smelled stale like he'd been in there for several days. And he'd be really abrupt and angry. So you'd come in and go, 'Hey, how's that DOOM port going?' and he really didn't want anybody in his office. So I remember saying to Gabe, 'Hey, I don't know what's going on with your guy here, but he's not responsive, and he just seems holed up in here, and I have no idea whether he's working on it or not, or what he's doing.' A few days later, he turned up dead… drug overdose."

As dark as this story is, St. John still remembers how he got dinged for being late with his DOOM port and lost points on his performance review. "So the feedback is that I didn't deliver DOOM on time because my engineer died."

St. John managed to enlist Robert Hess, a senior engineer who he describes as "in a career stage well beyond having to indulge in coding." Together, Hess and St. John approached the minefield of porting DOOM to Windows 3.1. "I mean Windows 3.1… Oh my god."

Each time Hess would identify a problem, St. John would endeavor to figure out what was causing it. "So what would happen is he'd say, 'I can't get sound mixing to work and synchronize.' And so then I would have to become an expert on sound mixing and synchronizing, and try to figure out why and who owned it at the company, and who was working on it, and was it getting dealt with in Windows 95, and so forth."

Networking DOOM

Another issue that came up while trying to port DOOM to Windows was networking. At the time, the only networking protocol available in Windows was TCP/IP, and the problem with TCP/IP was that when it sent out a packet of information, it waited for confirmation from the recipient system that it had been received. This was a serious problem, as St. John explains: "To be nerdy, TCP/IP packets are guaranteed to be delivered.

That is, if I send a message to your computer, nothing else gets sent until your computer replies that it received that message. For games, that's a problem because, if a message doesn't get delivered, it's irrelevant anyway. I've got to deliver the next frame anyhow. The game can't pause for several seconds to make sure a packet arrives. It just gets the next one. So you needed the ability just blast packets over network and have them received without responding."

Jawad Khaki was the engineer in charge of Windows Sockets API, known more commonly as Winsock, which defined how Windows applications accessed network services. The problem was, the current implementation of Winsock only supported TCP/IP, and what St. John needed for DOOM networking was the User Datagram Protocol, generally referred to as UDP. St. John had worked with Khaki in his previous Microsoft incarnation in the Publishing division, and he knew that UDP was necessary for networking printers because using TCP/IP caused printer sharing to grind to a halt in the early days before print spooling.

What made UDP preferable over TCP/IP is that UDP didn't require any confirmation, handshake, or even previous contact with a recipient. It could send data continually and fast—exactly what was needed for fast-paced games like DOOM. Games always had to move on to the next thing immediately, and if one packet got dropped, it didn't matter. At the refresh pace of any game, a dropped packet, or even a few packet losses, wouldn't be noticed.

St. John was able to persuade Khaki to expose the UDP protocol in Windows 95, which opened the door for networking games like DOOM to work on Windows, and for many games to come… such as almost every Windows game today.

Another problem with networking was how difficult it was in those days to link people together. Early multiplayer PC games required physical computers to be sharing a local network, but St. John wanted to be able to let people play over the internet. The problem was that the process in place for such connections was what St. John called a "fucked diddley mess". "If you wanted to play one other player in DOOM over the internet, you had to call them on the phone—call your friend on the phone—agree on the IP address, do something to route the IP stack through to a modem, then you call each other with your modem and hang up, and the game would synchronize."

The solution, which became part of the DirectPlay API, was to use a lobby server. "The way to find other people and play DOOM and connect over a modem, was you called an internet server with your modem. The game would just do it from DOOM. It would call the lobby server, find players, get their modem information, disconnect from the internet, call their phone directly, exchange the information, and you were playing. That was state of the art network gaming back then."

An early game networking service called Dial-Up Wide-Area Network Game Operation—DWANGO—used this technology with support from Microsoft to set up DOOM tournaments all over the world. Microsoft worked with DWANGO to promote online tournaments like the Death Match 95 DOOM tournament that was conducted online and in various local venues around the country and even helped DWANGO expand into Japan, where they were very successful.

DirectPlay was important for its time, and it formed one of the core technologies behind the formation of the Microsoft Game Zone, with several ex-DRG people, such as Jason Robar and Adam Watts, going over to help form it. St. John even brought in an old friend from Harlequin—Ian Robinson—to help write the DirectPlay API.

Virtual Memory

Even when not networking, many games need to move data very quickly, but Windows was not originally designed to move data particularly fast. It was designed to run simultaneous processes, however, so there were generally many drivers running simultaneously without time constraints. "So everything waited for a driver to finish whatever fucking around it wanted to do before it would respond. So drivers in Windows 3.1 and Windows 95 could really shape a game's latency. Even if you had fast video graphics—you could draw the screen at 60 frames a second—you could get a one- or two-second lag just because the network driver or something decided count its fingers and toes for a while before it returned control to the operating system."

St. John's solution was to put into Windows the ability to hard lock a chunk of memory "so that the OS couldn't just decide to do some virtual memory shit and slow down," as well as the ability to allocate a much higher priority to specific processes.

The Mouse

St. John brought Ian Robinson from England to help with DirectPlay, and he also brought another Brit to help build DirectMouse. As was so often the case, using the mouse in games such as DOOM was a nightmare in Windows. "The Windows 3.1 messaging architecture was so slow that you would move the mouse to spin the screen around, and even though the screen could spin in WinG at 60 frames a second, the mouse queue might check messages three or four times a second, so you'd aim at somebody, click the mouse button and they'd move out of the way before the game got the message and fired at them." DirectMouse once again cleared away the competing processes and allowed for realistic game performance. For joysticks, Craig Eisler wrote DirectInput for similar reasons.

The original name given to the suite of APIs Eisler was developing was the Manhattan Game SDK.

Sneaking in Changes

"You're not in charge. You have to sell everybody on anything you want." –Cameron Myhrvold to Alex St. John

Knowing that Windows 3.1 was soon to be history, St. John's bigger concerns centered on Windows 95, which was still being completed. Working on the DOOM port exposed several problems, which St. John was trying to fix in Windows 95—code-named Chicago—before it was too late, even though, officially, it *was* too late. At that time, no new features or changes were allowed, only official bug fixes.

One of the problems that showed up was in how Windows handled CD drivers. The Windows 95 driver architecture had been designed to assume that CD ROMs would be used to play videos, and so they used a cache to load data serially. "It just was slow as hell. Everything just bogged because this cache loaded everything serially, and I needed to turn it off for games."

At the time, St. John had no official status on the OS team, but that didn't stop him. He had learned from the beginning how his job worked. "Cameron Myhrvold said this to me when I took the job to lead strategy for all of publishing. I said, 'Oh boy. That sounds important. What authority do I have to do that?' And the answer was, 'None. Your job is to persuade them. You're not in charge. You have to sell everybody on anything you want.'"

"I used to try to do it by process," St John says, "but I quickly gave that up and what I really would do, I'd secretly find the actual individual engineer, and I'd go into their office and say, 'Hey, I need you to fix this. Can you get right on this for me?' And bypass their management, their process and everything. Remember, it was too late to make changes to Windows 95. Features were banned. Everything was banned. So if I want something done, I had to slip it in under the rug."

This is exactly what he did to fix the CD problem. He convinced the engineer in charge of the CD drivers to implement two changes—adding the Autoplay API that St. John had written himself, and some code that made it possible to disable the cache and run games directly from the CD, which also used code he had written. Humongous Entertainment's Freddi Fish was the first Autoplay CD ever published. It was also a WinG title.

Once the changes had been made to their DOOM port, he would have Hess test them to see if they were effective. But despite their efforts, the port was a failure. St. John says, "It was a disaster. Hess was brilliant. Years later he got upset with me for saying it was a disaster. He took it personally. But it wasn't you, Hess. Everybody knew you were trying to do something impossible."

St. John saw the problems, but there were no available solutions at the time. "The problem was the latencies were just huge. The audio just drifted out of sync with the sound effects and out of sync with the network, and there was nothing Hess could do to fix it. You know, it ran enough to go, 'Well, you can almost run DOOM on Windows, but it's clearly not as good as the DOS version.' *Obviously* not as good as DOS, and that was a problem. Even knowing it wasn't up to the highest standards, but still respecting the work Hess had put into it, St. John did show it to Carmack, who, predictably, said, 'No. I can't publish that.'"

-9-
The Games Division

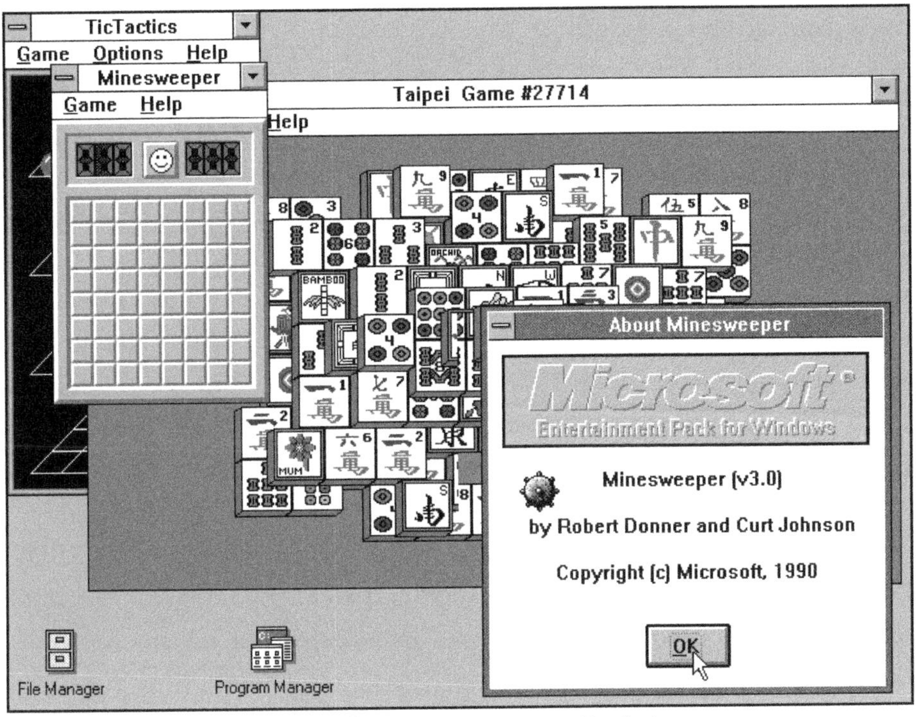

Windows Entertainment Pack 1

Tony Garcia came to Microsoft in 1991 after having worked previously at several game companies, most recently as a producer at LucasArts. Garcia was originally hired to work on the Windows Sound System, Microsoft's first sound card for computers. According to Garcia, Microsoft's hope was to incorporate sound into business software, but he was hired because Microsoft knew that sound systems were already an important aspect of games, so they needed a "game guy". Even so, Garcia says, "Microsoft's main objective was to introduce audio as a concept onto the desktop, so you could cross over from games into productivity applications like Excel and Word and do voice annotation and stuff like that."

This idea of voice annotations in business applications prompted Garcia to take liberties with the Microsoft mouse. "I took one of the Microsoft mice and I cut it open and I integrated a microphone into it and created this little dongle that you would plug into, between the RS232 port and the sound card microphone input, and so literally, with this small piece of software, you would lift up the mouse to your mouth, where the microphone was, you'd click the button to start recording, you would make your voice note, you would release the button, and it would auto-embed into your document." Garcia patented this concept.

Part of Garcia's early work was to evangelize the sound card both internally at Microsoft and externally to game developers. In terms of Microsoft's entry into the world of games and multimedia, this was early, in the Windows 3.1 era, and about the only game Microsoft was known for at the time was Flight Simulator. When the Windows Sound System 1.0 shipped in 1992, Garcia had become familiar with the essentially nonexistent state of games at Microsoft, and he wanted to do something about it. "I suggested that we should get focused around games because it was a great way to lure people onto Windows and get them using it in places other than the desktop." He found support from Bruce Jacobson, who at the time was one of the head managers in the consumer group. "Bruce got it from day one. They gave me five people, and that's how the Games Division (initially called the Entertainment Business Unit or EBU) started inside of Microsoft." At the time, other than Flight Simulator, Microsoft had little to show beyond little games like Minesweeper and Solitaire.

With such a small team, it was clear that they needed to find third party developers to support Windows, and also to build up a marketing team and distribution channels. Garcia worked as the head of the games group for nearly five years, slowly building the team from five people to about 150 full-time employees and outside contractors, and making positive steps toward a gaming presence at Microsoft. "We decided this will be a slow burn. This will take some time, but there are things that we can leverage that nobody else could back in the day. And that was monster distribution, huge demand—anything Microsoft. Anything that we were doing had a great amount of visibility and to some degree, demand and desire for. So we leveraged the hell out of that. So you'd be surprised at the kinds of numbers we did with these little games."

Like all division heads, he was required to report and do internal reviews with Bill Gates and Steve Ballmer. "Bill got it," says Garcia. "He was such a quick study on this stuff, and he saw that what we were doing was essentially enabling Windows users to think beyond just the desktop and think the living room. Think entertainment. Think media. And so he really got behind us and supported us in the very early days."

Is This a Real Job?

One of Garcia's early employees was Kathie Flood, already a four-year Microsoft veteran who had spent two years in operating systems and two years in an eight-person team working on interactive technologies. "And we'd talk about games, but we mostly used them to look at the user interfaces. So I got assigned to play Wolfenstein for example. And I couldn't play it. I eventually had to go to my boss because I could shoot the Nazis, but I couldn't shoot the dogs." In addition to studying user interfaces, Flood's group was envisioning online communities and looking at creating a 3D online world. "We had a little town, and we built a little King Dome where you could pick out Seahawks tickets, and we built a little Elliott Bay Book Store buy your books online, and looked at how you'd navigate inside the bookstore."

When Flood was "re-orged" into what she called the "itsy-bitzy game group," she asked her new boss, "'Do they still pay me for this?' We genuinely didn't know," she adds. "'Is this a demotion? Basically is this a real job?' And he just laughed and said, 'They're going to pay you. You like soccer, we're going to put you on that.'" Because she liked soccer, all of a sudden she was a game designer, and getting paid to do it.

Although Flood played real-life soccer, she knew nothing about game design. Fortunately for her, work had already been done by an outside development group, but they had failed to meet their deadlines, so she took the code and working with "two and a half programmers, a tester, and a localizer" she was given three months to complete the game and localize it in six languages. The result was Soccer 1.0. "It was terrible," she admits, "but it made money because it was in all different languages and it was shipped along with Works."

A New Concept—Fun

Kiki McMillan came to Microsoft as a technical writer in 1990, and, like Flood, she found herself working in the games group in 1994. She talks about going to the company store. "It was Word and Excel, and DOS stuff, and then they had the track and field game, which was the dumbest game. But they encouraged us to play these little games in the lead-up to releasing operating systems because they helped expose if there were problems."

Typically, a lot of projects were started but never released, such as a Hockey game and a women's soccer game ("Like they were really going to consider that back then," remarks Flood.) But Microsoft wanted the sports games to make money, thinking that they should be able to attain the kinds of revenues that EA's perennial hit, the Madden franchise. So the team pushed back, claiming that the only way to get even close to Madden numbers was to publish their games across multiple platforms, at the very least on Windows and PlayStation. But they were told no. Microsoft would only publish games on the Windows platform. Once again pushing back, the designers would ask, "Do you want to make money or use games as a strategic way to push Microsoft platforms?" And the answer was, "Both." And so Microsoft games ran only on PC platforms, with few exceptions, until Xbox provided a console that was also a Microsoft platform.

Another problem with the early games efforts came from trying to fit standard Microsoft methodology onto game development. McMillan says, "when I worked on Works, we went through a whole task force and talked about how we could refine preproduction, production, and all that other stuff. And we tried to do it in the games group, and it was impossible because we were trying to take a very disciplined software development process and apply it to games. The problem was that games are not like productivity applications. They are subjective, and often require a lot of iteration in the development process to get the best results, and this was especially true when most of the people doing the work had little to no previous experience. "When we came up with our development plan for Soccer," says Flood, "that very first game, we checked all the items off, and all the stuff was in… kind of. But we knew it wasn't fun. If you're making something bold in Word, nobody says, 'Was it fun? Did you enjoy it?' It either works or it doesn't." As it turns out, fun was a new concept at Microsoft. So was the concept of a game designer. There was no such category, and it was up to the program managers to fill that role.

Growing the Business

Even with support in high places, it was generally believed at Microsoft that games were peripheral to their central mission. For the most part, games were seen as an outlier, and not a core business. In spite of that, and even despite the general lack of support for the game projects, the games division grew. They acquired Access Software, makers of the Links golf games, around 1994, and Flight Simulator developers, the Bruce Artwick Organization (BAO), in 1995.

"It became clear that the Flight Sim guys were just tired of trying to run the company on their own, and they had been approached by Sierra On-Line," says Garcia. "And so, out of courtesy, they called us up and they told me, 'Hey, I just want to tell you that we've had a pretty compelling offer from Sierra, and we're at this stage now, and…' Bells went off in my head! Oh my god. What are you talking about? 'Oh don't worry. I'm sure they'll still let you publish it.' Aahh. I don't think so. So basically we got in there and we derailed that deal by giving them our own deal."

The funniest part of the story, according to Garcia, is when he had to go tell the Flight Simulator team in Champlain, Illinois that they were now part of Microsoft. "So I go to Champlain with my legal guy and my HR person and we just show up. We tried to do it low key. We thought about what do we say and how do we do it, and all of that. But then, when the time came to let the employees know, the founders of the company decided that they're going to get everybody together at a pancake house that's around the corner, where I guess they would take people every once in a while.

"So everybody gets in their cars and they go to the pancake house, and then they just basically say, 'So, are you guys going to tell them?' Without any prep at all. My face went white, and they said, 'We just think it would be better if you just let everybody know.' So in that setting, I had to stand up in front of… it must have been 40 or 50 people, all working at this company, and basically say, 'We're happy to announce that we've concluded negotiations to acquire the company and we want to welcome you all to Microsoft.'

"Now it was their turn, and their faces went white and all the mumble, mumble, mumble started out, and people start thinking, 'Do I have a job?' And for the three days after that we met with every single person to try to convince them to come—not just to become Microsoft employees—they had to come to Redmond. We were relocating everyone. And that took a lot of doing. The happy ending is that, of the 40 plus people that we tried to move over, almost all of them made the move, and many of them still live here." Ultimately, the BAO people became the nucleus of Microsoft's Simulation Group, which is responsible for the popular Forza racing franchise and other simulation-based games.

Meanwhile, developers like Flood, McMillan, and Russ Glaeser, who came over with BAO, continued to soldier on with little funding, and often without playtesting facilities, creating several entertainment and arcade packs, Close Combat, Deadly Tide, Fury^3, Monster Truck Madness (1&2), and many other games between 1995 and 1999.

Before leaving Microsoft in 1996, Garcia began work with Ensemble Studios and set the stage for distributing Age of Empires, Microsoft's first hit game.

Meanwhile, St. John and company were busy working in parallel to proselytize games at Microsoft, using their DRG tactics to push the envelope even further.

-10-
Pitfalls for Christmas

St. John was working with Activision to port Pitfall Harry to Windows 3.1 for Christmas '94. One of the problems they encountered involved the 320 x 200 graphics standard called ModeX, which was used by many DOS games at the time, including DOOM and Pitfall Harry. Simply scaling the artwork to a higher resolution would have been a visual disaster, so they needed another solution.

St. John gives major credit to another engineer named Todd Laney, who he describes as "one of those brilliant Microsoft giants" on the one hand, and also, "an unassuming nerd who just happens to be a huge influence in making it all work." Laney was helping Hecker with WinG, and he also helped St. John develop the Autoplay feature that ultimately became ubiquitous on removable media like CD-ROMs.

While Activision was trying to figure out how to port Pitfall Harry and still access ModeX, Laney saved the day by introducing St. John to a secret, undocumented Windows API called KillGDI. KillGDI literally killed the Windows Graphics Device Interface (GDI), which managed all the flow of graphics in Windows, and which imposed, from the game's point of view, unwanted overhead and other limitations to developers who wanted to use ModeX and who wanted to work directly "to the metal." KillGDI turned out to be the solution for Pitfall Harry. Later, KillGDI became part of DirectX, and so St. John refers to Pitfall Harry as "a proto-DirectX game that was done in the shadows, before DirectX really became a project."

What's the Opposite of Hakuna Matata?

"Ah the Lion King. To this day, I can't look at anything related to that product without getting sick."
-Rick Segal

"What started DirectX was the Disney Lion King disaster under WinG."

-Alex St. John

One of the most high profile Windows games coming out in Christmas of 1994 was Disney's The Lion King, which was also one of the early games using WinG. In theory, this should have been a big feather in the cap of both Microsoft and Chris Hecker, but instead it turned out to be a major FUBAR.

What happened is that Compaq shipped brand-new Presario computers for Christmas—a million of them—with The Lion King pre-installed on each one. Each of these computers had a new video chip and driver from Cirrus, which had never been tested with WinG. Say it again. Nobody had tested The Lion King on the new Presarios, even though it was pre-installed on the system. Nobody had noticed that when you launched the game it blue screened the system. Kaput!

And so it wasn't a very good Christmas for Compaq, Microsoft and Disney, not to mention thousands of children and their parents around the country. It was a disaster, and a very public one, at that. St. John remembers seeing a Wall Street Journal article about how Disney had spoiled Christmas for children everywhere.

According to Rick Segal, "As it turns out, this boiled down to a complete fuck-up of QA on the install process. In short, nobody took an Average Joe machine and tried a naked, out of the box, install. Surprise. It was a disaster of epic proportions. Drivers were missing, the install didn't properly catch missing drivers and adjust for it, and on and on. Disaster. Kids crying, parents screaming, just off the charts bad."

St. John adds, "Oh, it was a train wreck. It went Boom across Microsoft and everywhere. Because, think about the confluence. One, Windows 95 is about to ship. Two, for the first time ever Microsoft has somebody other than themselves making… big names making multimedia titles. And suddenly Disney is supporting you, and a number of other companies are supporting you and making games for Windows. And then you get this press disaster. I mean, that shook Microsoft to its core."

St John's role in all this wasn't trivial. After all, he was the one getting companies like Disney to use WinG. Once again, he expected to take the blame and, finally, get fired. "The funny thing is, that it was my fault in the sense that I made WinG happen," he says. "I talked Disney into it. Craig and I were the ones responsible for executing it. That was our disaster, baby." And the very real possibility of getting fired got even more real when a small army of Disney executives and lawyers descended on Microsoft in the aftermath.

St. John was never invited or required to attend any of the Disney meetings, but Segal was not so lucky. "Brad Chase on our side was chief punching bag with yours truly taking hits for Alex and the developers. After the yelling and legal threats, and swearing and such, we got down to the business of making it right for the customers. Nobody ever got fired or threatened with being fired simply because it was software. You couldn't pin any one thing on any one person to the extent that it was willful or incompetent. For instance, somebody would say St. John talked us into this crap, and the response would be, 'Yeah, he was supposed to be trying to help you find a kick ass solution for the Christmas season. He didn't code it, didn't test it; get off his back.' Then we'd move on to the next target and go through the same thing."

St. John was not-so-blissfully ignorant of what was going on. "Rick was in these meetings all the time, and he'd come back red-faced and perspiring. Nobody said a word to me. I remember sitting in my office going, 'OK. I'm fired, or I'm in trouble, or somebody's going to ask me what I did at some point, and I'll have to answer for it.' And nothing.

Even though nobody got fired, the humiliation and frustration he experienced caused St. John to seek a better solution, which included far more rigorous testing standards and a more foolproof solution to Windows game development.

-11-
The Manhattan Project

"The thing that I personally think, if you're going to tell a story like this, is it works because everybody's actually having a pretty good time. And that's what sustains you, that and the passion to build something. But if you can't stand the people you work with, you're not going to be able to do it."

-Eric Engstrom

Both Alex St. John and James Plamondon came from unorthodox, back-woods backgrounds. Eric Engstrom also came from rural Orville, Washington and never graduated from high school. Craig Eisler was a Canadian from Waterloo and well educated. Where St. John was completely non-religious—"my parents were classic hippies who attended Berkeley in the 1960s"—Engstrom's parents were Jehovah's Witnesses, and he even had to go on "missions" knocking on people's doors at one point, and both Eisler and Plamondon had very religious parents. When Eisler joined Microsoft, he was already famous in the tech world for writing Watcom's 32-bit DOS extender.

In addition to weight lifting, which they regularly enjoyed together, all three were, according to St. John, "100% D&D playing computer nerds, all big board game Diplomacy, Axis & Allies strategy game players."

And there was one more quality that they shared: a conservative tendency. According to St. John, "Many of the evangelists had conservative/religious backgrounds (that most but not all had rejected by the time they reached Microsoft). I wasn't religious but I was a conservative. Many were Ayn Rand fans. Big believers in free-market capitalism, competition, etc. Basically a lot of folks who had rejected religion (and liberalism) in favor of rationalism/conservatism. They were all very independent thinkers and inclined to reject whatever people wanted them to believe by that point in their lives. They also had an innate understanding of the power of influencing people's beliefs."

Even before the Lion King debacle, St. John recalls how he, Eisler and Engstrom had started working together to infiltrate and fix problems in the Multimedia Group, initially by moving Eisler over there after completing WinG.

St John describes Eisler as "our secret agent engineer over there that could actually get things fixed." When it turned out that Eisler was spending most of his time in "firefighting mode fixing the group's shit," they approached Engstrom, saying "Eric, can we sneak you over as a manager into Microsoft's multimedia group so that you can run political interference for Craig… so he can actually get some shit done on graphics?"

At the time, Engstrom was working in product marketing for interactive TV. "That was a big mistake. I'm not a marketer. Then Alex and Craig came and got me and said, 'Would you be a program manager for this games thing?' Craig was going to do the development. Alex was going to be the marketing guy. 'We need someone to do everything else.' So the program manager will figure out what exactly needs to be built and manage all the building schedules and all that kind of stuff. Craig was the guy who wrote all the code. He's god's gift to writing code. It just flows out of him like he was playing a concert violin or something. It's amazing to watch. And so I designed the API, Craig built it and Alex sold it."

Engstrom ditched interactive TV and became Eisler's *heat shield*. "He was great at that," says St. John. "You ever see those scenes in the movies where the monsters are chasing a group of people and the hero goes, 'OK. I'll lead them off,' and runs in a different direction, and bang, bang, bang go the monsters? That was Eric's job. He'd get them all engaged and distracted and entangled with themselves somewhere else, and we'd get work done on fixing the graphics."

This was the start of The Manhattan Project and the Manhattan Game SDK, AKA DirectX, but nobody really knew it at the time, other than St. John, Eisler and Engstrom. Why call it The Manhattan Project? According to Engstrom, "We named it The Manhattan Project, which was derived off of the movie War Games. 'Shall we play a game?' The kind of secret, build a bomb thing really resonated with game developers, so we got lots of immediate attention. They didn't believe that it would go fast, but they were willing to try because they were losing basically 70% of their revenue in installation and support costs and that sort of thing. So they were highly motivated to help us."

Part of finding an answer to their questions involved research, but when the Consumer group refused to share their research data, St. John admits to stealing it and turning it into a weapon against them, using their own data to show that their approach, which ignored games and focused on "stupid shit," was flat-out missing the point.

The Fine Art of Listening

In addition to stolen data from the Consumer Group, St. John had done his own research, going directly to the source—the game developers themselves. His approach was, from a Microsoft perspective, novel. St. John describes the standard evangelism model as "whatever the operating system guys hand us and told us to talk some poor sucker into adopting is what we sold." But what St. John wanted to do was just the opposite. He wanted the developers to tell Microsoft what they wanted. His goal, as he describes it, was "to define a platform whose sole function is to be crack for developers."

The majority of game developers hated Microsoft, viewing them as an evil empire, with St. John himself being an incarnation of Darth Vader, which St John made fun of. But what set him apart, and ultimately solidified his relationship with the game development community, was that he clearly was asking them to define the product they wanted. "I'd walk to game developers and I'd say. 'Yeahyeahyeah. I know you hate Microsoft. I know you hate us. I know you never want to use anything we make, and I think your reasons for feeling that way are probably totally valid. But just hypothetically, what could Microsoft possibly make, that you could not escape? If Microsoft made X, you'd fricking have to use it. Doesn't matter how you feel. If you don't use it, you're out of business. You're just done. What would it be?'" This was how DirectX began. "DirectX was started as an initiative to design a new type of technology virus whose sole definition is, 'What is it that game developers have to use?'"

"I think I came in for the first or second DirectX design preview in late '94," says Morris Beton, who eventually became St. John's manager. "There were maybe 50-60 in the room. Craig and Eric did a really good job of laying out what they were talking about to the developers. There was tons of feedback about what was needed, and I was really impressed at the degree to which the feedback was taken, noted… how much effort these guys put into understanding what the developers needed, and then I believe there was a follow-up to that where they incorporated a lot of that feedback and then played it back for the developers. I thought the process was fantastic. It was like a poster child example of how to do developer relations."

Taking Fun Seriously

"Alex took over on gaming with Windows 3, and what you could do there, and never looked back."

-Cameron Myhrvold

Right after completing the shipping version of WinG, St. John, Engstrom and Eisler began work on their manifesto, a white paper dated 11/18/1994, which was titled, *Taking Fun Seriously: or 'How to own PC games in two years, and take a bite out of the home game console market.'*

Taking Fun Seriously was a radical manifesto on the importance and strategic value of games—radical because almost nobody else at Microsoft, other than Tony Garcia's EBU, took games seriously at the time.

The Roadmap to Games

Taking Fun Seriously went on the attack from the first sentence: "The term 'Multimedia' among DOS game developers today is a euphemism for 'Poor game technology…'" What followed were detailed recommendations for how to win the consumer space by empowering games through well-thought-out Microsoft technology—technology that had yet to be developed—and in doing so turn games into a weapon against Apple.

"It's worth remembering that Microsoft was just paranoid about QuickTime, and multimedia in general, because it was clearly the way computers were going, and Microsoft just wasn't able to dislodge QuickTime as the *de facto* standard," says Plamondon. "And that played into DirectX and the eventual approval of the DirectX project because it took the competition to a

Taking Fun Seriously

or "How to own PC games in two years, and take a bite out of the home game console market"

by: Alex St. John, Eric Engstrom, & Craig Eisler

Date: 11/18/1994

What's important about games?

The term "Multimedia" among DOS game developers today is a euphemism for "Poor game technology", or put another way "the best game technology GUI OS's can support" It's lets graphic, less interactive, and generally less dynamic than the kinds of interaction found in most modern DOS, and console video games. We recognize that multimedia technology will be extremely crucial to the success of Windows in the home, yet our "multimedia" technology to date does little to substantially distinguish itself from the functionality provided by our nearest competitors in this area, Apple, and IBM. We place an enormous emphasis on video technology, but is this because video is really the most important component of multimedia, and demanded consumer feature, or simply that it's the easiest problem to solve on a platform like Windows, and the only efficient form of distribution for mass market entertainment until the computer came along? The fact that the arcade business was bigger than the movie box office last year would tend to indicate that interactivity is at the heart of today's consumer entertainment requirements.

To date most of the successful Windows based "games" have been little more than a series of beautifully rendered still frames, some animation, hot buttons, and maybe a video transition between scenes. Games that make serious money are consistently real-time dedicated applications. Ironically, Microsoft sells the number one PC based video game. Flight Simulator... a DOS application, and the folks who develop it for us steadfastly insist that it cannot be done as well under Windows. Further Sega+Nintendo titles pocket 87% of the revenue in the 4.5 billion dollar home entertainment market, while Windows is less than 1%... so consumer is writing Sega titles too.

Say why don't we fix that, eat DOS once and for all, grab a real chunk of that cash, and get a multimedia technology jump on IBM, SGI, and Apple a year wide, with a relatively minimal investment in solving some of the problems? Enter the Manhattan Game SDK, and a strategy for making Windows the premier game OS.

Executive Summary

Objectives

- Use Manhattan game SDK to enable Systems, ACT, and Consumer
- Kill DOS as game OS in two years
- Grow PC game revenue against console game machines

Market Observations

- Game market is huge
- Console market is in decline and must re-invent itself next year
- PC game market is severely suppressed because of difficulties with game installation, piracy, and little hardware innovation under DOS for games.

Prepared by Alex St. John,
Eric Engstrom & Craig Eisler *Microsoft Confidential*

different place. And this is all Sun Tzu right there. You don't attack their fortified cities. You do not attack the place where they're strong, which is QuickTime. You attack them in games, where Apple… all the personal computers were weak in games."

Taking Fun Seriously presents a roadmap to the technologies proposed to make Windows a dynamic and competitive platform for the games that the game industry actually wanted to make—as opposed to what many at Microsoft thought of as games or multimedia. In addition to the pilfered statistical data, the document describes specific problems and the solutions that their proposed Manhattan Games SDK would address, such as how to eliminate the overhead that Windows adds to the system, slowing down the performance of high resolution/high bandwidth applications like games. Another problem they set out to solve was the issue of working with different hardware and achieving device independence.

Here is a section taken from the document (including typos), further detailing problems they sought to solve:

- No major new technology innovation or standards for DOS games. Without device independence, hardware advances in DOS have been extremely slow and limited.

PC joystick model is antiquated, game developers code to it directly to get best possible performance from it, but this action prevents hardware vendors from introducing new joystick hardware architectures because it is difficult to get all of the individual game companies to support it.

Video hardware with graphic functionality substantially better than 320x200 Mode X in standard VGA has been available and in the installed base for sometime, yet games were not written to take advantage of it until VESA set standards for SVGA modes.

Most games don't bother to support sound cards beyond SoundBlaster. Although there are better cards with new sound technologies, they continue to support the installed base.

- Windows is an inadequate solution because it severely obstructs access to precious hardware functionality necessary to making PC games possible. The technology driven game market cannot afford to back up for Windows. Windows needs to support;

-Direct control of palette

-Page flipping

-Vertical blank synchronization

-Tight sound mixing
-Tight synchronization of sound and video events
-Raw blting performance
-Ability to set graphic mode

o -Windows consumes enormous valuable resources (RAM) for functionality games don't need

o –Socialist* OS model design is in direct conflict with needs of full screen real-time dedicated applications."

**Using the word "socialist" was a slightly tongue-in-cheek way of describing the way that Windows distributed resources to active applications and didn't allow one application to use all resources, which was necessary to achieve the highest level of game performance.*

Solutions proposed centered around key aspects of the Manhattan Games SDK, including DCI 2.0 (Display Control Interface), DirectDraw, 3DDDI, improved networking, and new input and sound driver models.

Here's another section from Taking Games Seriously that describes what DCI 2.0 and Direct Draw were intended to accomplish:

"Liability: Too much overhead, and lack of important functionality

Solution: DCI 2.0

DCI 2.0 and the associated Direct Draw interfaces define ways to get device independent access to hardware with very little overhead

o Asynchronous blting
o Transparency
o Translucency
o Page flipping
o Vertical blank synchronization
o Video memory to video memory copies
o Video hardware Display Contexts
o Palette Control
o blt ordering
o Antialiasing
o Color space translation
o Memory management, and hardware mixing of multiple video streams from 3D-DDI,and VFW.

Having looked at several internal Microsoft documents, I've noticed that humorous or very informal remarks and expressions often appear among otherwise very dry and serious facts, statistics, proposals, and analysis. Here is my favorite from the original *Taking Fun Seriously* (emphasis added):

ACT

"o Creates a loyal community of content generating ISV's on our platform and establishes credibility for Microsoft as a game technology provider. The cost to MS of evangelizing this market cold turkey when ACT is ready with new solutions will be enormous without very early efforts to get these companies to start regarding MS as a game technology provider today."

"o Establishes a community of knowledgeable real game **ISV's who aren't DOS bumpkins** to collect feedback from, and involve in new technology role outs, and beta programs. On DOS these guys are **low hanging fruit** for anyone who wants to introduce a new game console, or superhighway solution, early harvesting by Microsoft will leave nothing for the **Apple Maggots** when they come into season. (I'm sorry, I really couldn't resist this metaphor.)"

Don't Ask Permission

Taking Fun Seriously was completed only weeks before Christmas. They showed it first to Rick Segal, whose initial response St. John describes as, "Uh huh. Thanks but, you know… meh."

Then came Christmas and Lion King. As the dust was settling from the Christmas disaster, Segal approached St. John and asked, "What would you do?"

St. John handed him the white paper again, saying, "Rick, I've written this huge strategic document. I did the market analysis. This is what Microsoft needs to do in multimedia, and I just can't get any support for it. I don't know what to do.'

"And I remember very vividly, Rick saying something to the effect of, 'Do you believe that this is the right thing for Microsoft to do?'

"And I go, 'Yeah.'

"And he goes, 'Well why are you asking for permission?'

"I go, 'Well, don't I need permission?'

"And he goes, 'The answer will always be no. If it's worth doing, then it's worth risking being fired for.'

"And I don't recall the exact words, but that's what he conveyed very clearly to me. I have to say that until he said that to me… Let's just say that there were transition zones where I went from crazy to crazier, and that was one of them. 'OK Rick. Don't ask permission.'"

"I designed the API, Craig built it and Alex sold it."

–Eric Engstrom

St. John had been trying to be a well-behaved Microsoft citizen, at least when it seemed feasible. He was trying to ask permission, get support and resources the official way if possible. And that's when Segal told him, essentially, "Fuck that. Just do it, Alex. Do it and risk getting fired if it doesn't work." And so St. John got Eisler and Engstrom onboard, and the three of them started the Manhattan Project. Since they couldn't get resources or official support for what they were doing, St. John started using dozens of DRG contractors to help build the first prototypes for the SDK—what ultimately became DirectX 1.0. "So we started the Manhattan Project by funding it out of DRG, but managing it from the multimedia group. So we had them running it as though it was part of the systems technology group, but it was actually DRG budget that I was spending without permission to pay for it all."

When he needed new contractors on the project, he would go to HR and tell them that he had authorization from his manager. They never checked. "It would have been pretty extraordinary for somebody to lie about something like that." St. John also explains that DRG had an unspoken permission to shoot from the hip, encouraged by management, and put things on their credit cards that would be overlooked by the accounting department… things that nobody else could justify. And the cover for their activities went all the way up to Cameron Myhrvold. St. John claims that he managed to spend $1.2 million in unauthorized money to provide contractors for Eisler and Engstrom as they worked on their Manhattan Project.

Even though St. John had developed relationships with many game developers, it didn't mean that they had stopped hating Microsoft, and hating Windows even more. What St. John needed was a way to gain their cooperation and good will. He did so, in part, by organizing a distinctly un-Microsoft marketing campaign. Not only did he use the Manhattan Project name, but he told PC game developers that "the reason for the name was because we intended to take out the Japanese consoles that had permeated our living rooms with Windows PC games." St. John also designed T-shirts that featured a glow-in-the-dark nuclear cloud and the words, "SHALL WE PLAY A GAME?" Only 35 of these were printed, and they were handed out late in 1994 at an invite-only party at which Eisler and Engstrom introduced their plans for what would eventually become DirectX. It was the beginning of a long-term "anti-marketing" campaign.

St. John also worked hard to convince game developers that what they were doing was not from the typical Microsoft "We'll build it and you'll use it, whether you like it or not" attitude. He listened to their input and promised to build something that they would want to use. He positioned himself as their advocate and, in some ways, the enemy of the corporate Microsoft.

John Miles

One of St. John's original missions still remained: to counter Apple's dominance over video on home computers through its popular QuickTime application, and in fact the whole *Taking Fun Seriously* manifesto and the Manhattan Project were a part of that strategy. As of Windows 3.1, the Microsoft approach to video was just bad. As St. John puts it, "It was so bad that people have erased the memory of it." In addition to using a single 8-bit color pallet for the entire video, which could lead to frames displaying a paltry four colors, the audio tended to drift out of synchronization the longer a video ran. This even affected games, as St. John came to realize while porting DOOM. "As you played the game, when you pulled the trigger on the gun, a bang would happen a few seconds later. And there was nothing you could do about it because the OS just had no capacity to synchronize sound.

"The problem was that Windows 95 had the same sound APIs that Windows 3 did. So Windows 95 had the same problems running WinDOOM that Hess had. So we could not make DOOM work without a replacement for the Windows 95 sound system.

"Everybody in the industry pointed me to John Miles, so I did a contract deal with him." St. John contracted Miles, who hailed from Austin, Texas, to port his Miles Sound System to Windows, which was used to demo the next attempt at porting DOOM to Windows. Meanwhile, using Miles' work for inspiration, one of Eisler's engineers, Geoff Dahl, began writing a Windows API for sound, which ultimately became DirectSound. All of this occurred during the early stages of the Manhattan Game SDK. Meanwhile, St. John told Miles that if he would port his sound system to Windows and let Microsoft use it in their port of DOOM, then he could license it to everybody else. St. John even promised to help promote the Miles Sound System. "It was kind of an informal—hey keep the code. I just to use it for DOOM, but I'll pay you as a contractor to actually spend the time to make it work under Windows."

Scratching an Itch

As head of the internal games group, Tony Garcia was aware of what was happening with the development of new APIs for Windows, and the promise they offered for more robust Windows game development, but he had to work with the system as it currently existed. "There was a delta of time between what they were talking about doing and releasing, so what we had to do was find games like Golf and Flight Sim... and Microsoft Arcade. These were all games that didn't necessarily require a lot of graphics processing power."

Microsoft Arcade, which was released in 1993 with sequels in 1996 and 1998, consisted of five classic Atari arcade games: Tempest, Battlezone, Centipede, Asteroids and Missile Command. Garcia hired a contract developer to recreate those games from scratch. "We saw them as a good way to bridge between the early Windows games days to the DirectX days." But, according to Garcia, these little games were not trivial. In the early days of Windows, and were actually turning a profit. "Microsoft Arcade was just a huge hit. There were a lot of people who were coming into computing for the very first time. Getting into business, being set in front of a machine running Windows... these people were just like everybody else, they would get bored. But they didn't know how to get out of Windows into a soft prompt and load up a memory manager and all this crap you had to do to get a good DOS game running. So we leveraged that. We embraced that. Even though the games might not have looked as good or been as deep, they scratched an itch that a lot of new computer users had."

Garcia draws a parallel to the mobile games market. "A lot of people didn't want to do it at the time. They felt like it was not worth it, that the real market was the DOS players. Similar cycles have happened now on the mobile side where there was a lot of skepticism early on. A lot of people were just rolling the dice and investing in these new platforms, which ultimately won out because they unlocked a brand new set of users that weren't there before. So you can draw a corollary there, easily."

In retrospect, it's helpful to realize that in the early- to mid-1990s, video games were not really mainstream. Many people considered them "kid's stuff" and not suitable for adult consumption, and many adults who did play games didn't generally admit it in public. Things have changed a lot since then, but the introductions of these innocuous games from a company like Microsoft on a major platform like Microsoft Arcade very likely helped to legitimize video games to some people who for various reasons had not tried them, or at least it made them more accessible.

Meanwhile, Garcia observed that the work of the DRG was definitely consistent with his team's goals, and that St. John kept them informed about the goals and progress of The Manhattan Project.

Slipping the Hooks in

Using DRG budget, St. John had been supplying the manpower while Eisler and Engstrom were working to implement the elements of the Manhattan Game SDK within the multimedia group. With the intention of gaining easier access to the Chicago code, they both managed to maneuver their way into the OS group under Paul Osborne, who was, according to St. John "a nice, affable guy that we just ran roughshod over." Remembering Osborne, St. John told me, "I have a lot of guilt in my old age. I mean, I'm sorry I made you look bad or embarrassed or humiliated you, but we just had to win."

Following the Lion King debacle, Rick Segal started supporting the early DirectX efforts quietly. *Taking Fun Seriously* started to gain some attention, and Alex, Eric and Craig—the weightlifting buddies—were getting more and more serious.

According to St. John, "Windows 95 was done. It was shipping. You weren't supposed to be touching shit or making features for it anymore. So there was no putting DirectX into Windows 95. It was too late. So what we did was we touched it a little bit in the guise of fixing bugs. We put hooks in Windows 95 to make a hole for DirectX. So Windows 95, you could think of it like this: We treated it like a stencil, and we'd snip out a gap that we expected to inject DirectX into." Thinking about it from a project management standpoint, what they were doing was incredibly risky and would have gotten them in big trouble if they'd been discovered.

Of course, St. John had already been working on the sly, implementing AutoPlay for instance, but that was just the beginning. They put in hooks that would let them suppress the threading kernel and drivers to allow games to use all the system resources instead of sharing them with other applications. "We wouldn't tell anybody; it was undocumented—but we put in mechanisms to suppress the Windows kernel, and we put in mechanisms to lock RAM in place to prevent the OS from paging. And we put in hooks like KillGDI to literally shut off the Windows 95 graphics subsystem so it was possible to replace it. So we kind of mined Windows 95 with dynamite in anticipation of DirectX."

DirectX was designed to be its own standalone multimedia architecture. When a game was installed, DirectX would call its secret hooks to shut off the graphics subsystem, lock memory, reschedule the operating frame systems to put more processing emphasis on the game, and many other things. "It would all be set up so that if you installed a DirectX game, Windows would basically shut down and let our media operating system run. Nobody knew that but us."

Licking the Cookie

Chris Phillips came over to Microsoft with the acquisition of SoftImage, and was working on the business side to license technologies for DirectX APIs, such as acquiring licenses for MPEG and MIDI. He was also working with Eisler and Engstrom to figure out what APIs they would need in the future, and made sure they laid claim to those technologies even though they didn't really exist yet—what he calls, "licking the cookie." "You know, when we originally did DirectX, we kind of licked the cookie on a bunch of APIs that didn't exist. We just basically said we're going to have DirectMusic, we're going to have DirectSound, 3D, 3D sound, DirectInput… blah blah blah. Right? And DX 1 only did D-Draw. We didn't have D3D, even though we said we would. So we presented a roadmap, but we didn't necessarily have all the DLLs written."

WinDOOM

St. John hadn't given up on developing a working port of DOOM for Windows. In fact, he says that DirectX was designed specifically to make DOOM work under Windows 95 better than it ran in DOS, and it was the lessons they'd learned from Hess's failed attempt that led directly to DirectX.

To complete the Windows 95 port of DOOM, St. John hired an engineer named Fred Hommel. "He just looked like a drugged-out hippie." Hommel was an odd character, a Scientologist with bad hygiene. But a fine engineer who worked hard. Working with early versions of the game SDK that Eisler and Engstrom were creating, Hommel managed to produce a version of DOOM that played nice with Windows. This version of DOOM shipped in September of 1995 as DOOM II. St. John says, "DOOM 95 worked because DirectX was designed to make it work. The version of DOOM Fred worked on was the very first TRUE DirectX game."

St. John has many stories about Hommel, whom he used to tease a lot because of his Scientology beliefs, his hygiene (or lack thereof), and the time when Hommel witnessed a Microsoft manager having sex with his wife in the office across the hall. What Hommel admitted to St. John later on is that he had been sent to work at Microsoft in order to convert St. John to Scientology, with the ultimate goal of getting to Bill Gates. He obviously didn't do much of a job as a Scientology evangelist, but he did most of the heavy lifting on porting the version of DOOM that finally shipped. *(Sadly, at the time I was writing this book, Fred Hommel died from a long battle with cancer before we could complete arrangements for an interview.)*

Going Public

In the aftermath of the Lion King disaster, St. John, Eisler and Engstrom accelerated the pace of their development. They were working on solutions for graphics, video, networking, sound, and input simultaneously, and although they internally kept the name Manhattan Game SDK, at some point the project officially became the Windows 95 Game SDK. With Segal's permission to proceed without (official) permission, they put the efforts into high gear, and as the 1995 Computer Game Developers Conference approached, they were ready to start introducing people to the beta version of the SDK, and St. John was getting ready to put the "crazy" in overdrive.

The Tar Baby

As they prepared to launch the beta version of the SDKs, St. John wanted to be sure that their efforts wouldn't be wasted, and that involved making sure that Microsoft "owned" the collection of APIs they were creating. Referring to the famous Uncle Remus story about Br'er Fox and Br'er Rabbit, he describes his strategy. "I did something evil on purpose, which is that I went to the press and said, 'Microsoft is announcing a new API for gaming and Windows 95 codenamed The Manhattan Project. It's a feature of Windows 95. It's almost as though it was built into the OS on purpose.' So I glued DirectX to Microsoft right out the gate. I totally tar babied it." This was not the first time St. John had used the idea of tar babying to stick someone with an idea or project. It was just one of many tricks in his DRG arsenal.

The ploy worked to perfection, of course. Every major game magazine covered the story, and despite the fact that he had been told not to link the project with the radiation symbol they liked to use internally, St. John happily provided the symbol along with the story. And the press didn't stop with just the radiation symbol, but went nuclear—quite literally, at least graphically. There were nuclear cloud images on magazine covers and images of B-52 bombers flying over Nintendo and Sony. "Oh yeah," says St. John. "Microsoft's PR went apeshit after me over that. But Rick was running heat shield and I didn't care. I needed to sink that fishhook so deep into Microsoft's hide that they couldn't escape it. And so with Craig and Eric, we decided we're going to make a harpoon that we're just going to embed in this company. And, as we all know, it stuck. But boy did it get us in trouble."

Ground Zero

St. John had made waves throughout his career, and his amazing talent for disruption had already provided a roller-coaster ride of recriminations, censure and opposition, followed by accolades and promotions. In the months before the Computer Game Developers Conference of 1995, St. John, Eisler and Engstrom, along with small team of contractors, were busting their asses to complete the first beta of the Manhattan Game SDK—officially called at the time the Windows 95 Game SDK, but unofficially still called The Manhattan Project.

St. John wanted to make a big impression on developers at CGDC, which occurred earlier than usual, in April that year, at the Santa Clara Convention Center. The problem was that they weren't working on an official Microsoft product, meaning that St. John had no budget for a developer conference. Worse still, CGDC rejected all of St. John's proposed speakers. He remembers, "I was in serious trouble. I had no real company support for the product, no venue and no budget."

St. John's solution was typically over the top, and if the conference wouldn't cooperate with him, he would have to do something on his own. It happened that the Santa Clara venue was right next to the Great America amusement park. This fact might not have meant anything to most people, but most people are not Alex St. John, who decided to hold a massive event at the amusement park to promote the launch of his project. Pitching it as a giant party he managed to get sponsorships from a variety of hardware and software companies, receiving pledges totaling $1.2 million.

Not everything was rosy as the date approached. St. John had been unable to get many games using the new SDK, and had substituted several WinG games to round out the field of games to be presented. Eisler and Engstrom were exceedingly pissed off about it. They were busting their butts to complete the SDK and thought St. John had failed them.

The day arrived, despite the tensions, and conference attendees flocked to the park. Everything was free. The rides, the food… everything. There were three developer tracks in the theme park's theaters, each of which was capable of holding 1500 people.

The event was called "Ground Zero," and all the promotional materials featured the radiation symbol that the team had chosen to represent their Manhattan Project. Anyone with a CGDC pass was welcome. On entrance they received a Ground Zero radiation badge and a t-shirt St John had designed depicting a radiation symbol and the eerie green glow-in-the-dark image of a skeleton seemingly being blasted by an unseen force. At the top it read, "Windows 95 Game SDK," and below it read, "You'll be blown away." And, of course, it also had the Microsoft logo. There were also cans of "radioactive" green slime and glow-in-the-dark Frisbees. Meanwhile, all of the Microsoft developers were dressed in lab coats that featured the radiation logo and the slogan, "Shall We Play A Game?" on the back.

Attendees were packed into the largest of the three theaters to kick off the event, and while people were still filing in, they had an executive from Viacom—a major sponsor of the event—talk about and demo their upcoming game based on the Beavis & Butthead cartoon. St. John remembers what happened next. "I peeked through the curtains to watch the demo on one of the many giant projection screens and much to my horror the game crashed and the infamous blue-screen-of-death was emblazoned across every screen. The

theater roared with laughter and the developers began to chant… "DOS! DOS! DOS! DOS! DOS!" The Viacom executive was casting around widely for help."

The original plan was to fill the theater with a green "radioactive" fog at the end of the Viacom demo, and for St. John, Eisler and Engstrom to appear on stage as the fog cleared. That plan went out the window in a millisecond. "I grabbed three random people, told them to throw on lab coats and told them to run out on stage in a panic and ham it up like a bunch of circus clowns as though a terrible nuclear accident had just occurred. 'Quick, go pretend that crash is on purpose; make a big fake show of trying to fix it! Joan turn on the fog machine!' A minute later as the 'radioactive' green fog poured forth, three Microsoft folks ran out and tore the failed Viacom demo computer apart, ripped out its cables, tripped all over themselves and, thankfully, the audience began to laugh."

Then Eisler and Engstrom, veteran evangelists who were used to speaking to crowds, took the stage and first assured the audience that they were safe as long as their radiation badges didn't change color. Then they began to introduce the new technology—the first public glimpse of what DirectX could do.

Engstrom remembers the moment when everything shifted. "As we walked out on stage, 1200 DOS developers were chanting "DOS! DOS! DOS!" At the time, DOS games used a 320 by 240 pixel resolution. Windows games at the time were 640 by 480, but they were slow. Really slow. The display on the screen as Engstrom and Eisler walked onto the stage was a beautiful 640 by 480 image, and once it started moving, everybody naturally expected it to be glacial-

ly slow, like always. "That's why they were kind of laughing at the whole thing, but there was free food," observes Engstrom. "And then Craig started it running while I was standing up there with people yelling at me, and when it motion blurred there was a big gasp that went through the crowd. The first question asked was, 'How do I do that?' The fastest evangelism moment in technology I've ever heard of. It was just as fast as we could go."

What they showed was a customized version of Accolade's Super Bubsy at 640x480 resolution in 24-bit color, running at 60 fps. Just for fun, they then turned off the vertical blank sync and the game became a blur, running at 500 fps. Engstrom explains, "It was an Accolade title that they gave us the art

to. We fixed it up so that literally all it did was run sideways. It wasn't a game. We just made it show what we could do." But as St. John remembers, "The audience went wild; nobody had ever seen graphics like that on any platform of the time, let alone a PC."

Following Super Bubsy was WinDOOM running in 640x480 at 60 fps with multi-channel stereo and even a force-feedback joystick. And synchronized sound. Engstrom says, "Literally, in DOOM, put it on Windows, the gun would flash, come up, go back down… then you'd hear the boom of the rifle or pistol. It was terrible, and we managed to make it perfectly in synch."

Engstrom encouraged me to start my book with the story of this moment. To him, it was a "Steve Jobs" moment. "That's like if you've seen the Jobs movie where he says, 'I've got a thousand songs in my pocket,' where he's introducing the iPod. And then everything else is retro? That's the moment for DirectX. Everything after that was fun. That was the moment where it happened. Everything else was written after that." And he has a point. It was at that very moment that Windows gaming replaced DOS in the hearts and minds of developers—at least the 1200 or so who were present for this special moment. DirectX went on to be wildly successful, and it's not a stretch to say that Windows gaming might have been set back for years if it hadn't been for this moment, and Xbox might never have happened. *One thing leads to another…*

After snatching success from the ashes of the blue-screen; after the wildly euphoric demos, St. John and his partners were once again a happy team. And to top everything off, St. John had one last gift for everyone—a fireworks show that he got for only an extra five grand from Great America.

Of course, there were no written contracts between St. John and his sponsors, a detail that he had left for the event group to sort out after the fact. Getting it done was all that mattered at the time, and once again he figured he'd get fired once the bill made it to the accounting office at Microsoft. And once again, St. John dodged the bullet as Microsoft was able to recover at least a million dollars of the money pledged. So instead of being canned, St. John was given a great performance review and a promotion.

From April until September a team of engineers, led by Eisler and Engstrom, worked on completing the suite of Direct APIs, but there were still a few non-technical details to iron out.

Direct Gets its X

The Manhattan Game SDK enjoyed a brief period of being called the Windows Game SDK. For a while, Paul Osborne wanted to call it WinG 2.0 because somewhere along the way he had inherited the WinG project. The WinG option was unacceptable to St. John for a couple of reasons. The first of which was the association with the Disney Lion King disaster. But probably the biggest reason was that calling the new technology WinG 2.0 would mean that Chris Hecker would probably be involved, and St. John wanted to be sure that Hecker was nowhere near their project. He says, "In this case, I wasn't just being mean, because the guy was just making a mess. So he has to go. I need Craig to own this, not only because I can work with Craig, but because he can get it done. So I said, 'Look, the WinG brand is problematic. We should put that behind us.'"

In the end, after several battles, St. John got his way, and the WinG name was never used again. Ironically, WinG didn't ever truly go away. It lives on in Windows as an API called CreateDIBSection.

Whatever you called it, the software they were creating for the SDK was simply a collection of APIs with names like DirectDraw, DirectInput, DirectSound, DirectShow, DirectPlay, and so forth. People have different versions of how it got its final name, but according to Chris Phillips, the name was suggested by a journalist during an interview. "We'd go through and we'd say, DirectDraw, DirectSound, DirectInput… and somebody finally said, 'Well yeah. Ok, DirectX.' And we all just laughed. And we went, 'Oh yeah. That is so brilliant. We love that. We're using that.' And that's actually of how the X got on."

According to St. John, the first time he heard the name DirectX mentioned was from Eric Engstrom one day. Whatever actually happened, the name caught on quickly and DirectX remains today a key Microsoft technology.

The Politically Correct Logo

Microsoft corporate had already told St. John to ditch the radiation symbol in promoting their project, but he had persisted. It helped establish his anti-corporate cred. But eventually through persistence, they got him to comply—by adding another "leg" to the radiation symbol, essentially turning it into an X. James Plamondon remembers that the DirectX logo wasn't quite as simple to design as St. John likes to make it sound. "When we were trying to

Very early DirectX logo from "Microsoft Team Direct".

design a logo that included an X, he was having the hardest goddamn time with it because no matter what he did, it ended up looking like a swastika. You try to put something to make it look like it's active, like the X is moving, well that means something like putting wind turbulence behind. And a lot of the early designs of the DirectX logo were chucked immediately because they looked so much like a swastika. I love the solution they came up with, which was putting it on a 3D ball and rotating it slightly, so that it still looks like an X, but it doesn't look like a swastika because it's off center."

At the same time they changed the logo, St. John leaked to the press "that the poor DirectX team was being pressured by its evil corporate executives to

change its VERY popular logo." Again, St. John's strategy worked, and developers were coming on board to support the new project, and they were all eager to attend any new events or parties that the DirectX team threw. "With each new generation of DirectX I would craft a new politically incorrect launch theme, scandalize Microsoft with it and leak the scandal to the media."

The Beasty Boys

Brad Silverberg, as the head of the Windows division, ultimately had to approve the project that Eisler, Engstrom and St. John had been working on—making it an official Microsoft project—and he talked about what it was like working with the three of them. "Craig and Eric, and certainly Alex, especially back in those days, were high energy, really smart, and extraordinarily immature. I nicknamed them Beasty Boys. As smart as they were, they kind of went out of their way to antagonize people internally, and most of the fallout for that ended up on my lap. I knew their heart was in the right place. I knew they wanted to do the right thing for the company, and for gamers, and so I put a lot of energy behind the scenes, trying to clean up some of those messes and trying to counsel them on ways that they might be a little more—I won't even say diplomatic because that was too optimistic—but not really go poking sticks in people eyes just for the fun of it. They were brutal. They were really brutal. And they were righteous about it. They were right, but they were also righteous, which I'm sure was off-putting for a lot of people.

"I believed in the work that they were doing, so was kind of an executive benefactor and protector, and had to clean up a lot of messes and referee a lot of fights, and I had to make some decisions. For instance, I had to make the decision between work they were doing and the work that Hecker was doing. I decided correctly to choose the DirectX effort, but at the time, you don't know how it's going to turn out, and at the time, it was a decision I had to agonize over. I made the right decision. I'm pretty sure Chris Hecker was not very happy about it, and those guys had very little respect for Chris at the time, and there was a war of words and a lot of nastiness that came out of that, but in the end… You know, sometimes when you do great things, there's collateral damage that happens, and I was prepared for some of that."

But if Silverberg thought his "Beasty Boys" had been beastly in the build-up to DirectX, he soon discovered that he hadn't seen their total arsenal… yet.

~12~

3D Wars

It was obvious that any game SDK would need to support 3D graphics, and WinG had turned out not to be the ultimate solution. Microsoft had licensed SGI's 3D API, OpenGL, for the upcoming Windows NT, a platform that was meant to be a UNIX killer, primarily focusing on supporting enterprise and high-end business solutions. It was already known that Microsoft planned to switch everything over to Windows NT after the launch of Windows 95, and there was considerable rivalry between the NT team and the Windows 95 team. So, when St. John and his colleagues approached the NT team to let them use OpenGL as part of a gaming SDK they wanted to create, they were given a flat no. The NT group wasn't interested in supporting anything that might give Windows 95 more relevance. St. John remembers being told that they could have what NT had "when it's a consumer OS."

At the same time, according to St. John, Intel had announced that they were making software-based 3D APIs for Windows, and PlayStation was taking over the console market. NT, Intel, Playstation. Three almost simultaneous factors that inspired the DirectX team to develop an internal 3D API: Direct3D, knowing that this decision would place them directly into competition, not only with external threats, but with other teams within Microsoft. Engstrom didn't particularly care about Intel or PlayStation, but he took the NT group's flat refusal personally, and he saw it as his mission to give them the finger by developing their own 3D API.

Setting the Stage for Acquisition

In response to the NT group's refusal to share OpenGL, and their decision to create their own 3D API, Eisler, Engstrom and St. John decided that a smart way to approach the problem was to purchase a company with the technology, expertise, and engineers they needed. Leading the acquisition research, St. John saw four possible targets for acquisition: Argonaut, Criterion, Rendermorphics, and Epic. He decided against Epic because, although Tim Sweeney was a genius, St. John didn't want to hang everything on one genius when he could acquire several. Moreover, St. John had a deep respect for British engineers based on his experiences at Harlequin. For that reason, he favored Criterion, Argonaut, and Rendermorphics. "The British engineers, they were dedicated, hardworking, and their math expertise was way beyond what the US was producing. And so it strongly appealed to me buy a British engineering team… and Rendermorphics had eight geniuses. They were struggling; they were still early, but I liked their vision."

The way he sold the idea of purchasing a company at all was to frame it as a games-only solution, one which "couldn't possibly threaten NT's planned supremacy in the OpenGL-based professional graphics market."

Whose Idea Was It?

Even St. John's rather flexible DRG expense account wouldn't stretch to the point of acquiring a company; it was simply above his pay grade. Therefore, the first challenge was to find someone higher up the chain to authorize the purchase, but in typical St. John fashion, he didn't just go and make a request or use traditional channels to make the case for an acquisition. Instead, he formed a conspiracy with Eisler and Engstrom to get their boss, Paul Osborne, to have the idea himself. They did this by arranging for major 3D companies to come do presentations at Microsoft, and they would invite everybody to those meetings—except Paul Osborne. "I'd say, 'Hey, Criterion is in town. They're showing this 3D engine off.' The NT team is there. The consumer organization's there. The janitors are there. The busses are there. The only person not invited to the meeting is Paul Osborne."

They repeated this strategy with each visiting company, and Eisler and Engstrom would be sure Osborne knew about it. "Hey, you're not at the big 3D meeting?" they'd ask him. And so Osborne would crash the meetings, according to St. John, and say, "Hey, this is my charter. If anybody is acquiring a 3D company, it's my department. It's going to report to me." In this way, they forced Osborne not only to end up authorizing the purchase of Rendermorphics, but also to believe it was his own idea.

The Abrash Challenge

This next part of the Rendermorphics acquisition story involves Alex St. John and Michael Abrash. Abrash was, and still is, a leading expert on computer graphics. His expertise is unquestioned. And in the following accounts, he and St. John don't just disagree on certain details... they disagree on everything. As an author and historian, my job is to seek the truth, but with a clear understanding that truth can be subjective and, let's face it, people can sometimes have contradictory and yet valid beliefs. So, I will present the two sides of the story, and you can judge for yourself what you think really happened, keeping in mind that the end result is incontrovertible.

The second challenge that St. John faced in getting approval to purchase Rendermorphics was of a different sort. Paul Maritz, executive vice president of the Platforms Strategy and Developer Group, had told Osborne that the acquisition of Rendermorphics would only be considered if Mike Abrash approved of it. Abrash was at the time Microsoft's leading expert on computer graphics. Not only was he a published author on the subject, but he was widely respected throughout the graphics community. At Microsoft, what he said was law, and, in a very real sense, he was capable of stopping the Rendermorphics acquisition. In fact, he could squash any 3D graphics API on the Windows 95 side because, as part of the NT group, he was working on a 3D graphics API for OpenGL called 3DDDI (3D Device Driver Interface).

Unlike Paul Osborne, who was not very technical, Abrash was an expert, and there was no getting around that. But Abrash was also quiet and, by his own admission, a non-political man who really didn't play in the same devious sandbox as St. John, Eisler and Engstrom did.

St. John's Story

According to St. John, the tactic they used to persuade Abrash had similarities to the one used on Osborne... they claimed to know what drove Abrash, and they used it against him. "The thing that we realized about Abrash is that he really wanted to own 3D graphics," says St. John. "He was frustrated that he was the expert, and even in the OpenGL team he couldn't own the stuff. And so the song we sang to him was if you come over and help is with this, it can be your API. You can define it. You can be the visionary genius, and you can run a whole multimedia team over here."

Not content with simply appealing to Abrash's ambitions, St. John, Eisler and Engstrom engaged in a new tactic, which they called "Abrashing." The concept behind Abrashing was to steal his credibility by becoming his biggest, most vocal and most avid supporters. "He was like a religion. In the absence of anybody else knowing anything about 3D or graphics, whatever Abrash said was what went within the organization. You couldn't dispute his point of view, so if you criticized Abrash or tried to criticize him, you lost an argument immediately. 'You're not Mike Abrash. You don't have three books and aren't the famous graphics guy, and everybody likes him…'" So, every time they talked about anything related to 3D graphics, such as the acquisition of Rendermorphics or any of their Direct API efforts, they would refer to Abrash. "Abrash says this…" "Abrash… so brilliant… da da da." In other words, they would become the foremost proponents of everything Mike Abrash said or did. Being far more verbal and aggressive than the quiet and serious Abrash, they were able to get everything they wanted by using his credibility without having to argue with him "because we did a better job of pretending that we represented his point of view than he did himself."

Nobody can state definitively if having Abrash join the Direct3D team would have resulted in a successful collaboration, but there was reason to believe it would not have worked out particularly well. At one point, St. John said, "Abrash was brilliant, and we would have been happy to have him." He said that there was never ill intent toward Abrash. He was just in the way, and he could join them or oppose them. Abrash, on the other hand, was, quite reasonably, wary.

Abrash's Story

At the time the Rendermorphics acquisition was being considered, Abrash was a dev manager with four dev leads and "about 15 people, total, under me." He claims that Otto Berkes was working on 3DDDI under his direction, "and I gave one GDC talk about it, but it was very much a sideline for me."

Abrash contends that there was never any need to convince him to support the Rendermorphics acquisition. He had met the key people from Rendermorphics—Servan Keondjian, Kate Seekings, and Doug Rabson—when they first visited Microsoft. "I immediately hit it off with them and was impressed and thought they'd be a great way for Microsoft to move fast in 3D."

Abrash also recounts a meeting with Paul Osborne, Paul Maritz and several others—including Bill Gates. The subject of the meeting was the Rendermorphics acquisition. "Bill didn't see any reason it made sense, and was very dismissive for about 15 minutes, until I pointed out that 3D hardware was coming, and with it would come resources, like texture memory, that would need to be allocated and managed." At that point, he notes that the tone of the discussion changed and Gates came around to supporting the acquisition. "And of course Bill was right, as D3D ultimately showed."

As to St. John's assertion that his approval of the acquisition was contingent on promises they made to him, he replies, "Oh, please. This is fabricated from whole cloth. I never had any desire to lead anything. After leaving Microsoft, I never managed anything again for 20 years, which should be pretty good evidence for my level of desire to be in charge."

Of course, St. John questions Abrash's story, asking why he was so interested in Rendermorphics in the first place and how he came to be in a meeting with Osborne, Maritz and Gates if he had no stake in it personally. "Paul Osborne was only responsible for Windows video, Maritz had done the deal with SGI to acquire rights to OpenGL, Abrash was working on a driver model for OpenGL, and Bill Gates was already hugely invested in Talisman* and planning to make a Microsoft proprietary GPU and force it on the market... having recently acquired Softimage, an OpenGL-based 3D authoring tool."

**Talisman was a 3D graphics solution developed by Microsoft Research. Read more about Talisman in the Online Appendix.*

Rendermorphics

Servan Keondjian was one of many young people in Britain who became programmers on early home computers, such as the ZX80s and BBC Micros. Many of them got into programming assembly language games. Keondjian was no exception. He started writing his own 3D game early on, but got sidetracked developing the technology for games instead. He spent some time working for Magnetic Scrolls, a company that became popular by combining text adventures with nicely drawn still images. Keondjian met Doug Rapson while developing rapid high-end graphics software for them. Magnetic Scrolls did not transition into real-time games, however, and Keondjian teamed up with Rapson and Kate Seekings to form Rendermorphics, where they re-architected his fast graphics code for 3D and created an API. "At that time it was just Silicon Graphics' high-end 3D hardware doing 3D, and we were showing that we could do it faster on a PC, and also on multiple platforms. We were doing some really nice, fast 3D with very high poly counts."

Rendermorphics had competition, however. Criterion came out with Renderware and the game company Argonaut released their BRender engine. According to Keondjian, competition was good, because it started to increase awareness of 3D solutions. While most games at the time still relied on 2D graphics, 3D games were on the rise, and the time and effort it took to write a proprietary 3D engine was considerable. "It was right at that transition of game development, as it was beginning to move to more commercial teams, instead of the whole bedroom with a bunch of friends who could write good code. You just needed bigger investments, and that's where the 3D libraries started coming in."

Soon, the hardware makers began to develop graphics cards capable of accelerating 3D graphics, and they naturally turned to the major developers of 3D APIs, such as Rendermorphics and the others, who were already supporting 3D games. It became a race to see how many chips they could support, to write the hardware interfaces, and to make sure they could make them go really fast. And this, according to Keondjian, is where Microsoft came in, because controlling access to the hardware through Windows was important to their business model. "Suddenly there were these little companies like Rendermorphics and the potentially important business of the games industry that was beginning to do stuff through that 3D hardware that there was no way you could do it in Windows. So that was really why it was important for Microsoft to buy this technology and get it implemented into Windows."

Keondjian remembers that his first encounter with Microsoft was meeting Alex St. John at Siggraph in 1994. At the time, he was only aware that Microsoft was working with rival BRender on a game, and so he treated the first meeting as nothing more than a casual encounter. There was no indication at the time of any further interest.

Cute Little British People

In any case, with Abrash's approval—however it was obtained—the acquisition of Rendermorphics was able to move forward. Paul Osborne was the first to contact Rendermorphics in fall of 1994. Keondjian remembers, "We liked

Paul as a person and had a good relationship with him, but he was not very clued up on code or multimedia." After some initial talks, Osborne put Eric Engstrom, the program manager for DirectDraw, in charge of completing the acquisition. "Our first impression of Eric was that we really did not like him, as the ground was shifting through the negotiations and we could tell he was up to things. I liked Eric more, later, but it was not nice being on the side that has to deal with 'bad' Eric."

During the negotiations, Microsoft was looking to reduce the price of acquisition, and at one point someone told Keondjian, "Oh, you cute little British people. We're Microsoft. Don't you understand?" He adds, "I can't remember if it was actually Alex St. John that said that, but he was one of the people who were helping us understand that. That they were going to buy someone. They wanted to buy us, and basically, if they didn't buy us they were going to put it in Windows for free, and we'd probably go out of business. That was the approach, and we understood that. Well, it took us about 3 to 5 months to fully understand that because we didn't really want to understand that."

Keondjian's impressions of Windows at the time? "There was this big, fat, slow operating system that could just about barely do a window, and Windows 95 was the first step into making it cooler. So then after they bought us, we just had to get 3D in there."

Abrash to id

Meanwhile, Mike Abrash was done at Microsoft and gave notice to his boss, Jim Allchin, in January 1995. St. John claims that he was given "titular proxy" to Rendermorphics, but if so, it wasn't apparent to Keondjian or to Abrash himself, who continued to work in the NT division until he left toward the end of February to take a job at id Software.

Once again, St. John takes credit for influencing Abrash's decision, and claims to have steered Abrash toward id's John Carmack as the expert in all things 3D for games, saying, "I do recall that there was a period in-between the Rendermorphics acquisition and Abash going to id when I was constantly pressuring Abrash to do the right thing because he really didn't know anything about gaming, and I would bludgeon him with 'John Carmack says this' and 'John Carmack says that,' which he couldn't argue with. I did a pretty thorough job of making it clear to Mike that he really had no idea what 3D games needed and that he needed to educate himself. Abrash didn't enjoy having another 3D authority figure used to undermine his credibility." St. John also encouraged Abrash to engage directly with Carmack to learn more about the games side of 3D, figuring that if they met, the two might to get to know each other, which added to the probability that Abrash would leave Microsoft if things went badly for him. All of which Abrash refutes definitively.

Abrash contends that his relationship with Carmack was first initiated when Chris Hecker leaked him an alpha version of DOOM. "I emailed John saying how impressed I was. He said maybe we could get together next time he was visiting his mother in Seattle. We had lunch, and he offered me a job, and I declined." However, Abrash kept in contact with Carmack and ultimately went to visit id in Dallas. "I looked around the area, concluded my family could live there, and took the job. Alex only figures in the picture as a key part of what would become the Direct team, which was one of the factors making working at Microsoft no fun. He had nothing whatsoever to do with my relationship with John."

St. John also believes that Abrash was caught in a difficult position regarding his work on 3DDDI, and that he was opposed to the layered approach Keondjian was taking because it would have been far more advanced than the work he was doing, which was more suitable for CAD applications than games. "He would have had to re-architect his OpenGL driver model to be much more ambitious to keep it ahead of the driver model we were cooking up for consumer gaming. So Abrash quickly realized that he'd lost control and was stuck between a rock and a hard place so to speak."

Keondjian agrees that the OpenGL implementation was in need of considerable changes. "Doug and I did bring the cutting edge state into Microsoft. And Alex was doing the right thing to bring that in. DDI and OGL at that time really were not ready for where 3D for games was going and needed to go in the future. When I first started talking to Mike about DDI, there was absolutely no way it could even do texture mapping, and we were doing loads of that in software rendering already and could see 3D hardware on the horizon that would do that soon. But saying that, I could have found a home for DDI as an optional driver for D3D (optional as doing it under the hood so users would never see it or know, but just support all options). And D3D could have added all that layering. Mike was also amenable to putting in some of the innovations we had come up with at Rendermorphics to really accelerate triangle throughput, so I could have made it all fit together quite nicely."

As to why Keondjian ultimately made the decision to support the DirectX effort he says, "I wanted better software and I wanted 3D hardware for the masses as soon as possible. That's why I did it."

While St. John claims that he had no intention of making an enemy of Abrash, whom he respected, Engstrom was a different story. He was so pissed off with the NT group that he took a much more aggressive approach, making sure that everybody knew how they had intentionally given the middle finger to the OpenGL team, including Abrash. In the end, it seemed that getting rid of Abrash was the only solution left. Typically ruthless, St. John sums it up. "We were happy to have his talent helping us with 3D if he wanted to help us. But if he didn't want to help us, then fuck him… I feel terrible about it. I have blood on my hands. We got him to say yes. We dumped him. We stole his credibility. Got Rendermorphics and then just ran off with it. Dumped 3DDDI in favor of making our own 3D driver architecture. Then, what could Abrash do, but quit? And where did he go? Id."

Cameron Myhrvold, who had unleashed St. John on Microsoft, was aware of what was happening. "Basically, where they could, and people were in their way, they'd figure out ways to try to get them fired. Now Abrash was way too talented to ever get fired, but what they did is they convinced a game ISV, id, the guys that made DOOM, they hired Michael, and that removed Michael as an obstacle in the halls of Microsoft."

Whatever the truth behind it is, Abrash did ultimately decide to leave Microsoft and go work with Carmack, but when he told his boss, Windows NT head Jim Allchin, of his intention, Allchin asked him to reconsider. "Oh no. We'll figure this out." Next came Paul Maritz, who also tried to talk him out of it, followed, to Abrash's amazement, by Bill Gates himself, who spent an hour with him. "How much is an hour of Bill's time worth, trying to figure out how this can work? And they had me actually right on the edge of, 'Well, I guess maybe I'll stay.'"

After that, he didn't hear from any of them again. Instead, they sent Alex St. John to talk with him, and to tell him that they would hold his options open for six months if he changed his mind later. "It was such an odd misreading of the situation," he says, "because Alex had kind of made my life miserable.

It's just funny that they sent the one person who would be least likely to cause me to say, 'Oh well. I'll stick around.'"

To St. John, this was icing on the cake. "I couldn't wait to deliver that message on their behalf. I was sooooo sympathetic. Oh yeah, I think we were rolling on the floor for a couple days over that one. That was the ultimate proof that 'Abrashing' had worked brilliantly. Everybody, all the way up to Gates, who had approved the Rendermorphics acquisition, believed we were absolutely Mike Abrash's closest friends and biggest fans. Yeah... that must have really boggled his mind."

Many years later, Abrash is philosophical about what happened, but acknowledges that he was the victim of some kind of coordinated efforts against him. "I kind of got made a character in this because it's useful to have, I mean maybe not a villain, but somebody on the other side. So when Alex framed this story the way he did, it was that Chris and maybe John Carmack and I were against this. I mean, Chris is very straightforward. But there is no reason that OpenGL couldn't have been used, except that an open API is harder to evolve and didn't really fit with the way that Microsoft approached things at that time, as far as I could see. Alex and Eric Engstrom and Craig Eisler were on a mission to do this thing, and I'd been at Microsoft for a couple of years. I'd been the GDI lead for the first couple of versions of NT, and basically I think in some way I was an obstacle. I'm not sure exactly how. I was kind of on my way out anyway, to go work at id."

It may be impossible to know the entire truth, since both Abrash and St. John take such opposite positions, but it's clear that St. John's story is consistent with the many other stories in which he figures. It's even possible that St. John and Engstrom adopted tactics to force Abrash's hand, even if he already supported the acquisition. They left little to chance. As St. John told me, "We were TRAINED by Microsoft to be that way. At that time other people at Microsoft DID NOT KNOW that DRG was training charismatic engineers in *Art of War* tactics to be that diabolical and manipulative; that was a relatively closely kept secret. It came out in the DOJ trial, but it's worth noting that the people in this story at the time were not aware that they were dealing with Microsoft's own custom-trained mind-control engineers. We had been taught to manipulate entire industries... I think the surprise was that we turned inward on Microsoft. Most of the people we encountered at the time had no idea what we really did for Microsoft. There was another reason we got as far as we did without getting fired... we had special latitude in our jobs..."

Microsoft Announces Acquisition of RenderMorphics, Ltd.

Industry-Leading 3-D API to Become a Key Component of Microsoft's Multimedia Strategy

REDMOND, Wash. - Feb. 23, 1995 - Microsoft Corp. announced it has acquired RenderMorphics, Ltd., (London, United Kingdom the industry leader in 3-D programming tools and technology for personal computers. RenderMorphics' flagship product, Reality Lab(TM), provides high-performance 3-D graphics technology for a variety of personal computer-based games and multimedia applications. Reality Lab has been acclaimed by a wide range of developers, including Autodesk, Creative Labs, Kaleida Labs and Virgin Entertainment. Games incorporating 3-D graphics effects have proven to be immensely popular with consumers and are sales leaders in the rapidly growing games market.

"This acquisition adds a key multimedia technology to the Windows (R) portfolio - real-time 3-D graphics on the standard PC platform," said Brad Silverberg, senior vice president of the personal systems division at Microsoft. "Real-time 3-D graphics will enable the development of exciting new games and other applications that previously were only possible to run on high-priced, specialized systems."

Reality Lab, a real-time software-rendering library, has received accolades for its functionality, performance, easy-to-use features, and its high-quality application programming interface (API). Software that uses Reality Lab, such as games, multi- media, and virtual-reality applications, delivers new levels of performance, responsiveness and 3-D realism.

"We initially chose to license Reality Lab for probably the same reasons Microsoft chose to acquire RenderMorphics - it has a fast, robust API that offers a number of unique capabilities, allowing us to produce more scalable products in a shorter development cycle," said Christopher Yates, vice president of technology and operations at Virgin Interactive Entertainment.

"Virgin has a number of truly outstanding games coming out in late 1995 and 1996 that use Reality Lab for groundbreaking 3-D effects."

Reality Lab is modular in structure and transparently takes advantage of hardware acceleration at any stage of the graphics pipeline, further improving performance and responsiveness for the customer. Leading hardware-accelerator companies have worked with RenderMorphics and Microsoft to ensure compatibility.

"Microsoft's announcement marks an important step toward establishing an industry-standard 3-D games API," said Osman Kent, president of 3Dlabs, Inc. "In conjunction with Microsoft's 3D-DDI, this announcement will help accelerate market growth for both 3-D games and 3-D accelerators such as our GLINT chip and its derivatives."

Microsoft plans to enhance the Reality Lab product line and make it a general-purpose, real-time 3-D API in future versions of its Windows family of operating systems products (beyond the release of Windows(R) 95). The Reality Lab API will complement support for the OpenGL(TM) API, a higher-end API specially suited to professional applications.

"Microsoft's evangelism and pace-setting role will help bring 3-D to the mainstream of personal-computer software," said Kate Seekings, formerly vice president of marketing at RenderMorphics and now 3-D product manager at Microsoft. "The entire team at RenderMorphics, our existing customers, and new prospects are very excited by the opportunities that lie ahead."

Reality Lab product support, developer relations and sales will be transitioned to Microsoft's respective divisions. Customers will be able to order the existing Reality Lab 3D version 1.1 developer kit directly from Microsoft within the next 45 days. Sales and developer information can be obtained by sending a request by e-mail to Reality3@Microsoft.com.

The acquisition of RenderMorphics is the most recent of several important announcements Microsoft has made as part of its strategy to offer easy and powerful multimedia support to users of Windows. Other recent announcements include Multisession Compact Disk support for new audio-CD format; Surround Video, a technology that enables full-screen, interactive multimedia titles with 360-degree photorealistic scenery; AutoPlay, a technology that allows CD-ROM-based titles and games to start automatically; WinG, a technology for fast game animation; DCI, a specification for enhanced video performance; WinToon, a technology for creating interactive cartoons; and support for MPEG technology for compressing digital video.

Much later, in retrospect, St. John wrote to me saying, "I think it's perfectly reasonable to question whether or not the degree to which we attempted to manipulate Mike was entirely necessary. It was certainly cruel and unprofessional. We had, however, tested lighter approaches to navigating the Mike Abrash obstacle without success and we had been told unambiguously that his support was essential to acquiring Rendermorphics. Mike has every good reason to resent and deny the terrible things we did to him... and he did pay us back through Hecker and later by joining ID to help John become a vocal OGL advocate."

Stepping into the Middle

"Servan was the visionary behind our choice to commit to z-buffer support for D3D. That was a crazy leap for consumer 3D back then when memory was so expensive. He believed that it would be a driving feature in consumer 3D and was correct. The OGL drivers Abrash specified had no support for it. Neither did Talisman."

–Alex St. John

The Rendermorphics deal did not require the company to relocate to Redmond, but Keondjian was needed Stateside, and so he spent a lot of time at Microsoft. It took some adjustment. "I was actually surprised at how slow things actually went because of the politics. How much energy went into it. I mean fifty percent of my time, at least, became spent dealing with email, dealing with politics from everyone who wanted to be involved in the 3D stuff. And I knew absolutely nothing about it… Yeah. It was ridiculous."

A Few Seeds

On one of his journeys from Britain to America to present a new hardware device driver for Direct3D to vendors, Keondjian was detained at customs. A sniffer dog detected marijuana in his bag. On inspection, it turned out that there were some seeds at the bottom of the bag, which Keondjian claims was borrowed from a friend. His visa was revoked and he was no longer able to travel in the United States. However, Microsoft's lawyers quickly jumped into action and got him a new visa. Human Resources told him that they had no problem dealing with these issues as long as the work got done. Keondjian, none the worse for wear, nevertheless was forced to endure a bit of teasing at Microsoft.

Between Two Poles

Note: A lot of what follows in this chapter involves technical elements of 3D graphics rendering. You have been forewarned.

Keondjian worked mostly with Engstrom, but he enjoyed the company of Abrash, until he left, and Otto Berkes in the NT group because they were the only people who had any true understanding of 3D graphics. "So I was in this quite weird place, because Otto and Mike Abrash actually knew what they were doing, and I wanted to work with them. They really understood 3D, and I liked those guys. And there was Alex and Eric, who were really fighting quite a political battle, and they had a really uphill struggle to get this stuff in, and I'm not sure if Otto and Mike Abrash were friends, or even liked them at all, because they were competing groups within Microsoft. So I was really pulled between two poles."

The conflict even reached all the way to Bill Gates at one point when Keondjian replied to an email argument by the NT team saying that OpenGL needed to be absorbed into Windows. He wrote, "Well, I've been told I need to create the DirectX 3D APIs the way that fits with DirectX. That's who I'm working for in this … And there's a good reason for having it independent, controlled by Microsoft, because we can actually lead the features that we want." In the end, what Keondjian had to admit to the value of developing a proprietary 3D API with the features they chose, and with the flexibility to improve internally, rather than having to work with an open standard like OpenGL that they didn't control.

Technically, Keondjian's team made several improvements, such as building into DirectDraw a 32-bit calling layer, which allowed the 3D driver to be written in 32-bit code, where everything previously was in 16-bit. Rendermorphics software, which they called "Reality Lab," was a 32-bit system that provided very fast 3D, and so this calling layer made it possible to use their already proven technology.

One of the keys to Rendermorphics' speed was its revolutionary use of the Z-buffer, which actually enabled 3D graphics to run faster than even the current 3D hardware. "People did not believe this was possible, but with good programming and optimization I had worked out how to do this."

The new 3D API—still called Reality Lab—debuted in DirectX 2.0 and introduced the concept of an execute buffer.* This was the lowest level interface they could provide for the hardcore developers, but its implementation was rushed and confusing to many developers, who found it difficult to use. This, in turn, generated a lot of bad press.

* *Microsoft's website defines execute buffer as, "A fully self-contained, independent packet of information that describes a 3-D scene. An execute buffer contains a vertex list followed by an instruction stream. The instruction stream consists of operation codes and the data that is operated on by those codes."*

It took time, and several iterations of DirectX before Microsoft's 3D API was fully accepted by the developer community, but ultimately it was a success.

The Power of Naming

"Basically, we were Rendermorphics," says Keondjian. "We'd come in as Rendermorphics." And being Rendermorphics, they continued to call their API the Reality Lab, refusing to name it after the other "Direct" APIs being developed. On the other hand, there was power in the name, and Engstrom was trying to build a "Direct" API brand. The decision to change the name occurred after a meeting when Engstrom was urging Keondjian to change the name to Direct3D. "The big push from him and Craig was to get me to use the DirectDraw surface as a texture." This one technical change made all the difference. "As soon as the DirectDraw surface was a texture in Rendermorphics, we were basically heading the Rendermorphics API to be Direct3D, and we created the execute buffer structure and sort of hooked it all up and brought it into the Direct3D and DirectDraw interfaces." Keondjian was also suggesting that DirectDraw disappear altogether, and that everything should run through Direct3D, but at the time this message wasn't practical, as Direct3D was not yet proven and DirectDraw was. In time, however, that's exactly what happened, but not until Windows 7.

A DirectDraw Image is a Texture

Keondjian explains further: "DirectDraw was all about these surfaces that have images/pixels on them. You can copy them around and move images around very quickly on the screen. That's what DirectDraw was basically all about, whereas 3D is all about loading textures onto the hardware and then using them on 3D shapes. The 2D image is a subset of the 3D shape. In other words, a DirectDraw surface was an image buffer or sprite, but really in 3D speak this is just a texture. So what I was saying to them is that we don't need you guys because we've already got all that functionality here, but they were saying, 'But come in with our API specs, and we can form a more powerful offensive.' That was a political decision, and it was a big shift when I said, 'OK. We'll do it, but that means calling this thing Direct3D,' and that's when I sort of broke from the Otto and Mike Abrash lot. I couldn't work with them anymore because I was suddenly… I was very much a DirectX thing. So in the early days a texture was created from a DD surface, which was the right way to do it, but DD and D3D were still quite separate since we were only just beginning to bolt the two things together. It got cleaned up more and more over time."

Leaving Microsoft

Keondjian left Microsoft after Direct3D was completed. He didn't really have much interest in the politics. He was only interested in making a great 3D system for Windows. But, as much as he considered that politics at Microsoft had caused a lot of headaches for the industry at large—especially the battle between Direct3D and OpenGL—he had also come to understand how things got done at Microsoft. "None of that stuff would have happened without politics, so you have to have both, and I think that's what I really learned at Microsoft. That is why I supported Eric and Alex, because I thought they were doing the right thing technologically. I don't know if they did the right thing personally. I think they made enemies. I didn't want to make enemies, but I did want to do the right thing technologically. So that was the challenging place I was put in by then, and that's why I left in the end. That was not for me."

Other Views on Rendermorphics

More reactions and comments from 3D developers, see the Online Appendix.

Zack Simpson

The first version of DirectX was still in development during the time that the Rendermorphics acquisition and early Direct3D development were taking place—with all the associated drama. Meanwhile, St. John, in addition to working with John Miles on sound, had contact with another Austin, Texas company, Origin Systems. He and Zack Simpson, who was then the chief of technology at Origin, had met previously, and St. John knew that the people at Origin hated Microsoft… and for his purposes, that was perfect. His thinking was that they would be the ideal people to help him in his quest to make Windows a kick-ass game platform. "If they got mad at Microsoft, I'd bring them right in and put them in front of the engineer they were upset with."

Origin was well known in the PC game world for pushing the envelope, often requiring state-of-the-art graphics (and for some customers, major computer upgrades) to run their games. They had already hacked Windows to create proprietary technologies, such as their own Voodoo Memory System, which allowed them to access memory that was normally not accessible under Windows.

And so, in the summer of 1995, only weeks before the delivery date for the first version of DirectX, St. John invited Simpson, Frank Savage and Tony Braden to come down to Redmond and beat on Windows for a while. Origin founder Richard Garriott was happy to send them. "It really was on some level, an attempt to serve ourselves," he says. In fact, remembering previous Microsoft failures—he specifically names Memory Manager—Garriott went from, "Please call us before you implement any of this," to "Just let us do it." And Simpson, Savage and Braden were happy to go, says Garriott, "because they knew that it was not only going to make their work easier back at the home office, but also that they would set the standards that most any game developer would use."

St. John expected the Origin engineers to hate the early versions of DirectX, but more importantly, that they would be able to identify in detail exactly which parts they hated and why—parts that St. John could then fix. "So Zack would bitch to me and just rage on about how much he hated Windows. I would take everything he said, get it fixed, and then ask him to look at it to see if he was happy yet. I sucked him right in. So Zack in some ways was an unwilling accomplice because we got along great. He really liked the fact that, even though Microsoft would crap things up, I gave him access, and I would make people listen to him, and I would beat on them to pay attention to what he said… and that would produce improvements."

From Simpson's perspective, as much as he might have hated Windows, he also knew from conversations with St. John, starting as early as 1993, that the days of DOS games were coming to an end—a realization that many of his colleagues resisted. "I had a hard internal sell because I had to convince my programmers that DOS was going away, and that was not a popular view at the time. But it was very clear to me that DOS was going to die, and it was going to be replaced, so we had to do something."

Simpson, Savage, and Braden spent a month at Microsoft, living in a small apartment in Redmond, and hacking out various demos and small game prototypes to test out Windows 95, then called Chicago. They were not working for Microsoft, but for Origin, says Simpson. We were there to gain knowledge so that we could come back and spread knowledge of how were going to convert all of our stuff to Windows." He remembers Savage porting a version of Wing Commander 3 to Windows while Braden worked on some other projects. Simpson's most memorable game prototype was a "tile-based, overhead game that involved running down the corridors of Microsoft and trying to kill Bill Gates." This was perhaps inspired by the long-time tradition in Ultima of including obscure ways to kill the otherwise invulnerable Lord British (Richard Garriott's in-game alias), but Simpson admits it might just as well have been a way of expressing his real feelings about Microsoft.

COM Objects and Abstraction Layers

Simpson had his beefs with Windows. He really disliked the COM (Common Object Model) that Microsoft had adopted. He saw it as overkill for the game APIs, comparing it unfavorably against more direct Win32 APIs… "In other words, just a list of useful functions that weren't pseudo object oriented with droids all over the place. It was just very, very difficult to work with, and as far as I know, it's still difficult to work with to this day."

St. John's explanation of COM validates Simpson's opinion. "Making DirectX a COM (Common Object Model) API was another architectural abomination that we swallowed with some bitterness. COM was a strategy cooked up by the Office Products group to 'unify' all of the Windows Office products in a way that made them highly interdependent without it being easy for them to be accused of engaging in 'monopolistic' practices. The COM model had been foisted off on both OS groups as a grand strategy that everybody had to support. Every Windows API had to conform to the slow, confusing and cumbersome COM model. Half of the Developer Relations

Group was devoted to promoting it to developers. We got a lot of grief from game developers for it over the years, which I believe was rightly deserved."

In hindsight, St. John does credit the COM model for allowing future versions of DirectX to improve rapidly while preserving backward compatibility. "DirectX as a whole was in continuous development with subsets of functionality getting peeled off and 'productized' for release. Ironically <but intentionally> it was made possible by the early adoption of the much reviled COM model for DirectX, because it made it possible to ship one release of DirectX that was backwards compatible with all previous versions even when there were major feature differences between them. DirectX could evolve fast because it didn't have to worry about backwards compatibility, which held back development on all other platform APIs in that era."

One positive, Simpson notes, was that Windows made an attempt to improve on some major obstacles previously associated with DOS development. One such improvement was the addition of abstraction layers where it came to hardware interfaces for sound cards, joysticks and other hardware. "Before Windows, device drivers for DOS were like pseudo standards that weren't very clearly spelled out, and usually proprietary, and so instead of talking to an abstraction layer, and then the abstraction layer talked to a device driver that implemented that abstraction layer, it was more like you had to go talk to the device directly."

Simpson uses the example of sound cards in the old DOS games. "You'd have to pull down this list of sound cards and pick your exact sound card, right?" And in those days, the developers would have to write their own device drivers for nearly every sound card. The same was often true with joysticks. "We had horrendous testing matrices where we had to test every permutation of sound card and joystick." As for video, before the advent of dedicated video cards, he says, "It was run in this kind of driverless compatibility, hacked-up direct access mode where you had direct access to the memory buffers and you wrote straight into them."

At Origin they had to use something they called "slam," which entailed filling a back buffer with data and then switching it to the front buffer all at once… slamming it to the front. Another method, page flipping, he said was not as reliable a solution for Origin because not all people had hardware that supported that method.

The use of abstraction layers forced the hardware suppliers to create the device drivers specifically for their products, instead of forcing each company to create custom code for each and every supported sound card and joystick.

Simpson was very happy about the inclusion of abstraction layers, but not quite satisfied. As he puts it, "Windows 95 had abstraction layers for everything office-y, and nothing game-y. You couldn't write into a buffer anywhere and just get those pixels onto the screen. And the sound APIs had a whole bunch of latency. They were meant for mixing little dings and dongs, and stuff. They weren't meant for multichannel, real-time continuous, low-latency sound effects. The joystick basically wasn't even handled at all. I think there was just kind of like two button and X Y, and there was no dealing with the fact that there were all these other joystick devices."

On the graphics side, Simpson says that games needed the pixels to go directly to the screen. From the Windows point of view, graphics information might need to go elsewhere, such as to a printer, and having that ability created overhead. With WinG, Chris Hecker had created the idea of a device independent bitmap, or DIB—a solution that definitely sped up graphics under Windows. However, it was, according to Simpson, "all very complicated, and without going into tons of crazy technical stuff, there were these 16-bit thunking layers, and it's all very complicated to deal with because Windows 95 was a hybrid 16-bit, sort of pseudo, sometimes 32-bit operating system."

As for WinG, Simpson says that the performance wasn't terrible, but it wasn't spectacular, either. Moreover, he states, "It was still conforming to the Windowsy title bar with the limited size window." This was before the revelation of KillGDI. The Manhattan SDK, however, was designed from the beginning to provide full-screen, direct memory access. "It was implemented as a COM object, which was very difficult. It was a lot easier to work with WinG than it was with DirectX, but DirectX gave you lots of goodies that you needed."

Of course, this is what St. John wanted from the Origin team, and it's what he got. According to St. John, it was the feedback from the Orgin team that helped define what DirectX needed to become. "In some sense, DirectX is Zack Simpson's fault," he says. In retrospect, St. John laments the fact that he got Simpson and the people at Origin to be believers, to come to trust Microsoft to listen and respond to their needs as developers. That was St. John's credo, but eventually, after he was gone, "Microsoft would do what Microsoft did, which is take all that good feedback until everybody was sucked in and dependent on Windows, and then ignore them again, or let things go to hell when they didn't care anymore. I felt terrible about it, too, because, oh shit, what have I done? By giving these game developers the faith that Microsoft cared and respected and would listen to their feedback, I got them all dependent on Microsoft, which gave Microsoft the comfort to dismiss that and abuse them again."

But, despite St. John's expectations, Simpson isn't bitter about it today. "I don't have any regret. I think DOS had to die, and something had to be done to get the games onto Windows, and whether I was involved or not, even if Alex hadn't been involved, it would have eventually happened. It just wouldn't have happened as soon."*

Did Games Save Windows?

St. John was not as confident as Simpson about the inevitability of Windows gaming. "Windows was at an architectural junction between the old 16-bit Windows code base embodied in Win95 and the new Windows NT code base. NT was designed from the ground up as a giant monolithic, hyper secure, bloated enterprise OS. Its abstraction layers were so thick that any hope of supporting real-time anything like gaming was hopeless and DEEPLY entrenched in the NT architecture. Windows 95 was also badly broken for gaming BUT we were able to mine it with the DirectX booby trap before it shipped and the mine was that when a DirectX library shipped with a Windows 95 game, the GAME would virtually cripple Windows 95 in order to make the game run properly. If it had not been for the WILD and unexpected success of games on DirectX, the Windows 95 code base would not have survived all the way to Windows XP, and Microsoft would not have been forced to completely re-architect NT to support games. (Recall that the

**Here James Plamondon comments: "DRG was not brought into existence to 'sell developers on Microsoft's APIs'; it was brought into existence to assemble inconvertible evidence, from ISVs, that Microsoft's APIs sucked, and that they would suck less if they [were changed to do what ISVs wanted] -- and then go beat Microsoft's engineers over the head with this evidence. (That, and fuck the competition, of course.) DRG was in the "make Windows suck less" business. DRG's death knell was moving it out of the Systems Division into the Marketing Division, which dramatically weakened its 'improve our platform' focus, and over-emphasized its 'sell our platform' focus."*

DX3.0 that shipped with NT was a performance disaster, it just didn't work.) Without the market success of DirectX and Windows 95, Microsoft would never have been FORCED to deal with gaming. The PLAN was to bury Windows95 as fast as possible after it shipped and replace it with NT. Nobody imagined that Win95 would haunt them for years after it was released because of DX. I don't believe Microsoft could or would have ever overhauled NT if Windows 95 hadn't defined the standard that NT had to meet for gaming. Nobody in the NT org was ever going to call on id or Zack for input on how to make games work... the day would never have come."

Back at Origin

When Simpson, Savage and Braden returned to Origin, they found that their colleagues had removed the doors to all of their offices, boarded them up with sheetrock and painted over them—"just basically erased the existence of our offices."

Each of them responded differently. Simpson had somebody draw an outline of his body on the wall—"like a dead body outline"—and he took a reciprocating chainsaw and cut an exact-size hole in the wall, which he used to enter the office. Frank Savage made a small mouse hole at the bottom of the wall so that you had to wriggle in on your belly. He left it that way for months. Simpson finally asked him why he didn't fix it, and Savage's response was, "Oh, I like it that way because Chris* has to prostrate himself every time he comes to see me."

**Chris Roberts, the creator of Wing Commander*

Simpson says he's pretty sure that Richard Garriott was behind the prank, and when I asked him if that was true, Garriott smiled slyly and said, "But of course." In fact, pranks were fairly common at Origin in those days, in large part because of Garriott's mother. "My mother would do things like, when we'd go out to see a scary movie, in the middle of the night she would do something like come rub a hairbrush on our door, make a "Scraaaaaatch" sound on the door." Garriott remembers another of his mother's pranks, which perhaps helped inspire the one played on Simpson and the others returning from Microsoft. "When my sister was young, we got some brown wrapping paper—the kinds of paper my mom used to use in her art studio—and we sealed in my sister's room with paper painted as if it was a brick wall, so in the morning when she got up to open her door, she would find a brick wall there."

Back to Origin, it also happened that a building crew was onsite doing some remodeling, "So thinking back on the way my mother used to do these torturous things to us as a kid, we had the people and tools in the building at the moment to provide this crew of people an interesting time when they returned." In one case, they actually took out the door and put new studs in, with baseboard and trim, sheet rocked and painted so that there was no way you could tell there had ever been an office there. For that specific office, they also mounted a fire ax on the opposite wall. Garriott remembered the "person-shaped" hole and the crawlway solutions that two of the returning members used to gain access to their offices again, and when asked about the third he said, "Oh yes, third one really did use the fire axe to chop their way in."

Of course, revenge was the only reasonable response according to Simpson. "In retaliation, we bought like a bazillion packing peanuts and we went into Richard's office when he wasn't there, and we filled every single bit of volume, opened up every drawer, opening up everything, and filled it all up—100 percent packing peanuts all the way up to the roof. We built a dam, and then closed the door and pulled the dam so that when you opened the door it was like millions of packing peanuts came out."

Some Technical Issues Raised in This Chapter

More technical information about Z-Buffers, Cap Bits and other details about the development of Direct 3D, please see "Z-Buffers, Cap Bits and the Metal" and "The Problem of Capability Bits" in the Online Appendix.

-13-
Start Me Up!

Windows 95 launched on August 24, 1995. The launch was an expensive and grandiose affair. Microsoft paid the Rolling Stones a good deal of money (though possibly not the $8 or $14 million sums that were rumored) for use of their song "Start Me Up", and they also released a 30-minute promotional video featuring Jennifer Aniston and Mathew Perry. Jay Leno introduced Bill Gates on stage. They had the Empire State Building lit up with the Windows logo, and they hung a 328 foot banner from the top of the CN Tower in Toronto, as well as paying to distribute 1.5 million special editions of The Times in the UK (free copies for the first time in the 307 year history of the paper). They also gave away a CD that contained the game Hover! and some songs by Edie Brickell and Weezer. (*Source: Wikipedia*)

According to a Washington Post article posted on launch day, IBM, developer of the rival OS2 operating system, was unimpressed. "Microsoft is delivering the same features we delivered seven years ago," said company spokesman Tim Breuer. "We're moving on business as usual here."* Despite IBM's sour grapes, the lavish Windows 95 launch was a huge success worldwide, and ushered in a new era for the PC operating system.

http://www.washingtonpost.com/wp-srv/business/longterm/microsoft/stories/1995/debut082495.htm

DirectX 1.0

At the time of the Windows 95 launch, DirectX 1.0 was still about a month from completion, which assured that it could not be included with the OS. In fact, DirectX was not included in Windows releases until Windows 98. The SDK was completed in September, however, and was used by developers in their games for that year. "We had to beg, borrow, and steal developer cycles to put the hooks for DirectX into Windows 95 so that it could ship separately," says St. John. "That was the funny point about it. The world thought it was a feature of Windows, but in reality it was launched by the game developers themselves in their games. If game developers hadn't used it in droves there would have been no DirectX anywhere. It quickly became (and still is) the most downloaded technology on microsoft.com."

It was no easy path to get to launch. As Engstrom remembers it, "It wasn't clear it was going to be allowed to ship, but it was clear that the customers were going to use it if we got it out the door. That's the moment of product definition. And everything else was just fighting to make sure that no one killed it. I mean the OpenGL guys wanted it dead. They thought that having an SGI API would be smarter than having a Microsoft API. No one thought

**Plamondon notes that, while this statement was entirely true, "IBM tried to use PS/2 to exclude all other hardware vendors, and OS/2 to exclude most other software vendors. Hence, no one was willing to support it, whereas Microsoft spent a fortune on helping every ISV, IHV, and clone vendor PROFIT from supporting Windows. IBM (like Apple) was greedy in the short run, and failed. Microsoft was greedy in the LONG run, and succeeded. Moral: Short-run greed is bad, but long-run greed is good, because it COMPELS you to welcome and support the success of others."*

it needed to be bitmap, even though all the games used bitmaps. Nobody thought you should care about sound. It was a most interesting paradox at Microsoft, to have something that the developers and customers love, and the internal politics is just a nightmare."

Buggy

"It was all held together with chewing gum."

-Rick Rashid

The first version of DirectX was not without its flaws. It was a solution still in need of refinement, but it didn't cause any Lion King-scale disasters either. According to Rick Rashid, who was the head of Microsoft Research at the time, DirectX was not the only thing that was buggy. "Everything was buggy back then. Graphics cards were incredibly buggy back then. It was hard to get two of them from the same manufacturers that behaved exactly the same way. We forget that these days… even now hardware's still buggy, but we forget how much on the edge computing was in those days… The graphics cards barely worked. The software was built on top of things that barely worked. The Intel chips barely worked. I mean everything… It was all held together with chewing gum. And it worked most of the time. Miraculously."

In our fascinating conversation, Rashid elaborated on the role of the operating system in mitigating hardware instabilities. "A lot of the job of the operating system in those days, and even still today, was to mask over some of the underlying unreliabilities. One of the features that had to go into Windows was the ability to effectively reset the bus so that we could reset the graphics card on the fly (*see "The OS Illusion" at the end of this chapter for more on this subject from Rick Rashid*).

Meltdown

Meltdowns were a response to the Disney Lion King Disaster. Every year we started to organize developer and IHV events to ensure that new Windows applications worked on new PC hardware for XMAS hoping to prevent another fiasco.

Basically the IHV's would set up meeting rooms and scheduled meetings with the game developers to test the new games on their new software and

hardware. It was great for everybody because it gave the IHV's a great forum to promote their hardware to developers and the developers loved to get free hardware.

-Alex St. John

The Meltdown event was in part a response to the Lion King disaster, but it was also an important way for Microsoft to bring hardware developers together to test and discuss the new DirectX technologies. Meltdown was organized by hardware evangelist Ty Graham and software evangelist Jason White at the request of Eric Engstrom.

At the time, 3Dfx had the momentum in graphics hardware for the PC, but they had their own technologies that didn't necessarily conform to Microsoft's methodology with DirectX. Graham says, "We were definitely feeling like the underdogs in this space. Certainly in '95 and DirectX 1, we were scrambling madly." Together, Graham and White created the Meltdown events, which occurred prior to each major DirectX release, in August or September. According to Graham, it was a chance for all the hardware developers to do compatibility testing, "and then we started taking the entire DirectX team. It really turned into my platonic ideal of what a Microsoft developer event would be. We brought all our smart guys and they brought all their smart guys. People had a lot of fun, and there were great conversations and a lot of bugs got smashed, and we found out where the architecture was totally fucked up." In the beginning, there were about 100 attendees, but at its peak in 1997, Graham estimates that more than a thousand people came. "It became almost all that I did. I just became the Meltdown guy for a year."

How Did Meltdown Get Its Name?

According to Graham, Meltdown's name was inspired by St. John's anti-Microsoft campaign and his use of the radiation symbol. "We have this atomic theme," said Graham, "so it became Meltdown because that sounded appropriate in some way." Graham tells a story that illustrates the power of the Meltdown events and how the will of the developers actually changed Microsoft's strategy.

At Meltdown 98, he says, Deborah Black decided that Microsoft was not going to support DirectX in the upcoming version of Windows, but only in Windows NT. Game evangelist Kevin Bacchus was given the task of announcing the decision to a thousand or so industry folks from both hardware and software. Graham says, "We knew that they were just going to lose their shit when they heard this, and he worked so hard on how to say that in a positive way. I've never seen a guy given such a turd to present as Kevin announcing that, and of course everyone lost their shit, and it was like we had insurrection on our hands."

On the second day of the conference, the top guy in Windows NT, Jim Allchin, addressed the conference, in theory to take the heat and smooth things over. It didn't work out exactly that way. "Ultimately, when he saw the vehemence that we were dealing with, he retracted the position. It didn't make Deb Black many friends… I think that was her being decisive. She really didn't get the space. She seemed sort of clueless on this one." Allchin ultimately became the head of both Windows and Windows NT.

Hiring Jason Robar

"It was through my being a Dungeon Master that Craig and Alex thought I would be a good addition to the evangelism effort, based on the wild role I created for Alex to play as the secret villain of the entire campaign," says Robar. "Alex thought that was a pretty good understanding of some of the DRG evangelism concepts —along with my military background and passion for games and the game industry.

"One of the first things that Alex brought me in to do was to deal with more of the developers outside of the handful that he was able to deal with while dealing with all the internal issues. He had already arranged to do the port for Doom and had brought Zack Simpson from Origin to talk about importing Wing Commander, but outside of that, we still needed to get to the broader swath of developers. So if Alex was say 80% focused on fighting the internal battles and 20% focused on working with external developers, I would have that inverted, working 80% of the time with external developers and 20% coordinating with what was going on internally. So I was able to go to Sony's development team in Liverpool who were making a launch title for PlayStation called Wipeout, and I was able to work with them a get them to create a DirectX version for Windows. So what was seen as an exclusive and groundbreaking graphical title was suddenly shown to be just as possible on the PC with DirectX."

Talking about DRG's mission, he states that the goal was to help developers get measurable success through using Microsoft technology. He says there's a saying, "cradle to grave," and that for DRG, he thought to change it to "cradle to bank," because obviously the goal was to help developers with technology, but also to create successful products. "By that I meant that it's not very good if you convince developers to adopt Windows NT in 1992, and no one is adopting Windows NT in the workplace, so they make an NT version of their application, but then they can't sell it to anyone. What happens is, those people don't die—cradle to grave—they don't actually die. They lose their jobs. The company goes out of business… So my concrete example was that I thought, not only did I have to convince people to adopt Microsoft technologies as a win, I help them to win in the marketplace so that everybody else looks at those applications and says, 'Boy, that's how I'm going to get rich, too.' If they look at those applications and say, 'Oh, those poor fools. They listened to Microsoft and went out of business,' and then you show up, they're not going to listen to you. So I said that not only should we do something that highlights that we're winning—that we have these guys adopting our technologies—but we've need to do something that helps them sell more copies of their games than ever before."

A Simple Idea

One day Jason Robar had an idea. On the surface, it was a small idea. He thought, why don't we create a disk with some games on it? Games that used DirectX, of course. As a DirectX evangelist he decided to go forward with what he called the "sampler CD" concept, so he approached game developers and encouraged them to use DirectX and then create demos that could be featured on the disk, promising that Microsoft would distribute a gazillion of them.

Robar is humble when he talks about the disk, its overall impact and his role in its creation, but not so James Plamondon. "The game sampler CD became a product that Jason created out of whole cloth. And it was tremendously important because none of the technical innovations in DirectX would have meant shit if the consumer demand for the games using DirectX hadn't emerged. We did a great job of evangelizing the APIs and getting developers to support them, but we did an absolutely abysmal job of marketing the logo and general outreach to consumers to get them buy the products that implemented those latest APIs."

In fact, the Windows 95 Game Sampler CD ultimately became a huge consumer success for Microsoft, but it took the talents and imagination of several people to bring it to fruition.

Monolith—The Megamedia Artists

Ex-Marine Jace Hall was working for children's game publisher Edmark at the time. He and his friends had been writing some custom code for Windows 3.1 on the side, but compared with DOS programming, Windows was a nightmare. "Windows 3.1 just had so many layers," says Hall, "you couldn't really do anything fast inside of it in that UI." However, they soon became aware of Chris Hecker's API, WinG, and started using it to create some demo games and put them on CD ROMs. While working on these side projects, Hall encountered Jason Robar on Usenet, and they started talking. According to Hall, Robar told him, "I'm working for this guy named Alex St. John. We're trying to do this thing to make graphics faster in Windows because everybody knows that if you don't get the games over to Windows, no one's going to buy Windows 95."

Robar told him that their "little project" was unauthorized, but would allow him and his fellow developers to come over to Microsoft and do some secret contract work. That was good enough for Hall. "Long story short, I agreed, and I quit my job and some of the guys quit their jobs, and we literally went over to Building 6 as independent contractors under our overall moniker, Monolith, and started to get into this thing called DirectX. It was all just code, and we had to learn how it worked and why it worked because they wanted us to write example programs." While the DirectX team was working to complete the APIs, Hall and his Monolith team were busy becoming experts on DirectX and serving as an unauthorized private development and services department for St. John and company. For instance, the Monolith

Screen from the Windows 95 Game Sampler.

team came up with the nuclear symbol for the Manhattan Project, along with creating game demos and example code.

St. John often came to them and told them what he needed, but not how to do it, and so the Monolith team started thinking like the creative designers and gamers they were. "That's when we started to design the nuclear symbol flying around, the idea that it's in space and that you are in a space station. We built a totally 3D interactive user interface for the game sampler, all using DirectX."

So begins the Windows 95 Game Sampler CD in full 3D animation, the culmination of Robar's evangelism and the Monolith team's creative efforts. It was a clever and creative way to display the power of DirectX through game demos. As players explored the space station, they would encounter secret rooms and hidden stashes of radiation symbols. (Hall states that nobody has found all the secret rooms they hid on the station.) Players could also fire the radiation symbols, although doing so had no effect other than to show the symbols flying outward in the first-person view. There were signs on the walls with sayings such as "DOS is Dead," and information about the technology that powered the demo. One of the secret rooms contained a wall of black and white portraits of the main developers of the CD,

The DirectX Sampler Experience

"The time has come… to evolve," say the words on the screen.

FADE TO BLACK

Animated words appear: "WINDOWS 95 GAMES * NO LIMIT"

A radiation symbol animates onto the screen. It begins to spin, faster and faster, then explodes like a fist punching the screen. Back to black.

A dramatic (especially for the time) 3D model of a man appears and the camera revolves around him. He stands atop what looks like a mountain of lava, gesturing out into emptiness. A ship appears, chased by another ship firing green laser pulses. The two ships head toward a space station, and as they approach the pursuing ship is shot by the station and explodes in a ball of flame. The first ship lands inside the station, and as it sinks down on an elevator platform, the doors of the platform close after it to display the Windows 95 logo.

And now you are in a room inside the station. What will you do? A scrolling message along the bottom reads: "WELCOME TO THE MANHATTAN SPACE STATION! BROUGHT TO YOU BY MICROSOFT… AND THE WINDOWS 95 GAME SDK TEAM! DEVELOPED BY MONOLITH... MONOLITH… THE MEGAMEDIA ARTISTS!"

from right to left, Brian Goble, Bryan Bouwman, Brian Waite, Jason Hall, Toby Gladwell, Garrett Price, and Paul Renault.

Along the bottom of the screen was a function bar that included the Windows logo and the keys to operating the demo using the Esc key and function keys F1 through F6. Options were Exit, Help, Demo, WWW, 2D Menu, Map, and Teleport. To the right of the function list was a display that showed the current frames per second and the resolution of the screen.

The real meat of this sampler disk was found in the Entertainment sections, which featured animated screens along the walls. These screens represented 31 demos—some playable and some non-interactive—from companies such as Activision, id, Maxis, MicroProse, LucasArts, Virgin Interactive, Time

Warner, 7th Level, and several others. Robar had done his job well. Notable games were The Dig and Rebel Assault II from LucasArts, MechWarrior 2 from Activision, Magic the Gathering and Sid Meier's CivNet, and Monolith's own Meltdown… and of course, DOOM 95 from id.

During the development process, St. John would stop by and offer ideas, according to Hall, seemingly enjoying his first experience in game, or game-like, development. Hall remembers St. John's visits and his design work. "He'd come in and we'd have conversations about the design and argue, because he was new to it. So there were a lot of design conversations." Hall adds, "Most of the time it was them (St. John and Robar) showing up and saying, 'Hey. We convinced this publisher. Activision is going to put Pitfall. Help them get it into the sampler disk. Help them debug any DirectX problems.' And then they'd wander off somewhere."

Celebrating the Launch

There was no great event when DirectX was officially completed in September, but that didn't stop the DirectX team from celebrating. At this point in time, St. John had managed to piss off a lot of people, but there was one group that he hadn't offended… yet. "Yes, I even pissed off Microsoft's janitorial staff. We celebrated the launch of DirectX with a food fight in the conference room that just destroyed… thirty thousand dollars' worth of damage to the conference room, throwing Chinese food at each other. That was when Fred Humble got the hot mustard in his face, poor guy."

A food fight was not up to St. John's celebration standards, however, and although it had to do for the moment, the best was yet to come…

Taking Fun Seriously II

Along with the completion of the DirectX SDK, the team reissued a somewhat revised version of the *Taking Fun Seriously* white paper they had released 10 months previously, with a new subtitle: "A strategic guide to dominating electronic entertainment."

In *Taking Fun Seriously II*, they elaborate on old themes and introduce new ones, some of them visionary and predictive of the future, and others… non-starters. In their introduction, they state:

"This document is a comprehensive strategy from top to bottom for making the PC the ultimate consumer entertainment device, and creating on-line multiplayer entertainment experiences that will compete with everything but sex, and we want to address the WHOLE problem."

They go on to compare the computers of 1995 with Model Ts. They make the point that computers only worked reliably about 85-90% of the time, unlike automobiles and a lot of other common appliances. They then assert that the future of electronic entertainment is to be found in connectivity and interactivity, and they present a vision "to build a real-time on-line gaming service world wide over existing phone lines that would provide <~100ms latencies to anyone with a modem..."

A big part of their pitch was that Microsoft should build a huge infrastructure to support the coming age of online and massive multiplayer gaming. The new additions to the document examine additional subjects, such as existing consoles and their companies, the various competing technologies, the myth of "multimedia," and several subjects regarding what is required to create good, engaging and fun consumer products. They also coined the phrase "real-timely" to describe applications that work within certain parameters of responsiveness to user input and smooth production of sound and graphics.

At one point, they start using political and economic terms to describe what they envision. "'Directness,' as the GameSDK has come to define it, is more than just a set of API's and drivers exclusively for games. It's an architectural strategy for reconciling the needs of 'real-timely' applications with the existing 'communist' resource management for traditional business applications. Directness is a Libertarian approach to API design in which large memory and CPU sucking general purpose API's are pushed aside in favor of trim low-level API's that map closely to the hardware, impose little overhead, and do not conceal their functionality from the application."

They suggest free distribution of "DirectX 95" and talk about distributing the game sampler disk to OEMs as well as selling it for $10 at point of sale. On the other hand, their proposal for "DirectX 96" was to sell it to hardware vendors for $50 and incorporate it into Windows the next year.

In looking at the three console manufacturers, they identify only one company that could be influenced to become a Windows platform—Sega. They also propose the DirectX Global Arcade & Information Network (GAIN), which would attempt to enter the arcade business by replacing one-of-a-kind custom boards with Windows NT workstations with "on-line gaming, leveraged content development which is totally scaleable [sic] to Windows 95 based home PCs, and new content that is delivered in 'episodes' so the games are always fresh."

Among the ideas behind GAIN were online gaming, but also the idea of "internet pay phones" that would basically be dedicated Microsoft Network (MSN) terminals for net surfing, email and so forth. They might also become karaoke kiosks (claiming that karaoke technology was already part of the Game SDK.) GAIN was a project that James Plamondon evangelized, but, he admits, without success, "...because I forgot the cardinal rule of platform evangelism: the code has to work. The code I needed for GAIN wasn't in NT, and I didn't have Alex's skills at in-house evangelism. I couldn;t get the stuff I needed into NT, so GAIN collapsed. My fault (sigh).

The OS Illusion

Technical Section

These days, it seems that operating systems are fairly stable. Most of us don't see the dreaded blue screen of death as often as we once did. I know it used to be a relatively common occurrence on my systems in the past. But today, not so much. Microsoft Research's Rick Rashid figuratively provided me a glimpse into the world of operating systems that I found fascinating and worth sharing.

I pointed out that operating systems seem pretty stable these days and he replied, "If you don't do operating systems for a living, that's how you're supposed to look at it. I think for somebody who's built operating systems, built drivers, dealt with all these things, you see the memory errors that occur because of cosmic rays coming. Most computers, you have the illusion that they work. It's a well-crafted illusion, and you should be happy that you have that illusion. If you work on the other side of the fence, you don't have that illusion. You know all things go wrong and you have to build redundancy and build mechanisms for dealing with it.

"Our ability to build these complex systems has improved dramatically. Now there's software that actually can prove that large parts of the code have certain properties. Again, that's an innovation of this century, not the last century. In the old days, the whole process was much more seat-of-the-pants, you know? We didn't understand… we didn't have the right tools, we didn't have the right analysis software.

"I think that's a hard thing to say… There are always people who understand the details of systems. There are always going to be people like that. There is a vast majority of computer scientists that don't really know as much about the hardware as they would have 20 years ago, because it's just not taught. You don't need to. If you think of computing as software, that's one perception. If you think of it as, what is the fundamental microarchitecture of the machine doing? That's a very different perspective. If you think about what are the chips actually doing? What's the physics underneath it? That's a very different story. So at every level of detail, you have a different perspective.

Nuts and Bolts

"I'll give you a really simple story from when I was a graduate student at the University of Rochester. I built the operating system for the Data General systems that we used, and I can remember one of the younger graduate students coming up to me at one point, saying that his program wasn't working. And I looked carefully through his program, and it looked pretty good to me. So I said, 'Use the debugger. Let's debug it.' I could see that there was a point in his program where the result was coming back that didn't make sense.

"So I said, 'Maybe it's a problem in the operating system. Let's go into the operating system debugger.' So we went into the operating system debugger and I showed him how his program was calling into the operating system and he was getting back a result that was showing a bad value. So I said, 'Ok. Well, I don't see anything wrong with what the operating system is doing, but it's giving you the wrong value back. So let's just step through the microcode.'

"So we stepped through the microcode. 'OK. I see what's going on. It's taking a fault at this particular location, but it's returning a bad value.' So we went into the machine room, put the processor on an extension board, hooked up a logic analyzer. I said, 'Oh. What's happening is this driver chip is bad. Its logic is causing data to be corrupted.' So I took snips out. I took out the chip, got another driver chip. Soldered it in. Put the board in, and the program ran. Ok. So we had dropped four levels of abstraction below where he was comfortable. And I think that's sort of true with a lot of people. You don't necessarily know all the things that we are relying on, and when something goes wrong, your assumption is that you've done something wrong, or that the operating system has done something… It may just be something way down in the middle. The number of faults that cause things like blue screens that are related to hardware is actually quite high.

"I think it's one of the things that, again, there are just many different levels of abstraction in systems, and the same thing is true for graphics and graphics cards. There's the level that's understood by the programmers here, and then there's what's really happening at the DirectX level, and then there's what's really happening in the card, and then there's what's really happening on the bus. It's all different."

Graphics cards were always getting stuck. They were always getting into some weird state, and if you remember versions of Windows from back then, the screen would sometimes just go blank, and then it would come back? What we were doing was that we recognized that we weren't getting any data back, and then we had to reset the bus and reset the card, and cross our fingers and hope it would all come back again."

-14-
Judgment Day

It was 1 am on a typical night at Microsoft when Jason Robar ran down the hall to Alex St. John's office, burst in the door and said, "I've got it!"

"What have you got?"

"I've got the idea. I know what we need to do to launch DirectX."

"Well?"

"A haunted house," Robar announced. "It's perfect."

Robar's inspiration harkened back to his high school days, when he had assisted his step-brother in creating community haunted house events for charity. He reasoned that the timing, coming just before the release of Christmas games—the first crop to use DirectX—was perfect. Moreover, he said, "Halloween is completely not politically correct. It's full of ghouls and demons and blood and skeletons and scary things. And I thought, what better excuse could that be for us to be nonpolitically correct and embrace all the things about the game industry that our marketing teams really hated?"

Robar had no trouble convincing St. John, who also had a memorable haunted house experience when he attended one of Richard Garriott's very special haunted house events in Austin, Texas.

Richard Garriott's Famous Halloween

Richard Garriott is the son of an astronaut and one of the pioneers of PC gaming. In the late 1970s, while still in high school, he wrote a game called Akalabeth and distributed it in plastic baggies. After it was officially published by California Pacific, to his great surprise, he received a check for $150,000. Not bad for a high school student. What followed was the founding of Garriott's game company, Origin Systems, and the long-running and tremendously popular Ultima series, as well as the Wing Commander series, and many other great games.

Garriott is brilliant, affable and eccentric. His home, built literally around a full observatory, features hidden passages and knick-knacks such as a history of the world written in the 16th century, a full old-time diving suit as well as a medieval suit of armor. He also owns a space capsule that is inconveniently stored on the Moon, where it was left behind after the famous mission. Garriott even spent a year training to be a cosmonaut with the Russian space program and spent some time in a space station.

For eight years during the '90s, Garriott threw a semi-annual Halloween party at his Austin, Texas home and opened it to the public. Over time, his parties became more lavish, more colorful and creative, and more popular in Austin. Garriott gives credit to an early trick-or-treat experience where a woman had set up an entire witch's chamber. "It had all the dry ice and sound effects, had this thing called a Violet Wand, if you know what those are, that when you would come in contact with it would give you an electrical shock before we could get the candy. It was such an immersive and truly scary event, that that same year, even before the next Halloween, I began to build interactive, narrative adventures, and they were generally Halloween style in the sense of theme."

Garriott's haunted house experiences were unique and memorable, such as the maze that ended in a "squish/boom" experience where at the end the hallway itself would collapse on the participants, squishing them into foam-covered walls, and then the whole thing would fall over, "and you literally fall on your face—kabam!—but you're being held inside a padded wall, so it's actually not painful. But you don't know how far it's going to go. You don't know when the bam of the thing crashing down, whether it's going to hurt because we assume that it will." There were many other experiences, such as Faraday cages and fires, and any number of violent and scary activities—even swinging over chasms on ropes or walking across a river on floating bridges with monsters trying to pull you into the water. And St. John had attended at least one of Garriott's over-the-top events.

When St. John heard Robar's idea he knew it was a winner. He had already seen the concept taken to extremes at Garriott's events, and he instantly recognized a Halloween party as the perfect opportunity to continue the anti-marketing stance that he and the other evangelists had taken from the start. Like Robar, he immediately saw the opportunity to put on a party like none Microsoft had ever hosted—or even considered.

COMDEX

Initially, the marketing team wanted St. John to have the official launch of DirectX at COMDEX (Computer Dealer's Exhibition), which at the time was a pretty big event that took place every year in Las Vegas. The timing was about right because Comdex would take place toward the end of October or early November, but, while timing may be everything in comedy, it wasn't the only criterion St. John and Robar were considering. For one thing, as big as Microsoft was, games were not the big thing at COMDEX, which covered all consumer electronics and media, from car stereos to computers, and, for several years, also featured a section on porn films with porn stars signing autographs in the convention hall, until they were kicked out of the show in 1995 (responding by creating their own concurrent event at a nearby hotel). Launching DirectX at COMDEX simply wouldn't allow them to have the impact they wanted.

Also, they wanted it to be at Microsoft. They wanted the press and the developers to come to them. According to Robar, putting the show on somewhere else would be "an acknowledgment that Microsoft isn't the center of the universe." Their strategy was to have game people come to Microsoft *en masse* for the first time… to make Microsoft a destination and, according to Robar, "cement our place on the stage in the same way that Nintendo or Sony or Sega had."

The marketing team didn't see it the same way, and what resulted was a series of contentious meetings. Marketing argued that it was much easier and less expensive just to go to COMDEX, while Robar remembers arguing that they would get very little real publicity out of COMDEX. He recalled going to E3 and seeing the giant presence of Nintendo, Sega and Electronic Arts, and how Microsoft had a tiny booth showing off Microsoft Dogs or something equally unimpressive. "How is the press going to cover a Microsoft message when you've got Nintendo's latest news about Link or Mario?" he asked. And at COMDEX, "How is the press going to find your message when there's ten thousand messages to find? Of course we're Microsoft, and maybe we'd get some paragraph here and there, but if we create our own event, in our own time, when there's nothing else to talk about, well then the press would love to talk about it, because the whole point of media is to have something to say as often as you can to keep your audience." Not only would they be the center of attention if the event were to take place at Microsoft, but they'd be able to share the stage with their partner companies and promote DirectX and all the games that were in the pipeline. In addition to the DirectX SDK, they would be able to distribute the game sampler disk to all the press, as well as to the assembled development community.

Theirs wasn't the easy way, the cheaper way, or the traditional strategy, but it was the better way for the DirectX team. In the end, the Marketing gave in, and "Judgment Day" moved another step forward.

Stone Soup

So I bypassed PR organization, their events organization, all the structures the company had in place, the people, teams, large organizations, I just ignored them.

-Alex St. John

Of course the marketing people were right on one issue. Putting on the event that St. John and Robar had in mind was going to be much more expensive than putting on a typical developer event at COMDEX. The Halloween party was going to be an official DRG event, which in itself was nothing unusual. The DRG always had a budget for such events, but when St. John approached Brad Struss for the money, he was told that his budget would be $200k. Of course, he asked for more. He had something bigger in mind. Struss didn't budge. He told St. John to get sponsors if he wanted more money for the event, which is what he did—his way. "Ordinarily the way it was done when Microsoft did a big event, there was big budget like COMDEX, there were lots of PR people, whole organizations in the company were involved that planned these things. It was all a very formal process. Lots of legal accounts. And I pretended that was going on, and then played all the parts myself, and then, of course, pissing off and humiliating all of them, too."

St. John bypassed all the conventional red tape and personally approached Intel and the video chip manufacturers and said, "Hey. We're throwing a huge party. We're having a haunted house… all kinds of shit. And everybody's on board but you. Just two hundred thousand bucks." Telling each potential sponsor that their competitors and other industry leading companies had already contributed worked just as he expected it to. Nobody wanted to be left out. "It was totally stone soup," he says. Stone soup to the tune of $1.2 million.

The DOOM Strategy

St. John was counting on getting a lot of coverage from the hundreds of press people that were expected to attend the DirectX party. He also wanted to push boundaries way past any reasonable Microsoft limit. Knowing that id Software was planning an international DOOM tournament, Robar and St. John approached John Carmack and id's president, Jay Wilbur, and made a deal to host the tournament at Microsoft's expense. This gave him the cover he needed. When he took things too far, he could just say that it was id's party. "id, who I'm sure had no great love for Microsoft despite our great relationship with them, was only too willing to 'assist me' in going off the deep end in their name," he says.

St. John also wanted to involve Bill Gates in the event somehow, and he found a perfect way to do so. At the time, Microsoft had been making promotional videos featuring Gates and Steve Ballmer, so St. John came up with his own video concept for Gates, which would be used to introduce the DOOM tournament. The basic concept was to green-screen Gates into DOOM, and he sent the proposal to public relations for approval. Not surprisingly, it was rejected. As usual, St. John just ignored their rejection and went directly to Gates, who agreed to do it, "despite howls of disapproval from the PR organization. Their heads nearly exploded." The PR people did require that the video be shown only once, and then buried in archives forever. (Fortunately, a Microsoft employee smuggled a poor-quality version of the video out of Microsoft, so we can still view it in all its funkiness. Just search on "Bill Gates Doom" and it will pop right up.)

Gates' time was a highly controlled commodity, and so he was only able to offer 20 minutes for the video shoot. It was enough. St. John says, "As soon as he walked into the studio he got swarmed by PR people who were determined to micro-produce the soul out of the thing. Bill just turned to me and said, 'What do you want me to do?' I handed him a trench coat and shotgun and told him what I wanted him to say. He did it in one take with no prompter no notes and no rehearsal then left." Robar says, "It's funny because he doesn't even hold the trigger properly. But he did it in one take. It was pretty awesome. That's Bill's magic, right? That he could get the message right away. Within a second and a half he knew exactly what he should be conveying."

Sticking it to Multimedia

Naturally, the event coordinators at Microsoft expected the Halloween party to be a pretty tame affair, with some spook masks and some rooms set aside for the DOOM tournament. They had no idea what was to come. With several months lead time, St. John set in motion arguably the grandest—and weirdest—party in video game history.

The event, which would be called "Judgment Day," would be themed around Dante's Inferno. And St. John decided to bring back a slogan that had nearly gotten Brad Chase to fire him when he had demoed WinDOOM at the Windows 95 launch and closed the show with a slide depicting the DOOM shotgun blowing a "bloody hole" through the Microsoft logo and then fading into "Who do you want to execute today?" According to Robar, "Nothing was too far for Alex at that point, where he was like, 'Ok. I'm really going to go as far I can go, and I'm not going to stop until it just totally breaks.'"

Now that the idea was taking shape, St. John needed to find a suitable venue, and nothing ordinary would do. As it happened there was a perfect location that was not only vacant—and therefore fair game—but an opportunity to make more trouble at Microsoft by sticking it to the Multimedia Group. To St. John, Microsoft's forays into multimedia were pathetic. "The vision for multimedia was Microsoft Bob. Julia Child's Wine Guide. Microsoft Dogs and Cats. Encarta. You click on the text and see a video of a Panda bear." And he adds, "That's so fucking cool," in a voice dripping with sarcasm.

Sarcasm aside, his criticism had merit. The Multimedia Group was struggling. As St. John points out, Rick Segal had eight evangelists working to get other publishers to create multimedia titles for Windows, and they were striking out. He says, "Eighty percent of multimedia titles available for Windows were porn. Porn CDs. That's all we could get. I loved pointing that out to Bill. 'You know, Apple's got 90% market share from porn on Windows, Bill. That's your real problem."

St. John's disdain for Microsoft's consumer home group extended to its leader, Patty Stoneseifer, who had complained about the "creatively oppressive" Microsoft main campus, and managed to get Microsoft to build a new wing—Red West—just for her group. When Jason Robar showed him the new building, it was too much for St. John. "You had these spectacular, huge vaulted empty parking garages, empty offices, this giant new central cafeteria that was three stories tall. A three-stories tall glass atrium, empty. An entire campus built for that shitty group for their shitty multimedia titles, and it was under construction, and so everybody was really annoyed because you had all these gourmet cafeterias put in for all these just crap multimedia applications."

But Robar and St. John also saw an opportunity. In describing the scene, St. John said, "The Red West underground parking garages were concrete labyrinths abutting unfinished dirt walls, tunnels and pits where various bits of plumbing and wiring were still to be completed. Better still, the cathedral-like central cafeteria, which had not opened yet, connected directly to the parking garages. This would be the perfect setting for Judgment Day!"

As usual, bypassing the people at the top, St. John went to the Facilities department and arranged to use the new campus with its gourmet cafeterias and the garage still under construction, for his next event. Doing so had, from St. John's perspective, the added bonus of shutting down construction on Red West for a week.

When Stoneseifer became aware of what St. John was doing, she "screamed bloody murder to Bill Gates," but by that time it was too late to stop. Gates forwarded her angry message to St. John. "I replied, in my usual diplomatic fashion, that at the rate that the Microsoft Home group was losing money, every day I shut them down should save the company half a million dollars, which would easily pay for the party. Neither Patty nor Bill replied to that response, and the party went on as planned."

Two Downtown

St. John describes the event coordinators at Microsoft as "little event gnomes... These ladies are very sweet. They're all like 4 feet tall. Just the nicest people, and their idea of organizing an event or conference is you make sure that there's tables and nametags out and somebody at the counter

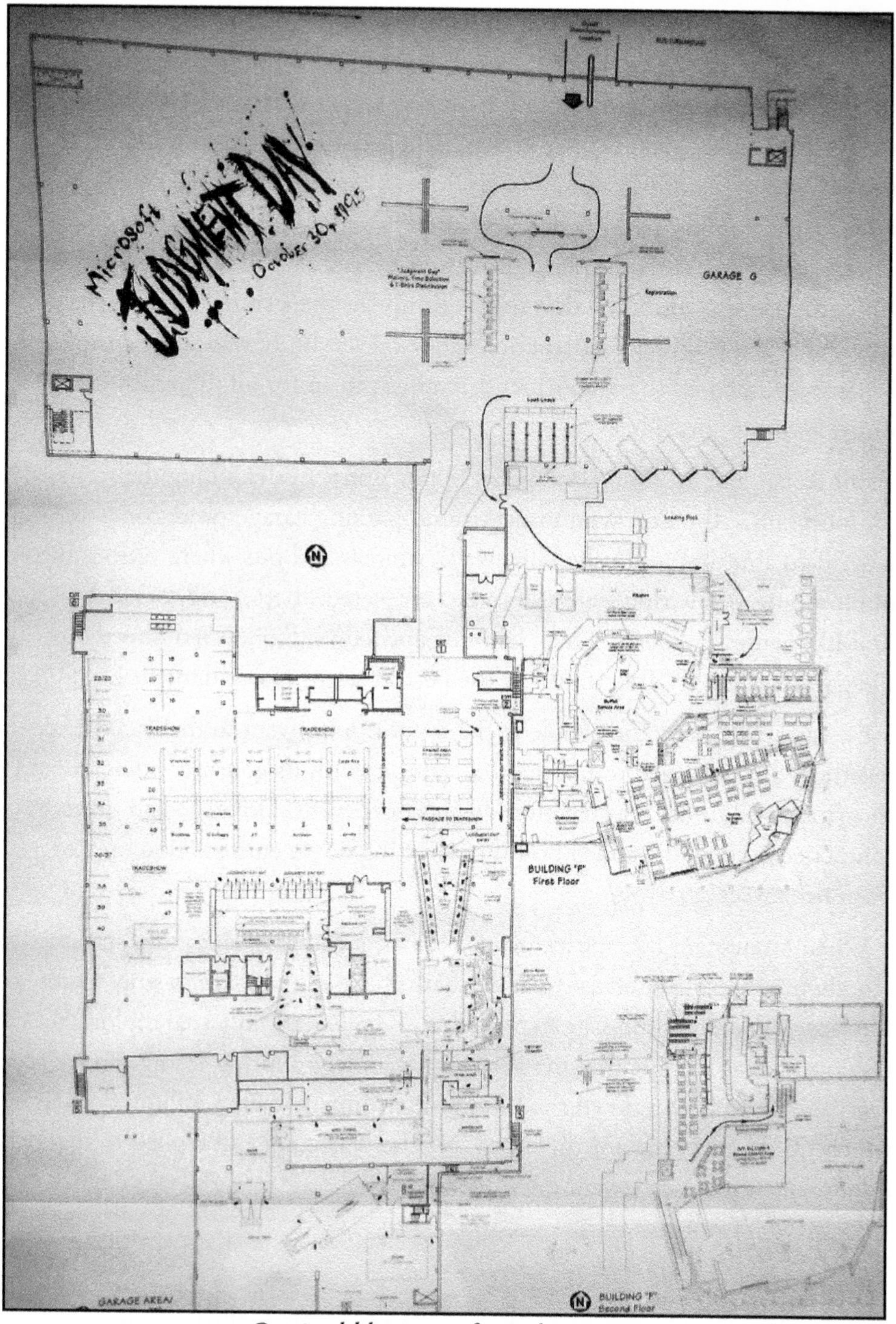

Original blueprints for Judgment Day

to register everybody for the boring presentations. So when I put them to work planning a three-story volcano and haunted house, I nearly broke their souls." St. John realized that his vision was far beyond anything Microsoft's event people could fathom, so he turned to a hip, two-person group in Seattle called Two Downtown. What Two Downtown produced exceeded even St. John's expectations. They turned the three-story atrium into a three-story volcano with an elevator in the back where devils and other actors would emerge at the volcano's cone. "It was magical. It was like a Broadway kind of thing," says St. John. The parking garage was turned into a haunted house/labyrinth.

Crazy, Obscene, Sacrilegious... Epic

As St. John describes the scene, two huge projection screens flanked the volcano and two forklift-mounted chairs were designed to lift the final competitors in the DOOM competition—the first of its kind—high over the crowd late in the evening, where they would battle to determine the winner.

In addition to the giant volcano, the cafeteria featured sponsor booths along the walls and a small stage where company reps could get up and talk about their products while the rest of the participants grazed at tables full of food and drink—and according to some, emphasis on drink.

Meanwhile, the high-dollar sponsors were trying to outdo each other in the haunted house/labyrinth, and heavy metal music was blasting everywhere from live bands.

On his blog, St. John describes the scene, which opened with what he called a "cheesy skit" that featured him, Engstrom and Eisler dressed as demons and standing on eight foot stilts, arising from the volcano's cone. The skit involved the demons judging a hapless Robar, who had been condemned for continuing to play DOS games. "We sentenced him to an eternity of futilely adjusting his media card jumpers to make his DOS games work properly. We then had our devil assistants march him off to the haunted house for tormenting." Next came the video of Bill Gates, which officially opened the festivities.

According to St. John, the haunted house and labyrinth created in the unfinished garage was truly hellish. The attendees were ushered through the "Gates of Hell" in groups of 12, where they would meet Virgil, Dante's spirit guide, who would lead them to the catacombs.

Bill Gates opens the show in DOOM with a shotgun.

Robar's Tour

Jason Robar had been involved in the setting up of the haunted house labyrinth, so he knew what it looked like from the outside. After his role in the skit, it was his turn to experience it from the inside, coincidentally, along with Windows top executive Brad Silverberg and Microsoft VP Paul Maritz as part of his group of 12.

Participants entered the haunted house on a stairway from the cafeteria down to the garage. At the entrance to the labyrinth, the participants would meet Virgil, who would tell them it was Judgment Day, and they were going to be judged. Then they were escorted to Hell. Here's Robar's account of his journey to Hell and back:

"You went down the stairs into this neoclassical entrance to Hell and, as you were guided into there, you had to crawl up… One of the first experiences was climbing up a couple of feet into a tunnel entrance, and then you kind of slid down back to the ground floor level, so it was only like a three-foot slide, but it felt weird because you were in total darkness. And you would crawl through a tunnel that turned and twisted and felt like it went on and on. And in that tunnel were bungee cords at various angles that you would have to crawl through, and in the dark many people thought they were spider webs, which is what we wanted them to think. And you're crawling on your hands and knees. And eventually, you exited the tunnel into the first of the sponsors' installations—Zombie Studios.

"One of the things Zombie did was fantastic. They created this giant Tesla coil, and being that Zombie was their name, they had a mad scientist using it to bring a zombie to life. Then there was another tunnel that twisted and turned around, and eventually you'd get into the Activision room, which had the giant pit of snakes you had to get across… rubber snakes, but there were some real ones in an area nearby. Even rubber snakes were quite enough for some people who had a phobia.

"Then there was another tunnel. The idea was that these connector pieces were supposed to be interesting in and of themselves, almost like a carnival ride. And so, we went through the Activision room (which I think was the one my step-brother did) and came to an elevator. The cool thing about the elevator was that it spun around, and so the crewmembers would disconnect it from the tunnel that you came from and spin it around and around and around until you were dizzy and couldn't tell what was going on, and they'd reconnect it to a tunnel that was exactly the same as the tunnel you came from, but was, of course, in a different spot. So it seemed like you were coming out the same place you went in, but in fact, you'd moved about 15 feet over to the left and were headed in a different direction. This tunnel led to the GWAR room, sponsored by id… and the dildo monster."

GWAR was a notorious group, known for over-the-top performances of extremely questionable taste. (If you've never heard of GWAR, look them up. Words can't adequately describe their act.) The guys from id first encountered the group, who were fans of DOOM, when they went to one of their shows together. As former id producer Mike Wilson remembers it, "We all went out to a GWAR show together once… the only time I remember John Carmack going out for anything remotely social in those days… to a bar in Deep Ellum <*the area with the highest crime rate in Dallas County and perhaps some of the most interesting acts*>. I remember my wife Melissa and Adrian Carmack's wife Ami being fed to a giant maggot onstage and emerging from it a few minutes later in just their jeans and bras. Fun times. I think John Carmack kept his GWAR-spew colored DOOM T-shirt unwashed for a good while."

The idea of bringing GWAR to the Microsoft party came in part because nobody at id had time to design or develop an installation, and if they wanted to make an impression—especially a not-Microsoft impression—what better than the spectacularly irreverent GWAR?

People experienced the GWAR event differently, some remembering specific details, and others remembering very little beyond the chaos. Alex St. John offers one priceless description of the scene: "So the id room in the haunted house was occupied by the GWAR band. OJ Simpson. An eight-foot tall giant vagina with fangs covered with penises with OJ's severed head for a clitoris was one of the monsters. They had a dominatrix there with a three-foot spiked dick that sprayed blood and semen on people going through the haunted house. You wouldn't fucking believe it. Oh my god. Of course, the Microsoft people were freaking. The irony is… think about this. They're going, 'Paul Maritz and Brad Silverberg just went into the haunted house.' By all accounts… Paul Maritz, Senior Vice President of Windows platforms reporting to Bill Gates, got whipped, forced to lick the demon dominatrix boots, sprayed with bodily fluids and finally eaten by the giant vagina monster… along with the journalists accompanying him from *PC Week* and the *Wall Street Journal*… He comes out of the haunted house laughing his ass off. So does Silverberg. They had the best fucking time ever."

Robar's first-person account depicts a slightly tamer, but still hopelessly chaotic scene where it was almost impossible to make sense of what was going on. "We got battered right up in the face. The giant dildo monster went up really close to everybody… almost hugging people, but I don't quite remember it actually spitting anything in people's faces at that point. That might be anecdotal. Some sort of crazy thing was waving appendages at you, and that's about all you could really tell in the dark and fog, and strobe lights flashing at you."

Jay Wilbur, who was there as part of the id contingent, recalls that the concept behind the installation was that you were coming through a giant birth canal to be born into this hellish world. "The idea was, you went in and the GWAR penis monster came on you, and you fertilized an egg somehow and you were born into this other world or something." There was apparently something resembling a script, but Wilbur remembers that the GWAR members kept going off it. "They would start yelling at each other, and they'd say, 'You fucked this up." "No, you fucked this up." And they'd start beating on each other. It was mania. It was like KISS on acid, or something like that."

In the midst of this chaotic event, Audrey Mann Cronin, id's public relations representative, was doing her best to conduct an interview with MTV. "We had to do 10 takes because the guys in the flesh column just couldn't get their words together. It was cringe-worthy." (The "flesh column" was what she called the giant penis.) Cronin also recounted an embarrassing moment in the haunted house tunnels. "I am a bit claustrophobic and it was dark as night and long. The CEO of GT Interactive, Ron Chaimowitz, was crawling in front of me. In my panic, I pulled off his shoe and ultimately needed to be rescued. One of my most mortifying experiences :-)" Clearly, the tunnels were not meant for claustrophobics, but there were safety hatches installed at various points and people on hand to bail out those unfortunates who panicked in the tight, dark passages.

Somehow Robar and his group managed to survive GWAR's treatment of them and continue through the labyrinth. "Then there was this giant room full of packing peanuts, but it was up to your waist, and what they had that was really clever is they had a couple with masks on so they could breathe swimming around underneath all those packing peanuts. So you didn't know it until you had waded out halfway into the room and suddenly there were things grabbing your legs, and you're trying to swim through this giant space—almost like a giant ball pit. I think it was packing peanuts—an enormous amount of packing peanuts in this giant, long hallway of a room. And then from there we came to the Mortal Kombat room, which ATI was sponsoring. If I remember right, ATI had paid to be able to show a port of Mortal Kombat using DirectDraw on their hardware, and so they had the guys from Mortal Kombat there.

"Finally, we came to the guillotine room. We saw them clearly, then were led up to them blindfolded, placed in the guillotine… and then we felt the guillotine go off, and there was that moment… the anticipation that the blade was coming down and you couldn't move. And when it landed, you definitely felt it because there was a bar right on the top of your neck, so you definitely could feel the WHACK! This part was for Eric. His whole thing is that he wanted people's heads to be cut off. He wanted it to be rendered in

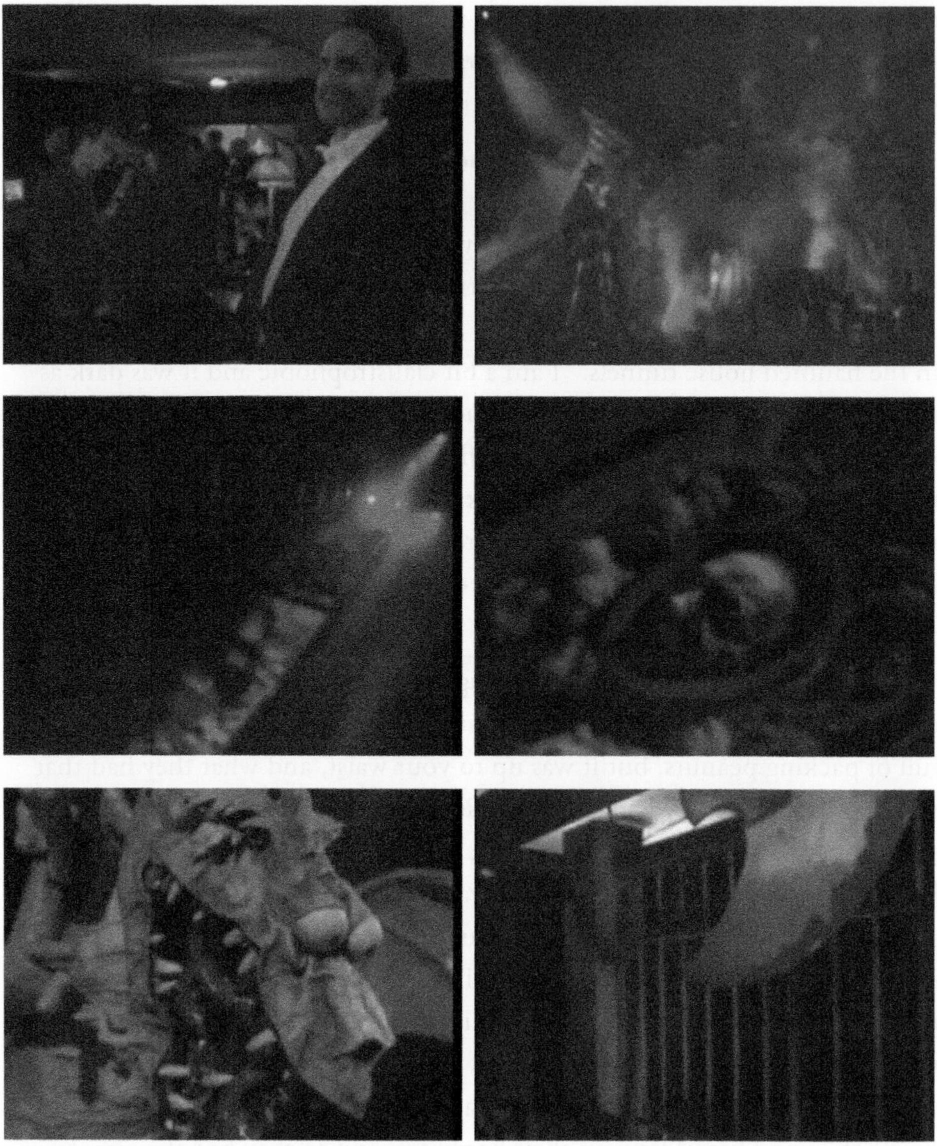

Some representative images from Judgment Day from a video by Computer Chronicles. https://www.youtube.com/watch?v=D9qAOblaRrA

full glory so you'd be looking down into some monitors, and you'd see your body fall away from you. We didn't quite achieve his vision of it, though, and to this day he'll bring that up when I see him."

From the guillotines, each participant was led into a closet-sized room and left alone in utter darkness. "The final thing was just this demonic voice saying, 'Get out.'" Then another door would open, leading into the brightly

Alex St. John, Mike Wilson, and friends.

lit show floor, where dozens of cameras would flash as people came screaming out. St. John recalls that, for many people, just standing and watching people come screaming out of the haunted house was the best part of the show.

The Battle of the Band

In addition to GWAR, id had brought along a thrash metal band, aptly named Society of the Damned, who were friends of id's Mike Wilson. Wilson and two of his friends, Rob Atkins and Harry Miller from Ritual Entertainment (also an appropriate name) dressed up as Mickey from Natural Born Killers, Jesus, and the Pope, respectively. They formed what Wilson describes as an "all-white mosh pit," saying that the band was used to having a mosh pit, "but were rather performing in front of a captive and very confused audience of MS suits. So we went and moshed." Comment of the night, according to Wilson, was when one of the party goers commented to Atkins (as Jesus), "Hey man! Loved your book."

Wilson remembers that the band took a break at one point and were told not to come back "by some suit, and that's what caused Alex to go code red, which was quite funny as he was dressed as Satan and painted red at the time."

Code red is putting it mildly. St. John went nuclear. He says, remembering the moment, "The Microsoft's people were going, 'There's 300 press here. Oh my god.' And so they were losing their shit over this. 'We're all going to get fired. Oh my god. It's the end of our careers.' And they cancelled the band and told them to go home without talking to me about it. The id people came running over and said, 'We just got told that Microsoft cancelled our band and sent them home.' And I was like, 'What?' I went to the event coordinators… 'What the fuck are you doing?' They go, 'Oh my god. They've got Jesus and the Pope and there's blood and they're holding crosses upside down in front of the volcano. And the press is… ahhhhh ahhhh…' I go, 'You can't fucking fire the band. That's id's band. They paid for it. You can't throw their asses out. It's too late now.' And they just screamed and fought over that.

"The situation was out of control. Microsoft's event people, they are shitting themselves. They are coming unglued. And I was just like, fuck it. I don't care. I kept telling them, 'Let them fire me. I made you do all of it. Just don't. fuck. it. up.' And I lost my shit with them. And Doug Henrick, my boss, finally came over to me. I made them put the band back on. 'Put them back on. Don't you fucking change a thing.' And Doug said, 'Yeah, Alex. You need to take a break. You're gonna kill somebody.' And I go, 'I'm sorry.' So he said, 'Go home. I'm not going to let them stop anything, but you're clearly overwrought.' And so I just went home and passed out. I'd had it. I couldn't deal with it."

It's important to note the amount of stress that St. John was under at the time. Doing an event of this magnitude and insanity was difficult enough. "I hated planning events like this. I just had to do it." Making things worse, his wife had taken the kids to the East Coast to visit family—and hadn't returned after two months. He didn't know it yet, but the signs were there. He was in the early stages of a very painful divorce.

The Competition

The DOOM competition and finale came off without any problems, although the final confrontation between Thresh and Paradox didn't begin until well after midnight—hours after it had been planned. According to Wilbur, the atmosphere was intense, with people cheering. "It was like you were watching the last game of the NBA finals, or the World Series, or the Super Bowl. It was bananas, and that was the point where I thought, 'Wow! This is really a sport.'"

People's memories differ in describing the scene, although everyone reported that it was an exciting event. St. John thinks the two finalists were hoisted up high on the volcano (although he was *passed out* at home by this time), but none of the witnesses remembered it quite that way. All they remember up on the side of the volcano were the two giant screens. The winner was Thresh, who easily defeated his adversary, Paradox. Paradox later complained about not being able to use his own equipment, but regardless of the outcome, it was an epic event and the first of its kind. Even MTV was there to give it some coverage, prompting Robar to comment, "I can't think that there was any possibility that MTV had ever said the word 'Microsoft' up until that point—October 1995"

One of the events that has probably been largely forgotten by almost everyone was Mike Wilson, wearing a long white beard and brandishing a gigantic hand-crafted bible, reciting his original poem, "An Ode to id: with apologies to Edgar Allan Poe." However, Audrey Mann Cronin not only remembers it well, but she still has the original poem. *(I kindly refrained from publishing it in this book. You're welcome. Oh, and did I mention that there was a lot of freely flowing alcohol at the event?)*

The Ultimate Irony

Although St. John missed some critical parts of the party, including the DOOM competition, he had done his part. He had put on a show that nobody would soon forget, even though many of the participants had a hard time knowing exactly what they had experienced.

The greatest irony of all was that, even though everybody told St. John later that it was the greatest party ever, people seemed not to have noticed some of the starkest and most disturbing details. He asked Silverberg and Maritz if they had noticed the giant vagina monster with teeth, and they said, "What?" He also asked some of the attendees from the press. They said stuff like, "All I remember was the haunted house. I was being chased by monsters, and the screaming and the lights and I was scared shitless and I got the fuck out of there, and there was shit going on. It was amazing. I don't remember seeing anything."

To St. John, this was a fascinating experiment in human psychology. "They didn't remember. They couldn't see that stuff. It was too weird and too traumatic and happened so fast that all they knew was that there were monsters and fluids and lights and scary things, and they're fucking freaked out, and they didn't know what happened. People did not see any vagina monster with teeth and OJ Simpson's head. They just… something grabbed them. There was biting and gnashing and monsters, and they got the hell out of there. And my theory is that it was so bizarre and so unthinkable for Microsoft to do something like that, whatever their brains saw was something that was not that bizarre."

Silverberg, however, remembers Judgment Day very well. "Microsoft hadn't done events like that before. It broke the mold. It was maybe a little bit over the line in terms of tastefulness… tastelessness. Definitely not politically correct, but it created a buzz. It was edgy, and it was fun. It was at a time of tremendous change in history, and we were leading that change… It was showing that this was not your father's Microsoft. It was a breakthrough. It was a breakthrough for Microsoft in transforming the way people viewed the company."

After the event, St. John took a couple of days off from work—something he rarely did—and laid there with an ice pack on his head, once again waiting to get fired. Jason Robar came by and let him know what a huge hit the party had been. They had succeeded in generating hundreds of positive articles in the press, and everybody, including Silverberg and Maritz, had a great time. With some trepidation, he asked Robar, "What about the GWAR room? Nobody mentioned the vagina monster?" "Not a word," was the answer. Somehow the toothed penis/vagina elephant-in-the-room had managed to go unreported.

Although St. John had left the party early, he was able to witness, if not enjoy, the incredible realization of his vision—expanded to the max. He credits the Two Downtown guys with taking it beyond anything he had imagined. "The Two Downtown guys went, 'You want to do Dante's Inferno? Well, we'll show you Dante's Inferno,' and they took that idea and really blew it up beyond what I thought was possible to execute under the circumstances."

What St. John and his team pulled off was not just a great party. It was an unforgettable event that people still talk about to this day. Even more importantly, DirectX was a huge hit, even though it was far from perfect and would go through years of refinements. But, where St. John's goal had been to have 25 Windows games on the shelves for Christmas '95, there were 90. Getting the word out, getting positive press, and getting games on the shelves were the real work, and for that, he received an excellent evaluation:

"You and Jason did a truly excellent job of closing out on Windows 95 titles for Christmas 95. You far exceeded the expectations for successfully evangelizing this community. Hosting porting labs and sending contractors on site helped secure a number of these wins. These efforts should hopefully also yield the remaining top tier titles in Q1'96. You, Eric and Craig have overseen an amazing industry movement over the past 18 months the time since you first went and visited game companies to collect feedback on OS features needed to when actual products shipped using the technology."

Another 4.5 evaluation dealt specifically with St. John's publicity efforts, and specifically the Judgment Day event and ended with an admonition:

"You helped Microsoft pull off an Impressive launch of Windows as a games platform. The event gained solid press in the targeted publications. The commitment to games it demonstrated and the strong vendor support were the highlights of the event. Unfortunately the event was more difficult to pull off than it needed to be due to several of your actions that we've discussed. It's key to your success moving forward that you avoid repeating these actions."

That final admonition is probably what prevented St. John from getting the ever-so rare perfect 5.0, although he did receive that coveted score in his next review.

DirectX Success

There's no question that DirectX was a huge success, and there's also no question that it was imperfect. Chris Taylor, founder of Gas Powered Games, was one of the developers who experienced some its early failures. "When I got the very, very, very first DirectX disk, the shit didn't work on the disk. I mean it was so buggy that I remember.... For instance, you had DirectPlay. DirectPlay was the communication protocol, and it was beautiful, right? The API said, 'call this function and you'll get a list of all the other computers that are on the network that also have a DirectPlay API' so we can just query and say 'Here's the game and what's your ping time, and do you want to play with me?' 'Yes I do.' And now we're playing, so we're handshaking, and now I can populate a structure with some data. That data would automatically and transparently in the background get propagated to the other clients. So everything was going to be magic. Well, none of that shit worked. And I was kind of blown away because it was the first time that I'd actually seen something that was advertising itself as a solution that didn't work. And I thought, is this normal?"

Over several software generations, the DirectX APIs were steadily improved, ultimately even incorporating ideas from other technologies, like OpenGL and Talisman, that it had originally rejected. Mike Abrash claims that the team creating Direct3D from scratch was reinventing the learning curve—starting from an inexperienced position and therefor having to make lots of mistakes in order to perfect the product, but he concedes that DirectX, and specifically Direct3D, were probably the way to go in the end. "The bottom line is that it enabled Windows gaming in a way that maybe wouldn't have happened with OpenGL, because it was possible for D3D to evolve faster than OpenGL could, and Microsoft put huge resources behind, not only evangelizing, but do doing *devrel* (developer relations) stuff and tools, and so I'm not saying it's the wrong way to do it."

Where Abrash offers qualified retroactive approval of DirectX, Brad Silverberg is unequivocal. "Of all the thousands and thousands of APIs that Microsoft launched in the latter half of the '90s, the only one that really had any major impact was DirectX. I even had that conversation with Steve (Ballmer) in '99 or 2000.

Like, 'Steve, I hope you realize that of all these APIs the company has launched, the only ones that really matter are DirectX.'

'Yeah. I know.'"

-15-
The Millionaire Club

St. John had taken to moping around and losing interest in just about everything. It was his personal life that was dragging him down. At one point in one of our many interviews he stated, "Had I not had the personal issues, I probably would have been on for another ten years of warfare. I lived for that stuff."

One of St. John's friends at Microsoft was Ken Fowles—one of the people who had originally interviewed him during his hiring loop. Fowles had become in some ways a mentor for St. John. One thing they had in common was their shared disdain for the Microsoft millionaires and their banana yellow or lime green Ferraris. Fowles rode a Harley—a loud Harley—and one of his favorite things was to drive it through the parking garage around 10am, after the parking lot was full of those Ferraris straddling two parking spaces because god forbid somebody might scratch the door, and set off all the car alarms. "Of course, the nerds got upset," says St. John. "They'd rush down to see if anything had happened to their precious car, and they'd bitch, bitch, bitch in email, and Ken loved every minute of it."

What St. John needed was a change of perspective, and he was about to get just that. One day Fowles came to visit, determined to pull him out of his depression. "I don't want to do anything," said St. John. "Just leave me alone." But Fowles didn't give in. He essentially dragged St. John to the local Harley dealership and told him, "Alex, we're going to cheer you up. I'm sick of this. You're pathetic. Now pick a Harley." But St. John said, "I don't want to ride a motorcycle. They're expensive…" At $21,000, they seemed like an expensive toy to St. John. And Fowles said, "Alex. Look at this dealership. How many of these bikes can you buy?" And that's when it dawned on him. With his stock options, he could buy the entire inventory of the store. At 28 years old, he was a millionaire. And he ended up "very badly wobbling off the lot" on his very own crimson red Harley Ultra Glide.

After the usual spills and embarrassment, St. John became familiar with his new toy and got his Class C license, just in time for Fowles to invite him to join him, along with Viktor Grabner, on their annual ride to Sturgis, North Dakota for the great convergence of bike enthusiasts from all over. The hysterical details of this ride can be found on St. John's blog at *http://www.alexstjohn.com/WP/2013/04/24/sturgis/.*

Hummer Time

Now that he freely acknowledged and embraced his millionaire status, St. John knew that he needed a prestige car, just like the others. "At Microsoft in that era, everybody was getting rich. All these kids out of college could barely wipe their own asses, and they were getting Microsoft stock options and becoming millionaires. The campus had thousands of them when I arrived in 1992. And there was a funny pattern to what these kids would do, people who had gotten insta-rich—all the kind of dumb mistakes they made with their finances… and one of the common things if you were a college nerd, never had any interests, you're antisocial, you can't make eye contact, and you've got a million bucks… What do you do? You go out and buy either a lime green or banana yellow Ferrari. That's the first thing you have to do. And you park that, and it's the most precious thing you've ever owned, and you park it as prominently as you can in the Microsoft parking lot after you come roaring into campus every day, and you straddle two parking spaces because you don't want anybody to park near you to scratch your precious new lime green Ferrari.

"And so you'd arrive at work at Microsoft and you'd see these cars scattered around the campus, and you just go, 'Oh god. I hate these guys.' I hate these guys not only because they're lucky enough to be millionaires at a young age, probably through no real productive contribution of their own, but they think that the cool way to express their success is to buy a lime green Ferrari and park it in public and straddle two parking spots."

The stories of Microsoft's early displays of wealth reminded Don Coyner, who had worked in marketing at Nintendo, of a time when Nintendo of America's president Minoru Arakawa visited Atari at its height. "He said, 'They are going to fail.' And that was at a point when they were doing relatively well. And I asked, 'Why do you think that?' And he said, 'Because their parking lot is full of really nice cars, and that tells me that their management team has lost focus.' They were enjoying their money more than they were focused on building their business. Just a little insight like that. He's just such a simple man in some ways, and he would say something like that, and you'd go 'Holy crap! That's really insightful.'" Whether Microsoft was destined to fail was obviously not an issue at the time, but sudden wealth did have its effect on the culture and performance of the company. *More on that later.*

Clearly, St. John's prestige car could not possibly be a Ferrari or lime green. It had to be something else—something offensive, if possible. As fate would have it, somebody in the porting lab said to him one day, "Alex, you should buy a Hummer. That's you. You're a frickin' bear. If you're going to buy a ridiculous car to signal your entry into the Microsoft millionaire club, then you should buy a Humvee." And, as he observes in his blog, since he needed to become more familiar with the Internet anyway—the newest, hottest thing at Microsoft next to lime green or banana yellow Ferraris—he might as well use it to look up the car mentioned. And it was the perfect anti-Ferrari. Huge. Bulky. Rugged. Expensive.

St. John was all in. He found a dealer online, examined the paint options and chose a crimson Hummer to match his Harley. He arranged to have it delivered to the Microsoft campus so everyone would see it and be impressed. His intended message was, "Fuck you and your lime green Ferraris."

And the day came when a big tractor trailer loaded with Humvees drove into Microsoft's campus and dropped off St. John's grape-colored Hummer. Yes, because there was no color correction on his monitor at the time, his carefully chosen crimson Hummer was actually a garish purple. And everybody who saw it assumed that he had ordered such an outlandish color just to mock them—which wasn't so far off the mark—and St. John decided that it was better to own the color purple than to own up to his foolish mistake… which is how he became the proud and unabashed owner of the purple beast. "I had to fabricate an entire fiction about why I'd pick a purple Hummer, just to show my contempt for the world, when really it was a complete failed effort to be cool, and to express my contempt for everybody with a properly colored crimson Hum-V."

Following Fowles' tradition of harassment, St. John took to wedging his Hummer a half an inch from the driver's door of a random Ferrari parked in two spots. Moreover, he made sure that his vehicle was as dirty as possible. "I'd drive onto campus dragging tree branches and swamp grass on the back. If it wasn't dripping gunk all over the parking lot right next to one of those Ferraris, I wasn't happy." He admits to being obnoxious and immature but adds, "That's the way we were making technology, too. In many respects, it's the same behavior that was taking place in the politics of Microsoft to get these technologies made."

Defacing SeaTac

St. John was almost literally hell on wheels now that he had the Hummer. For instance, the Hummer's tires could be automatically inflated or deflated to conform to road conditions, which had the side effect of increasing or decreasing the overall height of the car. St. John discovered the effect of this when he managed to tear down a "Maximum Height 6`5" warning sign in a Microsoft garage with his tires fully inflated. He also describes "that huge divot just above the right parking gate entrance" at Seattle's Sea-Tac airport as being his doing. "I got that Hummer so badly wedged in there trying to catch a flight that I had to let the air out of all four tires to get unstuck. When I returned from that trip I had forgotten where I had parked the vehicle and ended up having to report it stolen to airport security."

St. John got a ride from a highly amused female cop who had arrived at 2am to take his stolen vehicle report. "We finally located it on the very top floor in a distant corner of the garage, which spiked my memory that after wedging the vehicle in the garage entrance, unable to reverse out of the parking garage I had been compelled to try to drive it on its rims up the spiral ramp to another floor but the only floor I could get off on was the roof, which was also the only level where I could turn around to drive back down. I had parked the vehicle in a relatively hidden corner in the hope that the mangled roof rack covered with crushed concrete wouldn't get linked to the new divot in the garage entrance and result in the impounding of my vehicle before I could get back from my trip and try to make good over the whole thing. By the time I got back I'd forgotten the whole incident. The cop found this all very entertaining and sent me on my way with her phone number."

In fact, the purple Hummer was such a cop magnet that St. John was often pulled over on made-up pretexts just so the cops could check it out.

"It certainly wasn't for speeding," he adds. "I think that Hummer was able to accelerate to 60mph in four or five minutes."

Baptizing the Hummer

Word of the Hummer had gotten around, and a lot of people wanted to see it, or even better, to ride in it. Like a group of Intel executives who St. John was hitting up to sponsor one of his upcoming events. When he drove down the road from Microsoft to Intel and arrived in his purple Hummer, the executives asked for a ride, and St. John was only too happy to oblige… as long as he got his money.

So he piled these Intel executives, whom he describes as "responsible guys who actually wore suits to work and so forth," into the Hummer and off they went down the road. But it was a straight, boring road. They were all excited. "Wow. We're in a Hummer." But to St. John, driving down a straight road was not the Hummer experience—you had to do something "off-roady," so on a whim he veered off the road into a grassy park, thinking, "I've got to give them a shock and a bumpy ride. Something to remember. I'm going to take them off-roading in this park." The park was freshly mowed, so the tall grass was lying flat over everything, including a small stream that was all but invisible to the driver of the hurdling and bouncing Hummer. "The Hummer went nose first, straight into a swamp. Just right through the grass. There was no ground there… Embedded there with water about halfway up the driver's side window."

The Hummer was stuck at a 45-degree angle, nose first in the water. There were no wheels touching the ground. No way out. This Hummer was bulletproof and waterproof, and it had a snorkel extension that could keep the engine running even when submerged. But none of that mattered. They were stuck, and the water seemed to be rising… or they were sinking.

Meanwhile, people—Microsoft people—were leaving work, and a traffic jam had begun to form as people gawked at the ungainly purple Hummer nose down in the muck. In the back were freaked out Intel execs thinking they were all going to drown. It was not St. John's finest hour. Then two Redmond bicycle cops arrived. "They're riding their bikes, wearing their little latex stuff and their little goofy helmets, and they come pedaling up." St. John remembers lowering the window a little while the cops got as close as they could, leaning in and asking, "Sir. Are you in trouble?"

"Uh yeah. I'm in trouble. We're stuck in the swamp."

"Well. Is this a Hummer?"

"Yeah."

"Oh. Can we get in?"

"Are you kidding? Can you get us out?"

"Oh yeah."

By this time the Intel executives had lapsed into a panic at being confined in this sinking purple monstrosity, and the cops managed to get them out through the back door, following which, they climbed inside and began admiring the car and asking all kinds of questions while St. John is thinking, They're going to cuff me and drag me off to jail, and I deserve it. I'm such an idiot. And so, to get things moving, he asked if they needed to see his driver's license and insurance, or anything. "And they're like, 'Sure,' and they kind of glance at it and toss it back at me without writing anything down, and I go, 'You know this is sinking. I'm not sure this is safe to stay in.' And they go, 'Yeah, we called a tow truck. It'll be here in a minute. We'll get you out of here.'

The cops were having a great time with the Hummer and even when St. John admitted to driving intentionally off the road into this parkland, they didn't ticket him. Nothing. They just wanted a picture with him next to the purple Hummer while traffic was backed up as far as the eye could see.

When the first tow truck was too small to handle the Hummer, a larger one was called in. And all the while, St. John's co-workers from Microsoft are very slowly passing by, gawking at his vehicle covered in grass and mud and goo. "And of course there's nothing but this line of Microsoft people. Every one of them knows who I am, and I had to do the drive of shame with my dripping mud-covered Hummer down this huge line of cars with everybody I've had stuck in traffic for 45 minutes because I drove the thing into the swamp. And of course, the Intel people, they never spoke to me again, but they sponsored the event. So mission accomplished." Mission accomplished as only St. John could have done it.

-16-

Stories of Japan

After Judgment Day, St. John and Engstrom took the DirectX show on the road… to Japan. Among their entourage were James Spahn, who was in DRG and also fluent in Japanese, and former Softimage business specialist Chris

This page and next: Scenes from the Tokyo Game Show

Phillips, now working for Microsoft. St. John describes Phillips as "Microsoft's best-looking employee," and James Plamondon says, "Chris Phillips was a consummate negotiator. So they'd send Alex in to punch people, or imply that they were going to get punched if they didn't do what Alex wanted. Then they'd send in Chris Phillips and negotiate, and say, 'Here's the way to keep that maniac off your back, by doing these three things…'" Phillips also did a lot of work in Japan.

Spahn was a half German and half Japanese former Sega employee who had grown up in Japan. He functioned both as a fellow evangelist and a translator for the group. Partnering with MSKK, Microsoft's Japanese arm, they presented DirectX to Japanese developers. There were no massive haunted houses or crazy stunts, but there was a somewhat toned-down Wild West event and several successful presentations to large crowds of developers.

Japan was always a tough sell for PC games because their console companies were so entrenched and popular. However, DirectX did ultimately take hold in Japan.

Enter the Dragon

St. John tells a wonderful story on his blog about a last-minute meeting with Sega, arranged as they were heading for the airport at the end of their Japanese tour. The way he tells it, as they were headed out James Spahn noted that they had some hours to kill, so why not arrange a meeting with the president of Sega, Shoichiro Irimajiri? According to Chris Phillips and Eric Engstrom, the idea for the meeting came originally from Phillips the night before.

However it came about, a meeting was proposed, and it sounded like a great idea. The problem was, they had no real purpose, no justification for a meeting with Irimajiri. In St. John's version, that's when Engstrom blurted out, "Let's try to sell them on shipping a DirectX OS with their next console." In Phillips version, he told them the night before, "We should pitch them on doing something with us on the DX technology and putting it on Dreamcast."

Whichever version of the story you prefer, they both end the same way… with them presenting this off-the-cuff idea to Iramajiri, and to their collective surprise, he liked it.

As Phillips observed later, they were all running on the "do whatever you want and ask forgiveness later" model. Engstrom remembers getting back to Microsoft and having his boss get in his face right away. Iramajiri had already called to talk about it, and nobody at Microsoft had any idea what he was referring to. Engstrom's response was consistent with Phillips' attitude. "Hey, if I'd asked, you'd have said 'No' or been culpable. This way you can just be happily surprised and reward me."

Once the wheels started turning, Phillips was tapped to conduct the business negotiations. Looking back on the deal, he says, "The deal that I did with Sega was to basically produce this Dragon operating system with DirectX and Microsoft technologies for Dreamcast. And we were also putting our browser in it. They wanted a browser because Dreamcast had dial-up capability—so did Saturn, by the way—and they wanted to have the potential for online gaming. And they wanted to be able to have a device that could surf the web from your living room. Remember, by this time, we had bought WebTV as well. So that concept was already hyped. It would be a differentiator for the platform."

The idea was not that the Microsoft OS would replace Sega's altogether, but allow a different option that had access to Windows CE capabilities and to-DirectX so that they could write directly to the processor (to the metal) using C++ or C instead of C and in-line assembly.

This is how the Dragon OS for Sega's Dreamcast became a serious possibility, and what followed were the business and technical work to make it happen. Ted Kummert's CE division, already working on set-top boxes, was tapped to provide the core OS, and the project was quickly taken out of the hands of the DirectX team.

From St. John's perspective, this was a travesty. "What happened was once it became clear to Microsoft that a huge strategic deal with Sega to build a console OS might actually be possible, Bob Muglia stepped in to 'own' the idea. The deal to build the Dragon OS was given to the CE team which was a struggling group with no real multimedia skills. CE was Microsoft's original mobile OS, and it was going to be the OS for many presumed set top box projects that never panned out. The point was that nobody with our ambition and drive was chartered with delivering the technology for Sega and the lack of passion showed." In any case, the Dreamcast deal was in the works, marking Microsoft's first direct involvement in a game console, however minute.

Sega Negotiation Tactics

During the negotiations, Spahn says that Sega frequently changed negotiators. "That's how they negotiated. They'd send a different executive out, or have us meet with someone else, and try to get a better deal."

Spahn also tells a story of a brief, but unnerving, encounter with Sega chairman Okawa that occurred while he was waiting for another meeting to start. "He's in this room on the eighth floor, which is all loungy type, old school meeting rooms. And so he's sitting really low and deep in his chair, and he wants to talk to me. He's got this really, really low voice. He's sitting way back. He's got these half-tinted sunglasses on… probably in his 80s, and he's like, 'James. You've got to make this partnership work.' Something equivalent to that, but in a scarier voice, and that just threw me off. I wasn't sure what to say. 'Sir. Yes sir… We'll make it happen.'"

In any case, with rotating negotiators, the process dragged on, each executive trying to get a better deal, telling a different story. The deal was eventually struck, and the project executed, and although it was not an overwhelming success, it did give Microsoft its first console experience and a glimpse into the console market.

Spahn was actually working with both the DirectX team and the WebTV team, and he observes that Microsoft was successful in producing a WebTV box that hooked up to Dreamcast. "It only shipped in Japan, but it was cool because it was a disk that turned your $300 Dreamcast into that other $300 box, which was WebTV. You could surf the web and it had all these services that would reformat the web page. There was nothing on the back end at that point on specific websites, so it would reformat all the text and images for your TV screen. But to be able to do that on disk was very cool."

Spahn on Dragon OS

James Spahn had worked at Sega for three years and had a good relationship with some of their top developers like Yu Suzuki. He was at all of the Dragon OS meetings and spent a year in Japan helping with the integration process, particularly on the first title using the Microsoft OS, Sega Rally.

"It was a rocky relationship. The year I had to spend there was just for bug fixes and performance tweaking and all the stuff that I'm sure goes on in every new console title development, but having to work through Microsoft… I was feeling their pain, trying to get devs to change a feature, add a feature, or do any change." According to Spahn, the Sega engineers didn't really use the Dragon OS, "which is a shame. Strategically we tried to get some code into the hardware, but that didn't work. The Dragon OS was optional, and it was one where everything starts in English, versus everything starting in Japanese, so for Japanese developer, obviously the Japanese is going to be easier." He adds that Sega's developers had no previous experience writing for Windows applications, which was an additional barrier. "So you get the performance hit. You get the English documentation first, and then you get APIs that you're not familiar with. Having to choose between the two for a Japanese developer… not a hard decision."

The Dreamcast OS Team

Mike Calligaro was part of the Dreamcast OS team from Microsoft. A member of the Windows CE division, he describes the project as he remembers it. "We're going to have Sega of America design the hardware, and it was going to be 3Dfx, and it was going to be USB based – the input system was going to be USB, which was new at the time – actually it hadn't really come out yet, but it was going to be the next big thing – and it turned out to be. And this would all be great." However, the original Saturn team were writing their own OS for the Dreamcast. Their system worked with a different processor - the Hitachi-based SH4 - and a different graphics card. It also featured a different input system. "We learned that they had cancelled the one we were working on and swtiched to theirs from a press release. So now we're not the operating system, we are one of the operating systems. There is the Windows CE based one and there is the Sega of Japan one."

According to Calligaro, the negotiators on Microsoft's side managed to work it out so that they got a cut of every disk, even if it didn't use the CE version. "So we were getting paid, whether they shipped our stuff or not. Which was a good deal. But the worst of it was that our OS came with a connectivity model based on DirectPlay. It was like a precursor to Xbox Live. Our SDK used it, but they didn't push it very much."

Another little known, and apparently never used, feature of the Dreamcast OS is that it was built to run both Dreamcast and PC games. "We had the ability to write games for both PC and Dreamcast to play. In fact, my boss at the time did this DirectPlay demo for Bill Gates where they both got a controller and a spaceship. One was on a PC; one was on a dev board for the Dreamcast. And my manager shot Bill Gates down. I told him he should let him win. But he didn't get reamed for it. Gates was a good sport"

Typically, people in management didn't really seem to grasp what was most important about the work they'd done. As an example, Calligaro recounts an all-hands meeting that occured after the release of the Dreamcast in which the presenter says, "We're making a game system, and our executive says that the best part of it is you can browse the internet with it."

More Stories from Japan

While we're on the subject of Microsoft in Japan, there are a few stories I was told. They have nothing much to do with the technology or with video games, but they're amusing and provide more insight into the people who made this history.

The Official Conversationalist

St. John sometimes planned events for Bill Gates and acted as his "handler" for speaking engagements and appearances where it involved the game industry. He also entertained visiting game executives from Japan. In mid-1995, St. John hosted Masasyoshi Son, the billionaire founder of Sharp Electronics and SoftBank. Son was looking to start a strategic partnership with MSKK (Microsoft Japan) called GameBank. St. John introduced Son to some game developers and helped him understand more about the Western PC market.

Later, when Gates was scheduled to travel to Japan, Son asked that St. John come, too. Of course, traveling to Japan with Gates meant that he was also a handler, making sure that everything went right, but there was another job that he was asked to fill—that of the official conversationalist.

Gates didn't travel with any security detail in those days, but he also didn't want to get mobbed by people while in public. So, when they were at the Narita airport, he instructed St. John to carry on a very focused pseudo-conversation with him. It was the equivalent of someone reading a book or newspaper in a bus or train—a good way to keep people from finding an opening to engage.

Being Bill Gates

Having spent time with the man, St. John offered some observations about what it was like to be Bill Gates. "Playing the role of Bill Gates is an interesting job. When there are other people around, he has to be in that role. He was in a very formal, calculated social mode if he's in a crowd of people, so everything was very formal. But if you were in an informal context, he was very different. He was funny. Bill's got a sense of humor. He's kind of mischievous, actually. He likes to cause trouble and so forth when he's relaxed. So if you're in that situation where it doesn't have employees and executives around, he's pretty light. But in other situations, you're often dealing with somebody who is being very calculated about how they're interacting with you.

"One of the things he seemed to like about me, I think, was that I didn't care and I was just brutally honest, and I'd tell him he didn't know what he was talking about and stuff like that. There was usually sort of a reality warp field around him of people trying to control all of his inputs all of the time. And so, boy, there were people who, if you tried to have a conversation/interaction, they would jump in front of you, they would try to filter what you were saying, translate, interpret for you, be the voice for… whatever they could do to get between you and his ears. It was really annoying, and I think it annoyed him, too, a lot. So that's when you saw him being mischievous. I think he enjoyed letting me have my leash, just because I drove them all nuts... his listening to me and responding to me irritated everybody who was trying to constantly jump in his ears.

"And so I do remember, in retrospect, I think he had a kind of good time having me around because I think he enjoyed that I was such a trouble maker and didn't care if I was pissing off everybody around me. But he also wanted to hear what I had to say a lot of the time, so very often he would be picking my brain over things. What do you think of this, what do you think of that? He was very, very analytical… very eager to learn stuff. He was also very focused on efficient use of his time. So he kind of metered out his time. He tried to say and do everything as efficiently as he could. So you'd often have very systematic, clinical conversations with him when he was on a schedule."

Windows World, Japan

James Spahn first met Bill Gates at a huge event in Japan called Windows World, which he says attracted more than a hundred thousand people. "We were at the Nilatani in Makani and Alex and I went up to Bill's suite, just knocked on the door, and we invited ourselves in. Or Alex invited ourselves in. And I'm heads down trying to get the DirectX game demos ready for the keynote the next day, which is my job as an evangelist. But Alex is like, 'Hey Bill, let's go check it out.' And it's probably eleven or midnight—somewhere around there. So I asked all these guys to come back to the hotel and set everything up, and they did it pretty quick. And we showed him, and he was pretty floored. He had never seen anything like that running on Windows."

Crazy Americans

Spahn also tells a story about trying to cancel rooms at an expensive Japanese hotel. "I was talking to the manager. It was like $300-400 a person. So this is a big chunk of change, and she's like, 'I'm really sorry." And I'm saying, 'We had to cancel for these reasons. It's not our fault…' putting out every excuse in the world, and then I forget if it was Eric or Alex, but they both started doing it. There was a lighter on the table, and they started putting the gas into one of their closed fist and then lighting it as they opened it. And it's just something you probably wouldn't do anywhere, normally, but especially in a conservative country like Japan in a really traditional place like a Japanese *ryokan*. They kept doing this and the manager kept looking and trying to talk and I'm trying to get our money, and she said, 'It's all good. You guys can go.' And afterward, Eric and Alex said, 'What was that?' and I could have said, 'Hey, you guys did your part. We don't have to pay any cancellation fees.' But I didn't. I did not tell them anything, just 'Guys, let's go.'"

Tea Ceremony Revenge

Spahn was often the victim of practical jokes by St. John and Engstrom, but he had his ways of getting back at them. "On the last day in Kyoto, we took in this two-hour demonstration of tea ceremony and flower arrangement and all these kinds of things. I knew they hated Japanese *macha*—the really bitter green tea—and so on stage they were doing a tea ceremony demonstration and they needed two volunteers. And as soon as I hear that, I say, 'Eric. Alex. Raise your hands.' And quite promptly—boom—hands are up. They got called down to the stage. They have to sit Japanese style on their legs, which hurts, and then they get served this bitter green tea, and knowing those guys, normally they'd be like, 'Screw this. I'm not doing this,' but sitting on stage in a group of a couple hundred people, it's pretty hard to say no and just go back to your seat. So they drank the bitter tea, hated it, and I forget what they did to me after that. Something to get me back, for sure."

Dumb Americans

"There were so many times when we'd go into meetings and they would say something offensive," says Spahn. "I remember the original project name for DirectX was the Manhattan Project. I didn't think that would go over very well. So even if that did get cut out, or explained in some way, it was printed on the SDKs. So it would be like, 'Oh, I hope you don't know what that means.' But some people noticed in Japan, and that's where I would have to say, 'Just dumb Americans. Don't worry about it.'"

-17-

Bunnygate

Initial signs of the success of DirectX were revealed during the 1995 Christmas season where a whole new crop of DirectX-enabled games was released—and without any Lion King disasters. Riding high on success, and getting ready to release DirectX 2.0 (including the first release of Direct3D) at the upcoming Game Developers Conference, St. John began planning another Judgment Day extravaganza. However, one price of success was that it was far more difficult for St. John to work under the Microsoft radar than it had been during the DirectX development process and in the planning of the first Judgment Day.

Not only did St. John not want too much scrutiny on what he was doing, but he was also continuing in his anti-marketing campaign, and that meant that he didn't see himself as Microsoft's golden boy. He was the disrupter-in-chief. "I just like causing trouble. I admit it, especially inside Microsoft," he says.

In his blog, St. John gives a little Anti-Marketing 101 lesson. He asserts that people become tired and cynical of "positive" messaging. "It's so much easier to get people's attention when something negative is said about you, especially when you say it yourself 'accidentally'. Press coverage of 'negative' news is free." Since most game developers basically hated Microsoft for a number of legitimate reasons, St. John's strategy was to agree with them. "Nothing flips hostile people on their backs like agreeing with them."

But why do such over-the-top events? "The funny thing is, I didn't want to do them. It was all a weird kind of trapped-in-a-box-together kind of circumstance, because it all started wanting to host ordinary developer conferences and not having the budget for it, and the need to raise sponsors. And since I needed to raise sponsors, I needed to do something bigger than a developer event, and in order to do something bigger than a developer event, they'd turn into these crazy parties. And that's the irony of it." And for his next over-the-top venture, he needed something… a distraction to draw attention away from what he was actually doing.

Working with Robar again, they decided to create a party based on the Roman Empire, and even named the next SDK release using unconventional Roman numerals —DirectX II. Of course, to St. John, this was the perfect anti-marketing concept, because he was intending that people equate Microsoft with the Romans, and to further cement that idea, he named the event Pax Romana, which stood for "Roman Peace"… on the surface, nothing sinister. But anyone who knew the true meaning of the Pax Romana quickly got the joke, because the Roman peace was enforced at the end of a spear, analogous to the way many game developers viewed Microsoft's software domination and habit of forcing new technology on developers. The message to developers was, "Hey, we're going to have this party at Microsoft's expense. It's going to be like getting the Romans to host a feast for you. And it's gonna still be all about you."

As they were strategizing the next event and discussing sponsors, Jason Robar received a call from Gillian Bonner, the president and CEO of a game company called Black Dragon. What Robar didn't know at the time was that Bonner was also a centerfold for an upcoming issue of Playboy Magazine. "She was very professional. It wasn't like she introduced herself as a Playboy bunny, or anything like that. She introduced herself as the founder of Black Dragon Games, and she wanted to make sure her company knew what was going on." To Robar, just the fact that she was a female head of a game company was remarkable. Women were not often highly positioned in game companies back in the mid-90s. (Even though there are more women in the game industry today than there were, there are still far fewer in executive positions than there are men, but back then a female game company CEO was almost unheard of.)

Although Robar eventually learned of Bonner's association with Playboy, he was intrigued from the start. He thought that helping promote a woman game executive was enough of a hook. "We wanted to celebrate the fact that there were women in engineering. Hey look, the computer game industry isn't just a bunch of fourteen year old boys running around shooting people's heads off." What Robar didn't realize at the time was that Black Dragon's title in development, Riana Rouge, was an adult title with sexual content, but it probably would have made no difference.

Gillian Bonner: Playmate and game developer.

One day, soon after his phone call with Bonner, Robar told St. John, 'Uh, you know one of our developers using DirectX is a company called Black Dragon, and the president is Miss April in Playboy Magazine." Little lights started flashing in St. John's devious mind. Bonner could very legitimately be a sponsor for the event, but being a small studio, it was unlikely that Black Dragon could afford the level of sponsorship that big companies like Intel could afford. So St. John said, "Tell them if they promise 5K for the event as a sponsor, I'll get them all the Microsoft Office, equipment, development tools—whatever they need—for free."

The centerfold angle had set St. John's wheels turning. He realized that Gillian Bonner was the perfect distraction… that she'd make a great Cleopatra. "I liked the idea of causing some mischief and distraction... If people got all pissed off about something unrelated to the planning of the event, then I could do a lot of event planning while people were fighting with me over something unimportant."

Of course, one of the great aspects of the Roman Empire theme was: Everything in excess. St. John's fertile mind went wild, casting Bill Gates as Julius Caesar and Gillian Bonner as Cleopatra. He envisioned feasts and orgies and even vomitoriums. He had to have at least one vomitorium.*

**(Apparently, vomitoriums as places where the ancient Romans went to puke their dinners so they could return and eat more isn't historically accurate. The real vomitoriums were passages where people (patrons or actors) exited an amphitheater or stadium, coming from the Latin meaning "to spew forth". Nevertheless, Alex St. John wanted a historically incorrect vomitorium in his Pax Romana.)*

St. John claims that he and Robar had learned the lesson with Judgment Day that to get what they wanted they had to propose something even farther over the line and then compromise to end up with what they had really wanted in the first place. In the case of a Roman-themed event, they started out by calling it a Roman Orgy, which set off the expected alarm bells. "I milked that argument out for a good couple of weeks." He dropped the term "orgy" in return for acceptance of a "vomitorium with bird feathers… but as political pressure to 'tame it down' increased I knew I would need a fight with better staying power to keep the forces of corporate mediocrity at bay." And that's where Gillian Bonner came in. With the right "packaging" the idea of a professional game developer Playmate would definitely do the trick.

A popular idea that he and Robar had previously used at events was to have sponsors, who, according to St. John usually wanted to stand on stage and "bore your audience to death about your product," instead participate in a "stupid skit" in which they could insert some mention of their product. "The sponsors would get written into the event, and they had to deliver their message in character, in role. And that made it funny and self-deprecating."

For Pax Romana, St. John wanted Bill Gates to play Julius Caesar while people playing various merchants and generals would entreat him for favors. Then Gillian Bonner, playing Cleopatra, would be delivered to Caesar rolled up in a rug. They were confident that this plan would generate the necessary outrage and controversy, but to be certain that it did, St. John leaked a rumor about a Playmate at the event in a gaming forum, which ultimately morphed into a politically incorrect message that they had hired a Playboy bunny "to cater to the male dominated game industry's basest chauvinist roots."

St. John let the controversy grow as anger at Microsoft grew across the industry, while inside of Microsoft, St. John facetiously comments, "all 6 of the women working for Microsoft out of 20,000 employees at the time became incensed at the idea that Microsoft might have hired a Playmate as well. Of course, they all worked for the HR department so naturally I had to have my 'insensitivity' discussed." In reality, resistance also came from many other Microsoft women, including several female DRG evangelists.

Arguing with Alex

On his blog, St. John provides an example of the kind of conversation he had with HR, which helps demonstrate the futility of arguing with him.

HR: "So Alex, what's this about hiring a Playmate for a Microsoft event?"

Alex: "Oh that was just a rumor; she won't be a Playmate until April."

HR: "Well it has upset a lot of women at the company."

Alex: "Why, she's President of a game company."

HR: "…Really? So she's just attending the event?"

Alex: "Actually her company is one of the sponsors."

HR: "She's paying us to attend?"

Alex: "Yes"

HR: "Well we don't really think it's appropriate for Microsoft to be associated with a Playmate."

Alex: "So you're saying I SHOULD discriminate against a game industry executive participating in a Microsoft event BECAUSE she'll be a Playmate AFTER the event?"

HR: "What?"

Alex: "Well, what will people say when they hear that Microsoft kicked her out of our event BECAUSE she's becoming a Playmate despite being a game industry executive first?"

HR: <Confused Silence>

Alex: "People are just excited because she wants to play Cleopatra for the sponsored skit."

HR: "What?"

Alex: "Well it was just going to be Bill Gates carried up to the stage on a palanquin carried by slaves and hearing entreaties from various Roman merchants and soldiers for their products, but then Gillian said she wanted to sponsor the event so I wrote her in as Cleopatra."

HR: "Is that really necessary?... Did you say slaves?"

Alex: "Yeah, we hired a bunch of bodybuilders to play gladiators and slaves for the party."

HR: "You're going to have SLAVES at a Microsoft party?"

Alex: "Well, it is ROMAN themed..."

HR: "Oh my God! You don't think that might be regarded as pretty insensitive by any African Americans at the event?"

Alex: "There aren't any black people in the game industry, we hired the only one."

HR: "Wha.. who?"

Alex: "You know, from Nvidia, I think he's the only one I've met at Microsoft now that I think about it."

HR: "The English guy?"

Alex: "Yes, he's from England, that still counts doesn't it? Or do they cancel each other out somehow?"

HR: "I don't think you understand how serious this is."

Alex: "It's not a problem, all of the slaves aren't black. The Romans were equal opportunity enslavers."

HR: "Alex, Microsoft can't be associated with hiring African American actors to play slaves for you!"

Alex: "So I can only hire white actors to play slaves even if the black actors are clearly better qualified for the job?"

HR: ".....Look, I was told to have this conversation with you. You could get fired over this."

Alex: "I could be fired? I just had a Microsoft HR representative tell me to discriminate against female game industry executives and NOT to hire qualified black employees. I don't see how I'm the one who's going to get in trouble here. You'll understand if I want to document this conversation don't you?"

I never heard about it from HR again for some reason..."

The controversy over Gillian Bonner continued to rage outside of Microsoft to the point where one group of developers decided to boycott the event and hold their own "Direct Beer" party across the street. "You can't make this stuff up," quips St. John, and he recalls laughing his ass off with James Plamondon. "You can't get better branding that this." He sent Plamondon to the Direct Beer party to buy everyone drinks on Microsoft's credit card.

But to St. John the punchline was that while he was fighting this "bunny-gate" battle, the actual event was moving forward at full speed. "We're renting lions. We're bringing in gladiators. We're turning a stadium into a Roman orgy. Two Downtown's building a vomitorium for me. And all that stuff is happening. As the event is coming together, my management goes, 'Look Alex. You can do the party. You can do this event. But you can't have Gillian Bonner be Cleopatra.' And at the very end, after I've got everything else I want, then I go, 'Oh. All right. You guys win. I'll let you have your way.' So then I grudgingly concede the point. And everybody's just relieved. 'Oh. Thank god. That was such stress. Now we can just all enjoy the Roman orgy party Microsoft's throwing.' ...Live lions."

Robar freaked out. "What were they going to tell Ms. Bonner?"

And St. John said, "Don't tell her a thing."

"What do you mean?"

"We just do it."

"But we'll get in trouble."

"I don't care. We can have another meeting and my manager will say, 'You told me that she wasn't going to do it.' And I'll go, 'Yeah, are you ready to fire me yet?' 'No.' 'Then it's my way still.'"

And that's pretty much what happened. Gillian Bonner was Cleopatra, people got mad, nobody got fired. "It was comedy."

Pax Romana

Like Judgment Day, Pax Romana was built on a grand scale, again by the Two Downtown crew, in a sports arena near the San Jose Convention Center where GDC was taking place. Guests entered the stadium at the top and walked down a huge stairway, getting a great view of the "orgy" below: tables of full of food and drink, plus jugglers, dancers and other performers in the center and the sponsors' booths and gladiatorial events along the periphery. The bleachers had been removed and Roman themed wall coverings, jugs and other artistic details had been added, including living "slaves" painted like statues and standing motionless on podiums. At the far end of the stadium was a stage where various events would take place.

Upon entry, each guest was handed a Roman style toga, a bag of fake gold coins stamped with sponsor logos, and two cans of Silly String. Microsoft employees and sponsors would wear easily recognizable Roman senator's robes and would each be accompanied by two "slaves"—two women for male VIPs and two men for female VIPs. They would also be supplied with large quantities of the party's gold coins, which could be used to pay for entry into the gladiatorial competitions, and to buy drinks, various items of swag, and slaves at the slave auction. In the gladiatorial events, the winner would get a bag of gold and the loser would be marched off to the slave pit by Roman soldiers to be auctioned off later by Cleopatra (Gillian Bonner). Guests who were auctioned off were required to do the bidding of their "masters" for 20 minutes, and insubordination would be grounds for returning them to the slave pits.

In addition to the lavish décor, the excessive amounts of food and drink, and the various activities everywhere, there were two live lions, one in a cage and another with its trainer, leashed but loose behind a cordon of velvet ropes. St. John had been assured that the lion was tame, and says that patrons were even allowed to pet it.

In all, 12,000 cans of Silly String were distributed. The idea was to allow people to express their feelings about executives, self-important people and, of course, evil corporations like Microsoft. In retrospect, the Silly String was responsible for a host of headaches for St. John. "I was anticipating a great party! That fantasy lasted for about five minutes after we opened the doors to the event. Five minutes is how long it took nearly 2000 developers to overrun the registration lines, seize as much Silly String as they could carry and proceed to literally bury every "senator" present in so much Silly String that we all looked like Technicolor Cousin It from the Addams Family."

It seemed that his strategy worked all-too well. "Of course Microsoft people didn't get it. They didn't understand the psychology of what I was trying to accomplish. I had the Microsoft employees and sponsors wearing Roman senator robes, and they had slaves assigned to walk around and wave fans at them and serve them grapes by hand at the event. And the developers were all armed, and they were wearing togas, and they had cans of Silly String. And so, by the end of the evening, we were literally drowning in Silly String." At one point, St. John observed that due to the aerosol fumes from so much Silly String saturating the air, it seemed that "everyone was dizzy and euphoric before the bar even opened." St. John says that he asked one of the event coordinators to hide another 24,000 cans of Silly String "before things got really out of hand."

James Plamondon recalls a moment when St. John was being carried by four bodybuilder gladiators, and he had a big pot of gold from which he was tossing coins. "He's tossing these 'gold' coins, and the developers are diving for them, just fighting over these fucking little plastic tokens. And afterwards, he and I were just laughing our asses off. He says, 'This is just so unreal. We are creating our own reality in which the coins are worth something.' And you recognize that the word prestige, meaning honor and fame and everything, comes from the same root as the word prestidigitation. Sleight of hand. Fame is a trick. Prestige is a trick."

And so began the Roman orgy in a deluge of Silly String, people in togas stuffing themselves on turkey legs and wine, visiting the sponsor events and getting high on fumes and alcohol. After everyone had arrived and had a chance to eat, drink and be merry, the main event began to the fanfare of a Roman legion with trumpets blaring and various performers and slaves in procession, plus the two lions and a palanquin carrying Caesar. St. John says that he had "encouraged" a rumor that Caesar would be played by Bill Gates, although it was actually one of the managers who had the misfortune to be Eisler's and Engstrom's current boss. But with a passing resemblance to Gates and a good coating of Silly String, many in attendance believed it actually was Gates.

The skit involved sponsors offering gifts to Caesar in celebration of his "victory" over DOS games with Windows 95. One of the actors presented Caesar with a PlayStation, which got him thrown to the lions.

Being thrown to the lions was a particularly entertaining affair and an audience favorite. The lion pit was built to the side of the stage, with a wall sur-

Left to right: Raymond Chen, Eric Engstrom, Alex St. John, Craig Eisler.

rounding it to prevent people from looking down into it. The caged lion presided over this structure. At the bottom was an air mattress. The unfortunate actor (and later, people who received the thumbs down during the slave auctions) would be forced by centurions with spears to walk off the edge, where they would land safely on the air mattress. Meanwhile, there was a giant video screen showing lions attacking a wildebeest to the sounds of screaming and roaring, while prop people down below threw manikin body parts and "bloody" torn up clothing and rags up into the air above the pit. Meanwhile, the "victim" would walk out the back of the pit and rejoin the party.

The plan was for the skit to culminate with Cleopatra being presented to Caesar rolled up in a carpet, but that very nearly didn't happen. According to St. John, Gillian Bonner had arrived at the party early, but her entrance hadn't gone quite as planned. Bonner had designed her own Cleopatra outfit and put a lot of effort into looking the part, but when she entered the party, "the nerds turned her into Cousin It with Silly String." Bonner was pissed... furious... and St. John says he spent about a half an hour trying to calm her down and help her get cleaned up. In the end, she agreed that the show must go on. "She was looking very good, and she was not very happy with getting makeup ruined and hair ruined with the Silly String thing. But she was a trooper and played through it, and I gave her lots of free Microsoft stuff, so she was happy."

Once Bonner was calmed down, the slave auction began. Bonner, as Cleopatra, could decide the base price for any "specimen," and if someone successfully bid on them, they had to spend the next 20 minutes as the buyer's slave. However, Cleopatra could be cruel. She could, at a whim, throw somebody to the lions, a fate also meted out to anyone who failed to be purchased at auction. As for those who were auctioned off, St. John recalls that some people took their orders a little too literally. "It was necessary to inform a few that it was just a game and they didn't really have to do EVERYTHING that was demanded of them. You would have thought that getting fake-fed to lions was a dire threat to some folks."

The whole concept of having slaves caused all kinds of problems for St. John, of course, not only with HR, but with many of the women in attendance, who were not pleased at seeing all the Microsoft men and the sponsors flanked by two female "slaves" each. The fact that women were supplied with two male bodybuilder slaves did seemed to mollify them to some extent, but they were still displeased enough to exact some revenge. According to St. John, they entered their slaves into the gladiatorial competitions, pooling their money to buy more slaves. Next, they managed to get St. John himself onto the auction block by inciting the crowd to shout, "Alex! Alex" until he couldn't refuse. "I figured my fate would be similar to that of several of the other executive-senators who had lost at tournaments and been auctioned to developers and been forced to take business meetings they had been trying to avoid. I was not so lucky, instead my co-workers spent their accumulated wealth buying me and forced me to spend my 20 minutes... for some inexplicable reason... walking around the event and apologizing to all of the slave girls and female attendees for being a sexist pig... I had to go to every woman at the event and apologize personally for being a sexist pig."

There was still more hilarity toward the end of the party when someone poked the chained lion on the nose with a turkey leg, and it decided to take a stroll, nonchalantly ripping his chain loose from its moorings with no apparent effort. As St. John remembers it, "I was mixing with developers when out of nowhere I see a 500lb male lion strolling free through the crowd dragging a chain behind it and being pursued by a wild-eyed handler. Contrary to most rational survival instincts, nobody was running and screaming away from it. Instead drunk developers took the opportunity to spray it with Silly String and offer it their turkey legs." The lion was apparently the most relaxed being at the party. It allowed its handler to return it to its spot, where it promptly took a nap. Meanwhile, St. John was wondering what kind of press coverage he might have gotten if someone had actually been mauled by a lion at his party.

When asked if anyone used his vomitorium for its ostensible purpose, St. John answered, "I don't know. I sure as hell hope not," and adds, "I did get my vomitorium. I was very happy about that. It was just a big box that said 'Vomitorium,' but we didn't provide any feathers."

And once the dust settled, St. John received a $2000 bill for cleaning up the convention center parking garage at GDC, because, as he observed, "12,000 cans of Silly String can go a very long way..."

More Parties

Judgment Day and Pax Romana were only two of St. John's themed parties. In 1996, DirectX was introduced officially in Japan, and the launch party was themed around the American Wild West. "That was James Spahn's event, a Wild West themed event in which they hired look-a likes for famous American Western characters like... Dolly Parton. The Japanese were all kinds of fun." Also in 1996, at Siggraph, St. John orchestrated a Victorian-themed vampire ball at an old court house. The price of admission was to donate blood to the Red Cross, and despite that somewhat unusual requirement, the party was overrun and police had to be stationed at the entrance to hold back the crowds. Only 3000 people were allowed inside.

There were also some less grandiose events, such as the original Manhattan Project launch in December 1994 and the yearly, and ultimately twice yearly, Meltdown developer events. But St. John's next party promised to be his largest and craziest yet—Judgment Day II.

Dressing Like Brad

Following the launch of Windows 95, Microsoft did what Microsoft often does... it conducted an internal reorganization—a "reorg." For Eisler and Engstrom, things ultimately worked out quite well, but for St. John, the situation wasn't so rosy. In his case, DirectX operations were placed under Jay Torborg, who reported directly to Brad Chase, and the DRG was reorged out of the tools division and into the Systems Marketing Group, ("a disaster, foreshadowing the decline of Microsoft as a provider of market-dominating technology," adds Plamondon.) Meanwhile most of his previous senior management, including Brad Struss, Doug Henrich, Adam Waalkes, and Rick Segal were shifted to MSN. Struss offered St. John what he calls a "cushy General Manager role in MSN," even as Henrich warned him that we was unlikely to survive much longer if he remained in the DRG under Brad Chase. Chase had already tried to get him fired twice, once for having shown a "Who do you want to execute today?" PowerPoint slide at the Windows 95 press conference, and again for the "Bunny Gate" faux scandal.

According to James Plamondon, there were people at Microsoft who had seen St. John's potential early on and wanted to groom him for a senior management position, if only they could tone him down a bit. But Plamondon states, "You just can't tone Alex down. If he believes that he's right, he's going to run over you like the Mongol Horde. And there's just no compromise with that."

The reorg had serious consequences for the evangelists in the DRG. "Almost all of the DRG's best people left at that point because two things happened," said Plamondon. First, you got moved under marketing, which meant it was under Brad Chase, and secondly, it meant that part of the deal was Microsoft had just boosted the technical people's pay, like by 40% because it was losing all its best people to internet startups, so it gave a huge pay raise to anybody who had a technical job, but then it moved the technical evangelists under marketing, which meant that they were considered to be marketing slime and did not get this big pay raise. So basically Microsoft was telling every technical evangelist, 'Stop being a technical evangelist. Go do technical work if you're good enough, and if you're not, you must be a marketing slime, and that's why we're moving you over to marketing.'

"So most of the best people were pissed off at this and fuming and upset. I was working for Alex at the time, and he said, 'Hey guys. Let's do this. Let's go dress up in Brad Chase clothes. Let's wear his kind of pants and his kind of striped white and blue shirt, and let's go into this meeting that he's having with every DRG group and say how happy we are to be part of his team and what can we do to help, and let's make this new DRG kick ass.'

"And we showed up in that meeting with Brad and put this 'go team' face on it, and he was like stunned and confused for about ten-fifteen minutes.

And eventually he said, 'I have to say, I'm so happy to hear you guys say this, because nobody else is. They're all telling me this is awful. It's the worst thing in the world, and you guys are all up for it. What can I do to help you succeed?' And so Alex got everything he wanted from Brad after that because he made it clear he was going to be Brad's guy. And so when Morris <Beton> got shifted around, Alex had some air cover from Brad still because Alex had played that part of the game."

Telling the story from his perspective, St. John says. "Brad hated DRG and DRG people when he inherited it. It was a triumph for him to finally get control of us. He expected us to hate him. He expected resistance. He expected lots of integration contention. I said... let's not be those guys... let's quickly and unexpectedly conform. The less we stand out in his new org the less he's going to consider us the problem he has to spend time on and the more freedom we will have to go about our nefarious plans. I said be nothing but thrilled to join his org, happy to work for him, apparently happy to do whatever he asked. Be the group that talks positively about the whole thing when everybody else is bitching. I did that right after the re-org. Brad had a very funny reaction to that too. He'd come to meetings with my people looking all grim and ready for conflict, and they'd just be happy and cooperative in front of him and he would always seem bewildered by the experience... very entertaining.... doing the last thing he expected us to. I learned the trick from James. MSFT people were often evangelizing into a hostile community, James taught us that it is almost physically impossible to dislike somebody who apparently LIKES you and is openly supportive of you. We were taught it as a speaking technique, but I found it worked fine on an interpersonal level. Abrashing was the personal version of that technique used to co-op somebody else's credibility through support and admiration. Nobody expects that as a form of attack.

"Brad had to be suspicious of the incongruous warm welcome. I only needed it to hold during the roughest part of the transition. He was going to have all kinds of problems, I figured we'd make an effort to radiate that we were NOT a problem and let the conflict in other groups draw his attention off us. I think that it largely worked... until Judgment Day II imploded."

-18-

Judgment Day II

According to St. John, what kept him in the DRG—and at Microsoft—was his loyalty to his former partners in crime and to the developers whom he had championed for so long. Speaking specifically about Eisler and Engstrom, he said, "They needed me to keep the strong relationship between the developer communities and the new technologies they were building including Internet Explorer and Windows Media. I had told them that I was burned out and couldn't maintain the pace that I had kept through the early DirectX years, but agreed to keep their internal enemies/competitors busy to buy them time to build more successful products." And one way to keep attention away from his friends and onto him was to do something outrageous—again. At the time, he had no idea just how, and in what way, it would be outrageous.

Six months before the 1996 Christmas season, Jason Robar and Alex St. John began planning the next DirectX event. By this time, St. John's parties, in addition to being legendary, had now become a "cool" part of the Microsoft experience. His next developer event was already scheduled and budgeted, and coming about a year from the original Judgment Day party, it was to be called Judgment Day II. In this case, St. John actually did listen to his former management mentors and worked with Microsoft's event coordinators instead of doing everything on the sly—in part because now they actually seemed inclined to help him instead of impede him and also, perhaps, because he was completely exhausted. According to St. John, "My first big 'mistake' was letting them."

Robar had come up with the idea of an event inspired by the popular TV show, *The X-Files*. Their resulting plan was to put on the biggest event in Microsoft history. The first part of this vision was to be achieved by renting movie theaters all over the U.S. with live satellite feeds showing the presentation of the upcoming Christmas lineup. Admission to the theaters would be free to anyone (with the stipulation that the theaters could keep their concession stands open). In addition, Dell and Intel were going to supply thousands of computer stations where the theater goers could play the upcoming games in person and participate in a nationwide online gaming tournament.

The second part of the concept would be a live event following a two-day developer conference in the San Francisco area with an expected turnout of 4000. The original plan was to have the party on Halloween, keeping to the tradition of the previous year, but in this case, St. John remembers, "Microsoft's PR group would scream and cry about the date I picked as somehow being 'inappropriate' for the press," somehow forgetting the amazing success of the original Judgment Day. In his new spirit of cooperation, however, St. John agreed to let them set the date for the conference to begin on November 22nd.

The vision Robar and St. John had cooked up was anything but modest, and it required an exceptionally large space to realize it. At the suggestion of their event coordinator, Cheryl Bowles, they began looking on abandoned military bases, of which there were several in the San Francisco area. When they toured an abandoned base in Alameda everything came into focus. "I loved it," said St. John. "It was amazing. Just huge and military and abandoned. Everything was on a giant scale. It just looked like an *X-Files* scene."

Concept image for Judgment Day II.

They picked a giant airplane hangar for their installation, where they planned on depicting the inside of a giant spaceship, designed by the famed artist HR Giger, designer of the sets for the *Alien* movies and *Species*. "Basically it was just a giant tent, but the surface of the interior of the tent was designed to be projected on," Robar says, "It was made out of a fabric that allowed us to project from every direction. It's all draped fabric that you then project Giger alien textures onto." Looking up from below, it was designed to look like a giant dripping alien ribcage.

To round out the *X-Files* and alien themes, St. John had arranged for *X-Files* actors David Duchovny (Mulder), Gillian Anderson (Scully) and Brent Spiner (Data from Star Trek) to appear, along with a very special taped episode featuring Bill Gates.

If this all sounds large and expansive, but not necessarily over the top for St. John and company, that's because this is just the beginning of the concept.

The main conference schedule consisted of the usual technical sessions about DirectX—ironically mentioning DirectX 4 and 5, when there was never a DirectX 4—and various components of the DirectX family of APIs: ActiveMovie, Active3D, DirectPlay, Direct3D and DirectInput. However there was nothing "usual" about the invitation, the front of which had been conceived in a collaboration between Robar and Giger. Printed in red ink on Microsoft stationery to look like actual, slightly messy handwriting, it read:

"It's me. I wish I could give you more details, but I'm on the run. It's much bigger than I thought. I've seen military orders that scare me. So do these pictures. It's critical that you be at Judgment Day II. It's where everything is going down. I've enclosed information you'll need to get in and use once you're there. Fill out the form NOW and send it. I need you there. I'm running out of people I can trust. Special Agent Robar is missing. Listen to the tape. THE GAMES ARE OUT THERE..."

The accompanying tape featured Robar's voice giving various clues.

The flip side of the invitation was nothing out of the ordinary and began with, "Each year only the best game developers are invited. You have been selected to attend the world's most complete conference on DirectX™ and to learn about the newest Microsoft Interactive Media Technologies. Find out about new products, meet cohorts and gaming gurus, and try out the coolest new games." People who remembered the previous DirectX parties had reason to suspect that they were in for something memorable, at the very least.

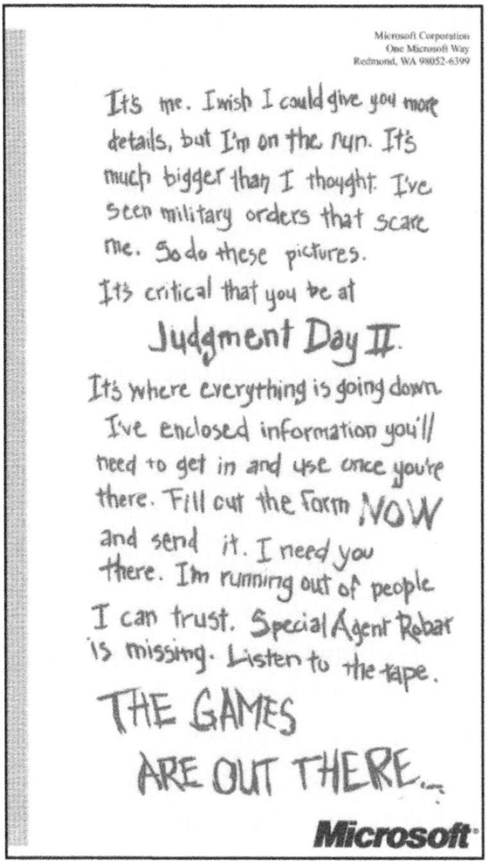

Microsoft Corporation
One Microsoft Way
Redmond, WA 98052-6399

It's me. I wish I could give you more details, but I'm on the run. It's much bigger than I thought. I've seen military orders that scare me. So do these pictures.
It's critical that you be at
Judgment Day II.
It's where everything is going down.
I've enclosed information you'll need to get in and use once you're there. Fill out the form NOW and send it. I need you there. I'm running out of people I can trust. Special Agent Robar is missing. Listen to the tape.
THE GAMES
ARE OUT THERE...

Microsoft

Judgment Day II
Oakland, CA November 22 and 23, 1996

Agenda

Each year only the best game developers are invited. You have been selected to attend the world's most complete conference on DirectX™ and to learn about the newest Microsoft Interactive Media Technologies. Find out about new products, meet cohorts and gaming gurus, and try out the coolest new games.

.C.O.U.N.T.D.O.W.N.
Developer Conference
Friday, November 22, 8 am to 5 pm

These hard-core technology sessions give you real, useable information and discussions with all our engineers who can respond to your tough DirectX issues. The agenda includes:

- Welcome and DirectX 4 & 5
- ActiveMovie™
- Active3d™ and Java
- DirectPlay™ I - Overview
- DirectPlay II - Drilldown
- Direct3d™ I
  - -Immediate Mode
  - -Retained Mode
  - -.xfiles
- DirectPlay III - Lobbies
- DirectInput™ Forcefeedback

Continued on reverse

Meanwhile, an online gaming competition would happen over three days, and the winners of the local competitions would be flown in to San Francisco to participate in the finals.

The plan was to complete the first day of the conference as usual, promising a big announcement at the last keynote of the day, where St. John says, "in the middle of my speech the doors would burst open and dozens of men in black carrying what look like alien weapons would burst into the conference and block the exits. One of them would come on stage and instruct the developers that the DirectX technology we were about to present was based on highly classified government research and that they would not be permitted to leave the premises with the CD's they had been given." Instead they were to proceed in an orderly fashion to the exits and board the buses (with blacked out windows) parked out front for "debriefing" at a top secret location. Once they arrived at their destination, the abducted developers would get a view of the giant hangar from the outside, "bright lights radiating from every window," and then enter the hangar, passing through a staged computer control room filled with scientists manning computers and people running around in environment suits. They would then enter the ship through what St. John describes as "a gooey, fog filled trachea-like passage…

"Everybody had to kind of make their way through this slimy hallway, full of vapor. We had it all set up so that dry ice-like vapor would seep through the fabric. The tent made from the projection material was set up so that smoke could also come pouring through it from every direction. So the whole thing was meant to be misty and slimy too. It was going to be so cool."

That's right. The plan was to abduct all of the conference attendees and spirit them away into this huge Giger spaceship. St. John does clarify that it was all voluntary and that nobody was forced to participate.

Inside the Spaceship there was a large stage, and the plan was to have presenters appear by rising out of the floor on a lift. Around the edges would be booths and possible themed installations. Scully and Mulder were scheduled to introduce the event.

All of the events within the hangar were going to be shown live to the theater audiences around the country, and at one point Bill Gates would take the stage. However, in this case, they would switch from a live feed to a taped event in which Gates, in the middle of some mundane speech would start peeling off a mask to reveal that he was actually an alien "grey". This idea had come from a UK developer who was launching a game called Drowned God. They even sent storyboards of the Gates reveal. To get Gates to participate in this little theatrical moment, St. John once again had to overcome a worked-up PR department's objections, but Gates, to his credit, happily participated. "Bill's a riot. He loved doing that shit," said St. John. "I think he sat/laid for half an hour, breathing through a straw to get his face cast made."

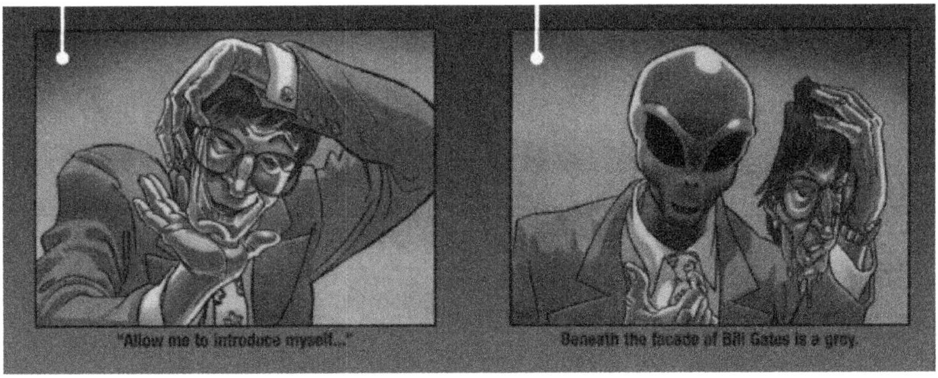
"Allow me to introduce myself..."
Beneath the facade of Bill Gates is a grey.

For once, St. John had a reasonable budget—$1.2 million from Microsoft and another million and change from sponsors. Everything was going as planned. A group called Area 51 was busy building the spaceship, and St. John was getting daily reports. Of course, there was the usual flack coming from various people at Microsoft, but St. John writes, "I was so accustomed to being constantly embattled over planning these events that I had acclimated to the usual whining about cost, organization, political correctness, etc. and just ignored it."

You'll notice that everything I've written about Judgment Day II is expressed in conditional phrases—what would have happened. Here's why:

A few weeks before the Judgment Day II event was scheduled to occur, St. John somehow acquired a new boss—Todd Neilson, whom he had never met or even spoken to. Neilson was the new head of DRG. Meanwhile, COMDEX was taking place in Las Vegas and it was at COMDEX, according to St. John, that Microsoft's senior event manager complained to Neilson about his "crazy out of control event that was over budget and doomed to be a catastrophic failure." The event manager also predicted that the proposed date of the event (which had been chosen by the event team itself) would somehow not allow them to coordinate adequately with the press.

On his blog, St. John recounts what happened next in considerable detail.

First, St. John received a phone call from Cheryl Bowles informing him that Neilson had issued a stop order, effectively cancelling the event and stopping further work on the spaceship. Second, she told him that he needed to call the Area 51 people immediately—before even calling anyone at Microsoft. Apparently union workers on site, concerned that Microsoft was not going to pay them, locked down the facility, with dozens of independent contractors inside!

What was going on? "I didn't want to believe that it was a serious hostage situation, but I couldn't discount the possibility that it was because when I asked direct questions about it I would get leading answers." He tried to contact one of the managers at COMDEX, seeking somebody in authority, but failed. He did finally reach one of Microsoft's lawyers, "who seemed as alarmed and confused about what to do as I was." Finally, he called the owner of Area 51, intent on negotiating the release of hostages on Microsoft's behalf. Here's his recounting of their conversation:

"Me: 'Hello John? I understand that we have a hostage situation down there?'"

"John: 'Oh, I don't know if I'd call it that.'"

"Me: 'Well, what would you call it?'"

"John: 'Well the contract with the union says that only union people are allowed to move equipment on and off the base, but obviously they can't move anything if they're not going to get paid by Microsoft.'"

"Me: 'What's that have to do with locking people in the hanger?'"

"John: 'Oh, they are in their voluntarily'"

"Me: 'What do you mean, voluntarily?'"

"John: 'They're not allowed to leave their equipment behind for insurance reasons and they're not allowed to move it, so they have to stay with it.'"

"Me: 'They're not locked in the hanger?'"

"John: 'Oh, they're locked in… we're required to lock it after hours.'"

"Me: 'And what would these union guys of yours do if these contractors tried to leave the base with their equipment?'"

"John: 'Well I can't speak for them but I suspect that they would not react well to it. It's not a problem really if you just get payment for their services down here asap.'"

"Me: '…and how much does Microsoft owe you?'"

"John: 'About $250,000'"

"Me: 'You know John, I don't have the authority to sign checks like that and all of Microsoft's executives are at Comdex for the next three days, I don't have any way to reach them.'"

"John: 'Well, I suggest you get some food and blankets sent down here.'"

For the next three days, which he refers to as "the longest days in my life," St. John called and sent hysterical messages to any senior Microsoft executives he could find, meanwhile checking for any mention of this situation in the press. To his relief, the story had not gotten out. At one point he called the base commander, who told him that everyone could be escorted off the premises with an escort from the military police, but first he'd have to pay the rent that they had contracted for.

Finally, on his third panicked day, he managed to reach Brad Chase, fresh from COMDEX—or more likely burned out from COMDEX—who did grudgingly agree to a meeting. On his blog, St. John recounts the story as follows:

"I started to explain the situation but he just put his hand up and said, 'I don't want to know, just tell me how much it will cost to make it go away.' I replied, 'I think $60,000 will end the current situation, but I don't know how I'm going to stop them from talking to the media if I have them forcibly removed…' Brad waved me to silence, 'Just tell me that if I sign this check I'm not going to hear anything more about this.' I shrugged and said, 'Okay.'"

In a later interview, St. John recalled a slightly more detailed conversation. "I explained that Todd Nielson's remote action to cancel the Judgment Day II event had caused a hostage situation and that the company responsible for coordinating construction of the venue, called Area 51, had told me that they wouldn't release the contractors or equipment locked in the hanger until their union employees were paid 250K. Brad said that he had heard from one of his event coordinators (Tanya Dressel, who was reportedly still fuming over Bunnygate) that the event was out of control and over budget. I recall readily agreeing and pointing out that this had been the case for all of the successful DirectX launch events from the event team's point of view because they were never budgeted and that coordinating my crazy launch parties always put them well outside their comfort zone, nothing going on was out of the ordinary for a DirectX launch event. I had always raised sponsorship dollars for DirectX launch events and had around 1.6 million dollars in sponsorship commitments.

"Brad said that Microsoft's PR team had told him that no press would attend the event. I pointed out that they said that every time to try to prevent a DirectX launch event which is why I had allowed Microsoft's PR group to pick the date for this event to ensure that they would have no excuses this time… but they were also always wrong and that the press never missed a crazy DirectX launch event. I told Brad that if Microsoft PR had told him they wouldn't be able to deliver press, it was their fault as they had chosen the events date and venue. (Northern CA)

"Brad didn't seem to enjoy that turn of the conversation especially after I pointed out that Todd canceling the event unexpectedly two weeks before it was supposed to occur had also saddled Microsoft with the expense of thousands of hotel room guarantees. The unexpected cancelation left us no opportunity to try to negotiate out of paying for them.

"It was clear that Brad was quickly losing interest in hearing about it. 'What do I have to do to get you out of my office and make this go away?' he asked. I laid a Microsoft check for $60,000 down on his desk. 'Sign this.' He looked at the check sourly and asked, 'And if I sign this I'm not going to hear about hostages or see you again for several months?' 'Well, the union guys want $250,000, but the base commander says that if we pay what we owe for the hanger he'll have the base MP's escort everybody off the property…' Brad held his hand up impatiently.... 'Yes or no?'… 'Yes.' Brad signed the check and I snatched it off his desk and made a hasty exit."

After meeting with Chase, St. John sent the check to the base commander, and within a few hours the military police had escorted everyone off the base. Despite assurances from PR that there would be no press about the event, St. John remained obsessed that news of this debacle would leak, imagining the headline reading, "Military police invade alien spaceship kept by Microsoft sponsored Alien abduction event. Microsoft denies all knowledge," and other scary headlines. Soon it became clear that there would be no stories about Microsoft and alien abductions, hostages, or military police. "For once, I was glad that Microsoft's PR folks were right."

St. John received his lowest review ever following these events, which he views as the ultimate irony. Unlike his previous events, Judgment Day II had been scrupulously planned and budgeted, with the full cooperation of Microsoft's event coordinators, full participation from the OS group. He'd done everything right, as far as he saw it, and succeeded at one of the most important goals from his previous review—"to plan the next DirectX event in advance with better coordination with other groups at Microsoft"—and was suitably punished for it.

Looking back in retrospect, St. John thinks that it's not at all unreasonable to suggest that Brad Chase met with Todd Neilson at COMDEX and put him in charge of DRG in order to sabotage the event and its architect. He says, "It's not a big leap. Chase was almost certainly complicit in it." Still, he was relieved to have escaped without the situation becoming public knowledge, but there was some financial damage—several million dollars' worth. Everyone had to be paid, including the hotels, which had reserved 1500 rooms for visiting developers.

The alien ship was taken down and apparently stored at Microsoft. According to St. John, it was only reassembled once, at a DRG 10th anniversary event. However, the spaceship and the details of the event had been kept top secret so successfully, even within Microsoft, that to this day St. John says, it is seen as a legend within the company.

For what it's worth, Neilson left Microsoft a few years later, apparently poaching dozens of employees while supporting platforms and products that were in competition with Microsoft, which resulted in a well-publicized legal action that shut his venture down forcing all of the ex-Microsoft employees to fire themselves after being sued under the non-compete clause in their previous contracts. (*http://www.businessweek.com/stories/2001-02-04/cross-gain-vs-dot-microsoft-mooning-the-giant*)

Dodging a Bullet

Yes, I was aware... not as aware because he didn't work directly for me; he worked for Cam for a while, and then he worked for Brad Chase... At that point, Alex was doing everything he could to get fired, and essentially daring the company to fire him, and ultimately they did. These guys were radioactive. They... ended the war but they caused a lot of damage in the process. They created an industry. I went out of my way to help them, support them, let them be successful, as much as I could to help them grow up a little bit, and help them at least be a little empathetic for the positions they put other people in."

-Brad Silverberg

St. John had survived many bosses and more than a few lectures about "toning it down," and he had also survived more than a few close encounters with being fired. At the end of the Judgment Day II debacle, St. John muses on his blog, "To this day I can only speculate as to why, even with this incredible disaster on my hands, I wasn't fired on the spot. I was certainly eager to take the blame for it."

Ask Morris Beton.

Fire Alex St. John

Morris Beton

Morris Beton joined Microsoft in 1994. "My job was to spin up the server side of Microsoft's business." This was around the time when Windows NT came out. Doug Henrich was in charge of the Windows side of the server operations, but Cameron Myhrvold intended that Beton take over for Henrich when he left. "Doug had the game stuff at the time. My stuff started to expand and even included things like the first handheld devices that we worked on, the first IE content…"

Then something happened that took Beton completely by surprise. He didn't know why, but suddenly it was decided that Alex St. John be transferred under him. He knew that something had happened—that there had been a big problem of some kind—but he didn't know what it was at the time.

"And then, immediately after that happened, I distinctly recall this day when I walked down the hall and in the room were Brad Silverberg, Brad Chase, Todd Nielson, and somebody from HR. And I just happened to be walking by this conference room that was all windows, and two hands go up and they wave me in. I come in, and the discussion was, 'What the hell's going on with Alex?'" I had no idea what they were talking about and made that clear. "They proceeded to tell me about a spaceship he was building, and about all this money that was being spent on it, and how I needed to fire him immediately."

Beton said, "No way." Then he went somewhat ballistic on them. "First of all, you just turned the guy over to me. Secondly, I have watched you, and I have watched this whole thing occur, I have watched you reward him repeatedly for doing crazy things and spending all sorts of money that you didn't know about, including having games built without your knowledge, having a toga party in the Bay Area without your knowledge, having a big Halloween party in the parking areas of one of the main buildings in Microsoft, and a host of other things, where you have rewarded him, given him stock, and promoted him based on these antics, and now you're telling me that because he built a spaceship, you want to fire him? It's not right. He just started working for me. If you want him to work for me, then I'll manage him the way I'm going to manage him, and I'll manage his performance. If you want to fire him, then take him back."

Apparently, what Chase, Nielson and Silverberg hadn't counted on was that Beton already knew a lot about St. John and admired him. "I really thought he was an interesting, neat guy. Very bright. I really admired his antics. I didn't know how long that type of behavior would last, because typically those kinds of things only go well when the results are positive, and as soon as they're not positive they turn on you. But I did defend him."

And so St. John lived to fight another day.

Not Getting Fired—Again

In some ways, not getting fired was a letdown for St. John. "I was disappointed that they didn't fire me after Judgment Day II. I did everything I could to take the blame for it in the end. I largely checked out after that. Craig and Eric really wanted me to stay and divert Torborg's energies* while they built the Chrome browser. (Ironically, it was called Chrome until later when MSFT lawyers said they couldn't get the trademark for it and they renamed it ChromeFX.) I mailed it in and spent more energy on dating and trying to deal with my divorce. So much of my memory from the post JDII period was about trying to sell my house, trying to find homes for the kids' pets, trying to find a bachelor pad, trying to figure out how to date again, etc. Oddly, even during a period when I recall being mostly disengaged, there was a ton going on."

** Jay Torborg was in charge of the Talisman project—more on that later—which was in conflict with the DirectX team's goals for Direct3D.*

St. John offers another story to illustrate just how strange his life had become. "The apartment building I had moved into was scheduled for demolition. The landlord didn't care what people did to their apartments at that point so I got into my head that I would paint a Sistine Chapel mural on my ceiling. I had no furniture. The entire time I lived there the floor was covered with black plastic and I was using projectors to project the image on the ceiling so I could paint by numbers. I'm sure I'd gone a little more mad than usual."

Despite his claims of being checked out, St. John wasn't entirely done at Microsoft, and, not being used to sleeping much, he still worked 60-80 hour weeks. There was more to come… wars over 3D graphics standards, the Internet, and new technologies to create.

Comments about DirectX

The idea for DirectX was to make something that everybody had to use. And then not to impose it on the poor developers, we were going to impose it on Microsoft, and that's what got me in so much trouble and caused so many interesting stories. Because, boy was that an antibody reaction, to have the fucking evangelists—the sales guys for their crap—come to them and go, 'No. You're not making that shit anymore, and I'm not talking about it. You're going to do this for me.' That caused a complete polarity reversal in the flow of technology at Microsoft, and caused a great number of very interesting stories, but the result was that it was tremendously successful. And it was successful in ways… again, I'd love to say, I anticipated it was going to work that way when I did it, but I didn't."

But it's fascinating why it worked in retrospect. Clearly the core strategy was absolutely right, but the thing that was amazing was that once you broke down Microsoft arrogant, hobbit engineers who hid in holes and didn't want to listen to anybody, once you broke them down and got them cooperating in building something that developers really wanted, that became tremendously rewarding for them. Up until that point, they made some crap that was strategic to Microsoft that maybe their peers appreciated but nobody used, and they got their validation from each other at Microsoft, which was I think very destructive, and a lot of why Microsoft's products are so buggy and often seemed so disassociated from what people wanted. And suddenly they were making technology that developers wanted and would give the accolades for. For the first time developers would go, 'I love this Microsoft stuff. You guys are the best.' They never heard that before. They never got that feedback. And it chain reacted inside of Microsoft.

Developers at Microsoft wanted to be associated with that feeling. What's funny is that DirectX was an idea virus both ways. It was an idea virus going, what kind of crack can I get developers that they have to take… they have to get addicted to, and interesting, at the same time, it was an idea virus at Microsoft that took over the company, because I couldn't do it by myself. I couldn't win every battle. I wasn't an executive at Microsoft. My influence was purely personality, which apparently was significant, but I could not have talked everybody there into doing the things I wanted them to do. They came to it themselves because they loved the adulation and the fame and the popularity that came with developers suddenly liking something Microsoft was doing on a huge scale.

And the press was loving it. The first time the press would talk positively about Microsoft without a PR flack having to bribe them to do it or write the release for them. And so that was what really caused DirectX to infect backwards into Microsoft. ***So when you step back and look at the whole Xbox story, I would definitely pin it to that root event of gaming as a strategy infecting and overcoming an enterprise—we sell spreadsheets and databases—company, and suddenly everybody at Microsoft wanted to do gaming. They wanted to be a gaming platform.*** *"*

-Alex St. John

You'd need to wear asbestos underwear to deal with those guys. And you have to show them tough love. They are intimidating and brilliant and relentless.

I can also immodestly say, had they worked for anybody else in the company at the time, they would have been fired. They were lucky that they were working for me. I'm a little crazy myself, and I like crazy people and believed in what they were doing. If I look at some of the other groups and people that they might have been working for at the time, I think they would have been fired, and we would have never seen DirectX.

The job of a good manager is to identify great talent and do what you can help them be successful, and it's not always easy, but the results are worth it.

-Brad Silverberg

Craig Eisler and Eric Engstrom really had an excellent insight into the problems that the game developers at the time were facing, particularly the ones who were trying to do software implementations on top of the Windows platform, and they did a great job of steamrolling that through the whole Microsoft development path. A lot of things that they were trying to do were against the general mind-

set of the Windows developers, where they were trying to shield the hardware as much as possible from the software, and Craig and Eric really were trying to do the opposite... trying to make the hardware as accessible as possible to the software developers so that they didn't have to worry about any extra overhead associated with going through the software layers. And I think they did a great job at that.

-Jay Torborg

PC gaming, if those guys hadn't been pushing to have something happen under Windows 95, PC gaming would have stalled from 1994 to ninety... I don't know. It would have stalled until, I don't know... god knows... 99? 2000? Who knows? Eventually they would have figured it out, but what probably would have happened is that we would have moved toward more console games.

"Consoles had very bad network I/O. They didn't' catch on to networking, really, for a long time—until the 2000s. So, yeah, I think our gripe with Microsoft was that DOS in particular, and Windows 3.1 especially, were just buggy and kludged together, and they didn't feel very well thought out or designed. So, they also didn't really think like gamers. Those APIs—things like the message pump and other sort of similar stuff—just didn't think the way we thought. It was difficult to wrap our heads... to get people to convert to that way of thinking. So, yeah, without those three guys, it would have stalled, ***and my guess is that the Xbox would not ever have happened. Of course there would be massive multiplayer online games on consoles, just like there are now, but the Xbox would not have been a real player.***

-Zach Simpson

There is no way that DirectX could have happened had not Microsoft already had a culture of the DRG... had there not been an organization that not only welcomed a personality type like Alex, myself, Craig, Eric, and many others, but fostered it and encouraged it. The number of debates that went around on emails on just random topics on the DRG lists; it was purely there for people to hone and sharpen their rhetoric and debate skills. That kind of activity would be looked at in another organization as a complete waste of time, where you had guys arguing about politics when they were supposed to be talking about operating systems. No topic was off limits, because ultimately it helped shape and refine almost a Renaissance man approach.

-Jason Robar

You had to make noise. You had to catch people's attention because people weren't looking at this, thinking about it really at all, and if they were, it was sort of a, 'well, we'll see.' And those guys went out there and really made some noise. It's not my style—it never has been—but that doesn't mean it's wrong. It was probably the right thing to do for the kind of audience they were trying to capture. It's all about salesmanship. It's all about getting out there and getting people excited. My charge was to create games for Windows, make money, grow the awareness of gaming for the desktop… for Windows, and we did that. I'm very proud of what we were able to do, but it was within the confines of Microsoft and our efforts there. The harder thing to do, really, was to go out there and convince the rest of the industry because they had no vested interest in this. And that's why it took some tactics, it took some time, and took some cajoling, but it was the right approach.

-Tony Garcia

I mean the thing about DirectX, it's a look back that none of us realized, that in some ways we enabled a ton of content, and we also enabled a ton of really bad content. This is going to sound maybe worse than I mean it to sound, but we made it so much easier to do games and multimedia content that it kind of lowered the IQ hurdle for someone working on devices. Now you look back and you smack your head and go, 'Of course,' but at the time, I don't think any of us fully grokked that we would unleash on the world a bunch of crap content. As a famous guy at EA once said, 'I could sell an empty box.' In those days, if you had a cool box cover and everything, it would sell.

-Chris Phillips

Of all the thousands and thousands of APIs that Microsoft launched in the latter half of the 90s, the only one that really had any major impact was DirectX. From 95-2000, we launched thousands and thousands of APIs, and the only ones that really mattered were DirectX, and I even had that conversation with Steve (Ballmer) in 99-2000. Like, 'Steve, I hope you realize that of all these APIs the company has launched, the only ones that really matter are DirectX.' 'Yeah. I know.'

-Brad Silverberg

I designed the API, Craig built it and Alex sold it.

-Eric Engstrom

-19-

Reorgs

At Microsoft at the time, the review scale was on a 1 to 5 basis, with 5 being the best, and 1 being terrible. And the highest realistic review score you could get would be what's called a 'four-five' (4.5), and a 'two-five' (2.5) is one where you'd be put on a performance improvement plan. In my years at Microsoft, I maybe gave out two or three fives.

-Brad Silverberg

When the DirectX team broke up during the post-Windows 95 reorgs, many of them migrated into new roles within the company. While some ex-DRG moved over to MSN, St. John remained in DRG, now under Todd Nielson—the guy who had pulled the plug on the spaceship—and Jay Torborg. Meanwhile, Eisler and Engstrom were expecting to be promoted. Given their critical roles in the success of DirectX, they each deserved recognition and new opportunities, but their promotions, unlike St. John's, were not a given.

Hot-headed, Arrogant Loose Cannons

In one of his performance reviews after the Judgment Day event St. John had received a very rare perfect 5.0 for his work, along with a promotion, and Eisler and Engstrom went into their review expecting to get at least 4.5s, which were extremely good. Their boss at the time was Joel Siegal, who had come over from Apple and was, according to Brad Silverberg, a great guy, but not someone able to handle personalities like Engstrom's and Eisler's. "They basically steamrollered Joel."

According to St. John, "We were all considered hot-headed, arrogant loose cannons for some mysterious reason, but felt entitled to management promotion. They were even more irritated that I had been promoted above them first... But I recall that Eric killed off something like eight of his own managers by various means and told Silverberg he wouldn't stop destroying his management tree until Silverberg stopped putting idiots on top of him."

Where Eisler simply disdained speaking to people who he saw as intellectually inferior, St. John says that Engstrom loved to engage with people so he could torment them. As effective as they were in their jobs, their behavior left a lot to be desired.

As Silverberg puts it, "You're in the middle of an important meeting and you get a message that there's a fire, basically a triple alarm fire that Craig and Eric caused, and you've got to go leave the meeting and go and try to put it out. Flashback of panic… oh jeez. I've got to deal with another one of these and calm them down." Silverberg had immense respect for Eisler and Engstrom, and believed in them. "They had unbelievable potential and vision and I wanted to support that. And I'm really proud of what they've done. They created an industry. And the benefits they brought to Microsoft… but there was a dark side to it, too. They made my life joyous and they made my life miserable at the same time." It was a dichotomy that required a solution, and Silverberg's solution was to use what he calls "tough love." "They were like children, and that's the approach I had to take with them."

So when review time came, Siegal came to Silverberg for advice. Both agreed that for their work on DirectX both Eisler and Engstrom deserved a 4.5, but for all the headaches and collateral damage they'd done that Siegal and Silverberg had been forced to deal with, they deserved 2.5s. Silverberg suggested that they average it and give them 3.5s, with the message that six months later, when they were up for another review, "there won't be a middle score. You'll either get the high score, if you learn to clean up some of your behavior, or you'll get the low score, because with all that you're doing it's just too much damned trouble."

Siegal was afraid to give them such a review, convinced that they would destroy him in their fury. "They're going to take my head off." But Silverberg said, "Yeah, what's probably going to happen is that as soon as you give them the review, they're going to come storming into my office and start screaming at me." So Silverberg arranged his schedule so that he'd be free when the reviews were given, and, just as he had predicted, they both stormed into his office, and he said, "Hi guys. I was expecting you."

After much ranting and raving, which Silverberg endured patiently, he finally said, "Let's have a talk." He explained to them how their scores were derived, telling them, "Next time, you guys get to decide. It's up to you which one it's going to be. I really love the work you do, and I love you guys, but you can't break so many things and make my life miserable by your behavior… I'm doing a lot to protect you, so you've got to respect me a little bit more and clean up your act."

Engstrom and Eisler left the office still raging, but whenever they came back, Silverberg remained firm, until about a month later they returned once again, but this time it was different. Silverberg remembers them saying something along the lines of, "Brad. We appreciate it. Most people don't give us the straight story, and we really appreciate that, and we appreciate everything you've done to protect us and support us and be our sponsor, and we will try a lot harder to not make your life so miserable."

"They were young and didn't fully appreciate how many people were helping them be successful, and how many people were behind the scenes, cleaning up their messes to help them be successful," says Silverberg. "But that's the role of what management and leadership is: to help incredibly talented people go out and change the world."

Under New Management

To some degree, Silverberg's message succeeded and helped tone down Eisler and Engstrom, but they still had to convince one more person—their new manager in the internet division, John Ludwig, because even though they were moved over to Ludwig's division, they were still left low in the hierarchy, which royally pissed them off…. again. In fact, according to St. John, they went on strike and stopped coming to work.

Ludwig doesn't specifically remember them going on strike, but states, "Microsoft was an intense place in the 80s and 90s. It was not unusual for people to get overheated and stomp out of the office. I did it. I know others who did. Certainly I can believe that Eric and Craig did it. I just don't have a specific memory of it."

Silverberg had been ready to fire them around that time, but St. John recalls interceding on their behalf. "We had a very difficult time adjusting to 'winning'. We had been running in full berserk warfare us-against-everybody mode for so long that we didn't get the memo when Microsoft surrendered and basically said; 'Okay Okay! You guys can be in charge. Stop killing everybody!' That was an embarrassingly long transition period during which Ludwig got assigned the task of 'taming us' for management. Eric and Craig were slow to understand that Microsoft was trying to promote them. None of us knew how to take 'yes' for an answer; it was a completely foreign concept to us, and basically Eric couldn't be put in charge of anything important until he showed that he could get along with anybody, and that message wasn't well received at first. It took a while for Eric to believe that they were sincere about promoting him if he stopped being so lethal."

In addition to St. John's intervention on their behalf, it was very helpful that John Ludwig was probably the very first manager that Engstrom and Eisler actually respected. Under his tutelage, they reformed to the point that they were able to accept the message—that Silverberg and Ludwig actually wanted to promote them…

Working with Craig and Eric

You know, when I joined Microsoft, I was relatively young by most standards, but I was relatively old by Microsoft standards. I joined when I was 28 and I was surrounded by 25 and 26 year olds, and even younger—22 to 24 year olds—and I also had a 3 year old daughter by that time and a son soon after. I guess somewhere along there, between some combination of age and parenthood, I probably learned a lot of patience.

-John Ludwig

"I do remember those guys, when they started working for me, and they'd come storming into my office every day… everything was always a crisis and everything was always a disaster, and I just never reacted to that stuff," says Ludwig, who would respond to their histrionics by telling them, "Nothing is truly a crisis. Nothing is a disaster. Is someone actually dying? Is there blood on the floor, and is there somebody dying, and if the answer is no, then you do not have a crisis here."

Generally, the crisis or disaster *du jour* involved some spat they were having with a rival team—the NT group or Talisman or OpenGL. In other words, a political situation, but, according to Ludwig, "They would give you the 4000 technical reasons why their point of view was right…" They often came in together, although Ludwig was aware that, even when one came alone, they were talking all the time and planning what they were going to say—what games to play. For instance, they would come to Ludwig's office and tell him that Silverberg had told them something or wanted them to do something. "They never seemed to realize that the rest of us could play that game, too. They didn't realize that I had a really high bandwidth connection with Brad in those days. You can't jerk that chain on me because I have a better connection with Brad than you guys do. But yeah, they did love to come in together, and it was always… entertaining."

Ludwig remembers how Eisler and Engstrom would come into his office almost every day to tell him the ten ways he was failing as a manger ("fucking up as a manager" is how he put it). Instead of caving in or getting steamrollered, as every previous manager had done, Ludwig just listened to them tell him all the ways he was doing things wrong. "My general math on it was, of the ten things that were wrong, two of them were really good ideas, and we should talk about that and figure out how to improve there. Two of them were probably good ideas but for reasons they didn't understand that I would patiently explain to them, it was not the right time to do those things. There were other factors outside their purview that prevented those from actually being a good idea. And then six of them they were just wrong on. And you just sit and listen to them each day, and for things they were right about, you would engage."

In addition to the benefits of age and his experiences as a parent, Ludwig had learned from his mentors at Microsoft, such as Brad Silverberg. He learned one particularly important lesson when he and another manager, David Cole, had a major disagreement over something they both considered very important. So they took it to Silverberg. "Brad listened to us and he looked at us both. He said, 'Well, what do you think we should do?' And we both presented our views, and he said, 'Well, I can solve this for both of you, but neither one of you will like my solution.' And we looked at each other, and we realized that what he was telling us is that we need to grow up, and we need to figure out what the right thing is for the company and just fix it. Coming in here and making it his problem is not going to help us, not going to help either one of us in our careers, or in any ways. And so we kind of sheepishly left there and we figured out the answer… it's some stupid meaningless thing, I'm sure. And I never did that again with a boss. I never once went in someone's office and created a big fucking issue for them, because that's not what you do. And I probably tried to pass that lesson on to these guys, that storming into my office and trying create a big issue for me is not helpful, it's not going to work for you, it's only going to make your life worse, so you guys are smart guys, so why do you keep doing it?"

Despite the near constant barrage of interruptions, non-crises, and attempts to undermine him, Ludwig says that he figured out how to deal with Eisler and Engstrom—Engstrom in particular. "When Eric is underutilized and under burdened, then he gets busy doing all kinds of shit that's not very helpful," and so Ludwig piled on the work, adding more responsibilities and more challenges. "It calms him down, because all of a sudden he's busy. He's got shit to get done. He doesn't have time to stir up trouble and plot world domination."

-20-

Taking On the Internet

Let's be blunt, we were trying to hijack Windows with DirectX and we were hijacking Microsoft's browser strategy with Chrome. It was always about taking over... The minute they put us to work on IE the goal was instantly to own it. Everything else was just ground work.

-Alex St. John

J Allard joined Microsoft in 1991. It was his first job after graduating from Boston University with a degree in computer engineering. In the ensuing years, Allard discovered the Internet and, possibly even more importantly, the metaverse courtesy of Neal Stephenson's breakthrough book, *Snow Crash*. Allard was so inspired by *Snow Crash* and its vision of the melding of reality and a mysterious online virtual world that he later required people who worked for him to read the book, and expensed the copies he gave out to his division at Microsoft. Skipping ahead seven years, Allard also used the name of the main character of *Snow Crash*, Hiro Protagonist, as his Gamertag at the very beginning of Xbox Live.

There is an exchange in *Snow Crash* that possibly exemplifies what Allard understood about the power of the Internet and the power to shape it.

From Chapter 8, Hiro is speaking with Juanita Marquez, his ex-girlfriend:

"Did you win your sword fight?"

"Of course I won the fucking sword fight," Hiro says. "I'm the greatest sword fighter in the world."

"And you wrote the software."

"Yeah. That, too," Hiro says.

The message? He who controls the software, controls the world.

Allard is a visionary. He's unconventional, a risk taker. He loves extreme sports and would often show up to the office in a cast from one of his many injuries. But injuries were merely a setback, and he always recovered. He continued to seek the thrill of the ride and the risk again. Allard is a spinner of tales and a predictor of possible futures that few other people could conceive.

On May 26, 1995, Bill Gates wrote a pivotal internal memo called "The Internet Tidal Wave." In that memo, he outlined a new strategy for Microsoft. "I now assign the Internet the highest level of importance. In this memo I want to make clear that our focus on the Internet is critical to every part of our business," he wrote, further stating, "The Internet is the most important single development to come along since the IBM PC was introduced in 1981."

J Allard is often credited with convincing Gates about the importance of the Internet and inspiring this now famous memo, most likely through his combination of technical depth and story weaving. In any case, Gates' memo was a directive that helped shape the future of Microsoft.

Gates initially wanted to own the basic protocols and standards that governed the Internet, but according to Cameron Myhrvold, several people, including J Allard and Brad Silverberg told him, "You're crazy. That horse has left the barn… Our only chance is to fully embrace internet standards and to do so broadly, in broadly distributed products like Windows, and if we don't do that, we're a dinosaur."

So the focus of the company shifted after Windows 95 shipped. There were major reorganizations going on, and in the midst of that Silverberg started the company's Windows Internet Division. Starting with a version of the Mosaic browser technology, Microsoft created Internet Explorer and began positioning it to unseat Netscape Navigator as the preeminent browser. At the time, Microsoft was a nonentity in the world of browsers when, if they had been paying attention, they should have been in the forefront. Silverberg put it, "People have forgotten how to defend the castle."

Before Bill Gates refocused Microsoft on the Internet, there was exactly one person in the Internet support team, according to John Ludwig, who ran the team. Less than a year later it had grown to 700 people. This massive redeployment of personnel had a specific goal—to take Microsoft from last place into a position of dominance and control over the Internet as it related to Windows. In doing so, Gates also put Netscape directly in the crosshairs of the Developer Relations Group—most notably St. John and his accomplices Engstrom and Eisler. Since Netscape dominated the browser market, the idea would be to blow it out of the water with a super browser, and so a super browser was what they set out to create.

While St. John remained in the DRG, Eisler and Engstrom were strategically moved into Ludwig's group. Ludwig says, "We shifted from thinking about multimedia as a separate thing, to thinking about how can we use this as an asset in the Internet world so we can be more competitive there? And so, at some point, they joined my team and started to think about multimedia and graphics in the Internet sense." The fact that this move was strategic on their parts, that they were still working with St. John to further the DRG's mission, came as no surprise to Ludwig. "I always knew those guys were close and talked all the time. They didn't hide it that well."

Manipulation Practice

Craig and I used to tease Eric that his material existence was just an interference pattern generated between Craig and me because he was the perfect combination of Craig's technical execution power and my creativity and madness.

-Alex St. John

St. John, Eisler, and Engstrom had developed a unique partnership while they were developing DirectX. While St. John was running interference and working with developers, Engstrom would help design the product while also doing his part to distract people away from what Eisler was doing—coding. They would have discussions during their morning weight lifting sessions where they also planned and practiced their DRG-inspired techniques. The three of them would often stage seemingly "spontaneous" arguments in public, all designed to create a false sense of division in the ranks so that when all three of them did finally agree on a direction, it was notable. And to their carefully chosen audience, the theatrical and contentious disagreements, along with very cogent arguments for and against other technologies, gave special legitimacy to their well-planned conclusions and ultimate agreement.

"We met every morning at the gym for an hour to have fun, talk about the future, and figure out if we would have to do anything that day to protect ourselves," says Engstrom. "People talk about stand-ups and scrums and all that. We did that for political survival and feature set, both, every morning, five days a week. We just did it with weights in our hands at the gym." On the suggestion that they must have been in good shape, he answers, "Well, strong at least. Good shape might require some cardiovascular. I was the only one doing any cardiovascular at the time. I used to run around Alex and Craig when they went for their walk. But both of them were significantly stronger than me. Craig and Alex could both lift a hundred pounds more than I could. I could lift 275 pounds at the time, and Alex and Craig were lifting 370… 380. And I'm not a very tiny person."

DRG Tips and Tricks

Plamondon was Microsoft's secret weapon. The point was to be obscure about doing that stuff. If you look at my blog, I post these stories. Strangers will correct me going, "No. So-and-so was in charge of this." No. So-and-so had the title of being in charge of it, but the puppeteers were at work. DRG was like the CIA. They didn't leave fingerprints if they were doing their job right. Most people at Microsoft had no idea what we were. Sometime I'll tell you some of the techniques I used. I used techniques to get what I wanted.

-Alex St. John

Under Plamondon, Eisler, Engstrom and especially St. John had learned the essence of the DRG's philosophy, but they, and their fellow DRG operatives, took the essence of their early lessons and made it an art form, practicing and sharing their ideas. As promised, here are some of the methods they developed, according to Alex St. John:

Out of the Room

"DRG wasn't a casual operation. We did exercises in manipulating people. Training exercises. One of the challenges was, what is the quickest, most efficient way to get somebody to leave your office? And so we'd have this debate at DRG, going, Ok, what is the most effective technique to get somebody who has come to your office to demand or suck up your time or talk at you, to get out? And so, each evangelist came up with their best approach to getting somebody who didn't know what they were doing to leave their office.

"Eric Engstrom's was he brought a huge jar of jawbreaker cinnamon balls into his office, and what he'd do is he'd sit in his office, and somebody'd came in and sat down to talk to him, he'd offer them a cinnamon jaw breaker. And of course they'd decline because you can't talk with one of these things in your mouth. He would consume them until they didn't burn him anymore. Then he'd pop one in his mouth, and he'd just be sucking and jawing on it while talking to them. And he said, he'd leave the jar on the floor right in front of them, and he'd keep offering it to them —go, 'You've never had one of these before?' So whatever they were saying to him, he would just go, 'You've gotta try… these are the best,' until he got them to put one in their mouths. Five seconds after that thing starts burning the shit out of their mouth, they make an excuse and leave.

"Then it was Brian—funny guy—he had his office piled with junk such that the only place to sit in his office was three inches from him. He would take a huge Bowie knife out of his desk *<he says it was a Spyderco>* and pick his fingernails with it and wave it around, gesticulating while he spoke. And so claustrophobic, enclosed and perilous being there that you just wanted to get the hell out. He did that during the interview with me. And I didn't know that that was a game back then.

"So the one I came up with was shaving in the office while they were talking to me. I would put out a razor and shaving cream, and I would literally, while they were chatting… I wanted them to feel like they were literally sharing a bathroom stall with me. In the middle of the conversation, I would get some shaving cream out, spray it in my hand, and put it on my head, because I was bald at the time. I had no hair. I had just shaved it completely. And then I would just sit there and shave my head with a mirror, and go, 'Uh huh. Yeah. Uh huh,' and talk to them about whatever they wanted to talk about while shaving. And oh man, that got them right out."

Into the Room

"Microsoft people hide from each other. So, they have private offices, and you'd email and if they didn't respond, and they were in some labyrinth of offices and you didn't know where they were across campus, you'd never find them or see them. Right? But they were all Asperger's antisocial engineer types… couldn't make eye contact. So if I wanted something, what I would do is I would find their office. And I would bring a book with me. I'd knock on their door and walk in their office, and sit down before starting a conversation as close to them as I could. As close to their stuff as I could. And I'd say, 'Hey, I'm sorry to bother you.' I'd introduce myself. And while I was talking, I'd get close, I would be touching the stuff on their desk. Putting my hands on it, fiddling with a pen of theirs. Whatever. Ask compulsive engineers… they can't stand having their space invaded. Drives them crazy. Most of them would agree to anything to get me to leave. And it was totally friendly. And if they were hiding from me, and they weren't in their office, I'd sit in their chair with my feet on their desk and wait, and I'd pick up something from their desk and be handling it when they came in. Because compulsives can't stand that, and the social stress that touching their stuff and being in their space causes them makes them very agreeable to get rid of you. And so, I would be completely friendly. 'Hey, it's a little bug…' It was just this little thing, and maybe this and that, and I'll be right out of your hair. And if they didn't do it after I left, then I'd come back and do it again until they'd just go, 'God, what do we have to do? Please.' It worked very well. It's very funny, and I'm almost afraid to have it in circulation because I don't want people to know it, because it will lose its power." (Too late, Alex.)

Debating Challenges

"One of the other things we'd have were debating challenges, which were really argument challenges," says St. John. "It's funny. We actually got requests from people to have debates, because they were considered so entertaining. While working out in the gym together in the morning, we would pick a new topic to practice debate skills on. I remember I got handed, 'Defend the argument that black and white are the same color,' and you had to fight to the end with your best arguments, with the best case you could make, and try to win it, and you were not allowed to give up. And people witnessing us doing this didn't know that it was an exercise. They didn't know it was just today's practice debate topic.

"I think one of the funniest ones we ever had was Craig Eisler got assigned, 'You have to name two things that have nothing related to each other—at least two things you can think of that have the least in common.' I think he picked like asteroid and love. And then argued that they have nothing in common while the other two people have to prove that they actually are very related or very similar. And so these produced insane arguments. And sometimes we'd get really mad and passionate over these arguments and yell at each other and point and gesticulate. Sometimes we'd end up just breaking down laughing."

Teleporting

"Another one was teleporting, which Ken Fowles taught me. And teleporting was the art of getting past conference security without a badge. And so, it was a collection of techniques. What can you do to walk right into a meeting that has security on it without being stopped? We had a whole bunch of techniques that we'd come up with for doing that, so we used to have a lot of fun testing those. But years and years later, I was telling some Sony executives about teleporting, and they didn't believe me. And they were taking me to this huge secure party they were throwing to impress me because they were investors in WildTangent. And they challenged me to teleport past their amazing security, and I did, and it blew their minds.

"It looks like magic when it's done, but I had a big collection by the time I left. So you had to assess in each situation how you were going to mix and match approaches, but frankly, we really enjoyed the funniest ones. So I think it was Michael Windsor who came up with the broken badge. You know you have a conference chain with a badge on it? He'd hang a chain with no badge around his neck. And then just go to walk in, and most of the time, just walking in without making eye contact works, but if the guards stopped him, he'd go, 'Oh no. My badge is right…' and then he'd look, like 'Oh my god. There's a chain hanging around my neck.' And the security guy would always let him by. Obviously the guy was stunned that his badge was missing and walked around with a loose chain around his neck. Another one that amused me most was Ken Fowles would draw badges. And they looked like shit, like a kindergartener made them, and they always worked. He would literally—he'd walk up to them and show them a hand-drawn shitty badge, and they'd let him by. Oh, it was funny as hell.

"The thing I did that amazed most people was a technique I came up with for getting a whole bunch of people in at once, and what I'd do is I'd walk right up to the security guy, and it's called a rolling walk. So you make eye contact with the guy at the door, and you keep walking around him into the conference slowly, while talking to him, so a dozen people behind you, while his eyes are following yours, are walking right by, behind you. And so you walk up to him saying, 'Hey, where's the bathroom. I've gotta take a piss.' And he'd go, 'Oh, that direction' without even checking your badge, and I'd roll right in and go to the bathroom, and ten other people went in behind me. And it wasn't to save money or anything. They'd always buy the badges, so of course it was just one of those exercises—practice. It was literally a kind of training exercise. Can you control minds? It's amazing what's invisible to people."

The Most Valuable—A Bar Exercise

"One of the funniest ones I remember was the bar exercise at conferences. Conferences were where all of DRG would turn out, so that is where we'd have these practice events. And one of them was in the evening. The rule was, you had to go talk people out of the most valuable personal stuff you could. And the rule was that you couldn't pay them or promise them any future compensation. They had to just give it to you. So you had to persuade people to give you whatever you could get, and the goal was to get jackets, shoes, cellphones, credit cards, girl's underwear, with no promises. And I used to win those flat out. So I'd come home from these conferences with people's Sony jackets, their elephant ties, credit cards, cellphones… all kinds of stuff.

"You know how I did that… got somebody's credit card? I was at the bar, and I was ordering drinks, and I bought everybody a round of drinks at the table. Because I'm not offering them anything in exchange for money, but buy them all drinks, they go, 'That's really generous.' 'It's my Microsoft credit card. Whatever.' And a guy goes, 'Wow. I wish I had a credit card that could do that.' And I said, 'I'll tell you what. If you give me your credit card, I'll give you mine.' And he says, 'Really?' 'Hell yes. Microsoft. I can expense anything. I'm a big shot. Go ahead. Try it.' And so he goes, 'Oh. Ok.' And he gives me his credit card, and everybody's 'What a sucker,' and I give him my Microsoft credit card. My Microsoft credit card was dead. I'd already paid the bartender before I sat down. So I gave him the dead credit card and kept his. Of course I canceled it later when I got home, but he tried to use the credit card and it's no good." So that was the technique: prepay the bartender, claim you'd used your Microsoft credit card, and wait for someone to bite

The Funny Thing About Food

Another of St. John's little exercises involved food.

"One of the things I love doing in social settings is, if you're just around, especially in a closed space like an elevator with somebody, nothing's weirder to people than talking to a stranger in an elevator, because you're trapped close to each other, and people always avoid eye contact in an elevator, like 'you're not here.' And so if you talk to people unexpectedly in elevators, it's always very funny. And if they are eating something, ask if you can have a bite, or if you're eating something, offer them a bite, and after they decline say, 'No really. Try it,' and see if can get them to take a bite. Or offer them a drink. It's really funny. People have the funniest reaction to that. Because after you do that, they become incredibly familiar with you. Whether they accept the drink or the bite or not, they suddenly become very familiar. There's something about offering or sharing food—even offering to share food—with a total stranger that suddenly makes them act like you've known each other for 20 years. 'You should try this. Have you ever had one of these before?' It's funny. People have a very funny reaction to that.

"And if you eat other people's food unexpectedly, it's very funny how that happens, too. Douglas Adams told me this story in person. Now I know he wrote it in a book, but… I hired him for a Microsoft event and I got to spend some time with him, and one of the stories he told was funny as hell, and it was a true story apparently. He was in a train station and he had some time to wait, so he figured he'd get some cookies or crisps and he'd read the paper. So he bought some crisps and the paper and he went set the crisps on the table and sat down to read his paper, and somebody else comes and sits across from him at the table. And while he's sitting there reading the paper, the person reaches across the table, picks up his crisps, opens the bag and eats one. And he said, 'Being British, we don't have any tools for coping with this.' And he goes, doing what any red-blooded Brit would do in a circumstance like this. 'I ignored it and pretended it wasn't happening.' He didn't say, 'Those are my crisps.' 'So I reached out and I ate a crisp and put it back, hoping that would indicate to him that these were my crisps, and a few seconds later the guy took the bag and ate another one of my crisps. I didn't want to make eye contact with him, but I took the bag back and ate a crisp, and we went back and forth this way until the crisps were gone.' And he goes, 'The entire time I was just livid. I couldn't believe this guy was eating my potato chips in front of me, and not even having the courtesy to notice that he was consuming my chips. And so finally the guy went to catch his train, and I sat there reading my paper in frustration that this had just transpired, and what could it possibly mean. Finally, I got up to go and I picked my paper up, and laying there on the table, under the paper, was my bag of chips.'"

Room Number Challenge

James Plamondon adds one more DRG game, which occurred whenever they checked into a hotel together. "We'd compete to see who could get the room with the highest room number. Every tactic was fair game, so long as it did not make the front-desk person aware of the competition."

Impossible

Engstrom had his favorite tactic, which involved just being impossible to work with. "Well, everybody had a hard time working with all of us. So it really depended on who you were, which one of us you found most impossible to work with. And we did it that way on purpose, so from the marketing side, I was impossible. Everyone had to go through Alex. And from the engineering side, Alex was impossible, so everyone had to go through me. It was all broken up neatly so there was always somebody that backchannel information could come through if we pushed too hard. We'd stage arguments among the three of us, all get mad at each other because I was being a prima donna, Alex was taking all the credit, blah, blah, blah. We wouldn't script them or anything. It wasn't necessary. It was just fun."

Ty Graham was one of those rare people who had no problems with Engstrom. "For whatever reason, I didn't flip Eric's bozo bit*. I found him useful, or he found me useful… something like that." But Graham does acknowledge that Engstrom could be difficult. "Eric was a big pain in the ass back in those days. Like if I wanted to get a picture of Eric for a speaking engagement at WinHEC (Windows Hardware Engineering Conference) for example, and I would show up with a shirt and a comb and a camera and the whole setup, I'd have to camp out in his office and cajole him into putting on a shirt with a collar, sitting down… just a big pain in the ass." Still, Graham acknowledges the pressure that both Eisler and Engstrom were under while completing DirectX. "They were just… besides being frazzled, they were prickly personalities at best, with the time they were putting in and how fast they were going… that was amplified, but Eric was never obnoxious to me."

**In this context, "bozo bit" refers to dismissing someone's input because they aren't worth listening to.*

Elite Manipulation Task Force

"The truth was, I used to be a magician when I was college age, so I learned a lot of that there. So DRG came very naturally to me. But I really didn't do that stuff maliciously. I didn't try to be a con man, but you just go, if you want to have influence and get what you need done, it was a very powerful way of being. So people didn't realize that evangelists were—how do you say it? Trained to that degree to be that way. One of the things I wish history would know is that we weren't just there to talk people into using the Microsoft APIs. That group was kind of Microsoft's elite manipulation task force." (And now they know, Alex.)

Boss Killing

One of Eisler's and Engstrom's—particularly Engstrom's—favorite pastimes at Microsoft seemed to be "boss killing." "They were definitely boss killers," observed John Ludwig, "and they would know how to hit those buttons, and they would identify those quickly in people, and they would know how to really get their bosses worked up."

Engstrom freely admits to his boss killing habit (meaning getting them fired, of course). "Paul Osborne. Heidi Brussels, 'Brussels Sprouts' is what we called her. Steve Banfield. He was the guy that tried to get me fired. Richard Best, who came and went quite quickly. The others were pre-DirectX 1. And then Joel Segal, who we really liked, but he just couldn't keep up. He was getting smeared like a banana over the front of the windscreen. And he brought in Richard Ness, who lasted eight weeks.

"Like one time they were going to fire me, and Alex found out who they were going to use to do it, and so I showed up and didn't take the bait. Of course they had a senior person there, a VP of something, to watch the explosion and realize I was impossible to work with, and yet nothing happened, so my boss got fired over that. At the time, I started collecting bosses that I could get rid of. One, two, three, four… I think it was six in a row. At one point, a former boss of mine went to the head of the division and maneuvered to try to get control of DirectX. And his boss's only comment was, 'Why would you want to put your head in that guillotine?'"

Engstrom explains why his bosses had to go. They would often take credit for the work that Engstrom and his teams did, but often as not, even when they did try to manage things, Engstrom believed they did so poorly. So, they had to be dealt with. "We would let them be in the room when we were having a discussion about something, and we'd just leave out something important. And then they would run off and explain this great genius idea they had and how they'd managed to win us over, and blahblahblah. And we'd just make sure they were dead wrong the next time they gave a presentation. And that was that. Goodbye. It was great. You know, like when you tell three different people you don't trust slightly different stories, and then we can see what pops up. It worked great… over and over again. It was amazing."

-21-

DirectX Media

I put DirectX in IE so that you could do the cool things that HTML5 does now—and you could do them in 1994—and then we finished by putting a 3D XML model together that would let you do way more than you can do in HTML5 now... Hardware accelerated inside IE4.

-Eric Engstrom

After Windows 95 shipped and DirectX became an established product, things began to change. Eisler and Engstrom, now working in Brad Silverberg's Windows division, were working on Internet media strategies under John Ludwig. They had big plans, but they needed to stay under the radar at first, before they unleashed their next bombshells. And so they appealed to St. John, who was apathetic and dragged down by his personal life, not to self-destruct, but to be their "heat shield" and help distract people from what they were doing. Out of loyalty, and knowing that he could do the job very well, St. John acquiesced. He would create such a distraction that nobody would pay any attention to what Eisler and Engstrom were developing until they were ready to show it.

St. John found the perfect distraction—a growing war over 3D graphics solutions that involved Direct3D, SGI's OpenGL and an internal project code-named Talisman. All he had to do was to keep escalating that war.

While St. John was busy supporting developers and fighting internal and external battles over OpenGL and Talisman, Eisler and Engstrom were working to integrate DirectX into web technologies. Despite his other activities, St. John started the ball rolling by helping create a prototype browser technology to open people's eyes.

The technology wasn't simple. It started with Java—which Microsoft had licensed from Sun Microsystems—and Microsoft's proprietary implementation: Microsoft Java Virtual Machine (MSJVM). There were technical challenges to working with Java, one of which being that Sun's original implementation of it wouldn't support the real-time, extremely high volume of API calls needed to do the heavy multimedia lifting in games that DirectX was designed for. "Microsoft made its own interface in order to do this, called RNI," says St. John. "So we basically bastardized Java. At Microsoft we took all kinds of liberties with Java, which led to the Sun/Java lawsuit*."

**Sun Microsystems sued Microsoft for "incompletely implementing the Java 1.1 standard." Even though Microsoft's JVM implementation was very fast—even faster than Sun's—it did not conform to the standard implementation for which they had a license. As St. John put it, they took liberties. Sun was also involved later in the antitrust lawsuit against Microsoft.*

Two engineers, Matt Wilson, who was what St. John referred to as a "junior monkey" in DRG at the time, and game industry veteran David Petchey, wrote a Java wrapper for DirectX and the team began demoing web pages using their prototype. To say the least, people were stunned. St. John remembers John Ludwig's reaction. "Holy shit. Yeah, not only are we glad we put you guys in charge of multimedia, but what else have you got to say?" Once again, the collaboration of Engstrom, Eisler, and St. John was opening eyes, and according to St. John, Ludwig instantly became a big fan of theirs, "even though we drove him nuts because we were immature."

Ludwig's positive response was in part due to his own long-term strategy for beating Netscape. "I was always thinking, 'How are we going to develop a distinct advantage over our competitors, and what could we do that they simply cannot do?' And it was clear on the internet that we had this deep asset called the operating system team, and one part of that deep asset was this great multimedia graphics capability that Netscape had nothing like. And because they were committed to being as cross-platform as possible, they would probably never have that capability. And so I was always entranced with the idea of how can we make all that rich multimedia stuff that we see in gaming that's just part of the Windows platform? How can we embed that into the Internet, because if we can do that, a) the end users will like it because they enjoy that kind of rich, beautiful, deep stuff, and b) it will be a competitive problem for Netscape."

Promotions... Finally!

It was shortly after the Java-fueled demo that Eisler and Engstrom finally got the promotions they both felt they deserved. Eisler was promoted and worked on building the Windows Streaming media server platform. Engstrom was also promoted and given responsibility over the Windows media client and media technologies for the web, specifically DirectX Media, which is what the browser demo ultimately became. According to Ludwig, it was only peripherally because of the DirectX Media demo that had so impressed him. He says that nobody was ever promoted at Microsoft just because of the success of a single event, but that Both Eisler and Engstrom had demonstrated that they could work effectively with these kinds of technologies, and especially in Engstrom's case, Ludwig reasoned that the extra responsibility would actually improve his behavior. "What's going to happen? Either he's going to handle it well, and it will calm him down, and he'll be productive, or he won't. In which case we'll know it's time to move on and move him out of that job." He adds, "I definitely think they did not learn good manners, but eventually, they did fine."

Managerial Styles

Clearly Ludwig's success with Eisler and Engstrom had to do with his managerial style and his overall patience with them and their respect for his deep technical knowledge of networking overall, but there was more to it. He contrasts his style with that of another highly successful manager with whom he had worked, David Cole:

"David is really good at running large teams and at communicating well in teams, getting them organized and getting everybody to step in line and working against the same goals. I see David as a great army general. I mean, when you're doing a really big effort, you need supply lines and chain of command, and plans, and David is really good at that stuff. He enjoyed doing it and he made people feel good about it. He was good at inspiring people.

"I suck at all that. I viewed myself as much more like the Marines, which is you send us in to an area—like the Internet—where we have nothing going on. It's a disaster. And damn it, we have to get a beachhead somehow. We really don't care about the cost. We just need the beachhead. And that's what I was good at doing. And I think that was just mentally better attuned with guys like Eric and Craig. Let's just go in, make trouble, shake things up, find a way—any way—to become relevant and gain a beachhead, and then we'll clean it up later."

And so Engstrom was offered a promotion to a general manager position where he would lead a team of 250 engineers, which from Engstrom's point of view was a good step toward his ultimate goal of becoming a Microsoft vice president. "It looked like there was every chance we were going to make the 'destroy Netscape super browser' according to plan," observed St. John, "and that became a big Microsoft initiative." But there was a catch. According to St. John, Engstrom was told by Brad Silverberg that he could be promoted to general manager of the internet media division, but only if he removed the Java binding to DirectX and embraced the work of Microsoft Research (MSR) rather than use the Java solution.

In commenting on St. John's assertion Silverberg said, "…there was a LOT of pressure from Bill and Nathan <Myhrvold> to use technology from Research, and it's possible that I asked Craig and Eric to play ball on this to make life a little easier and get Bill and Nathan off our collective backs, all the while expecting that research technology to fail and use theirs in the end." Ludwig adds, "I think the Research guys had some really grand ideas, and I suspected that when you actually tried to implement them in a product, that they would grind apart and fail. But sometimes you had to agree to try in order to move ahead."

Engstrom accepted the deal despite the fact that he knew it would have an adverse effect on the technology. Working with Jim Kajiya and a team from Microsoft Research, they axed the Java wrapper and added MSR's own API, DirectAnimation. According to St. John, it was cool technology, but utterly useless. He describes it as "just animation scripting for no clear purpose... which it carried on being useless for well into the modern Silverlight incarnation. Six generations of irrelevant Microsoft technology searching for a purpose. And it was no use for making games."

Although Kajiya was not the author of DirectAnimation, he does defend it, at the same time defending the point of view expressed by Engstrom and St. John. "I think DirectAnimation had a different objective than they wanted. They were looking for a small set of widgets that you could put on pages that would spice up a web page a little bit, and DirectAnimation was, at the time, like VRML a few years later… very much in that vein, which was a general system for making 3D web pages. So, it had a very different objective from what they wanted. I think their assessment that it slowed their project down and really didn't help them with their limited objectives is probably quite accurate."

At this point, the DirectX Java Wrapper prototype officially morphed into DirectX Media, a combination of the original low-level DirectX APIs with higher level media services, like DirectShow and DirectAnimation, that offered tools and cross platform DirectX support for creating all kinds of content in web applications. In a white paper from March, 1997, it's described as "Media Integration and Streaming Services for the Active Platform," However, according to St. John, the layers of technology they added to DirectX Media prevented the full implementation of the DirectX APIs.

Ludwig explains further: "The ongoing discussion between the core DirectX guys and the everybody else in the company was that a lot of people wanted to slap the Direct *blah* name on their technology, and because it had some success in the marketplace, but most of that technology was not philosophically the same as DirectX at all." DirectAnimation was an example of a technology not truly suited for the "Direct" brand. "They were about exposing a whole new rich API set to do a whole new class of behaviors. But was very different philosophically from what DirectX was about..."

Meanwhile, the goal of creating a super browser was still percolating.

Compensation Stories

When Eisler and Engstrom were transferred and given new responsibilities, they also received a considerable boost in their compensation packages. Not so, St. John, whose division was not in a position to raise his package. This is a story that even St. John probably never knew. Cameron Myhrvold tells it:

"It got to the point where Craig Eisler and Eric Engstrom left my group, left DRG and went over to work for Brad Silverberg, and I remember Brad calling me up and saying, 'Cam. What are we going to do for these guys during the review cycle?' I'm like, 'What do you mean?' And he goes, 'Well, obviously we should collude on how we compensate these people, or there's going to be dissentions within the three of them.' I'm like, 'Jesus, Brad. Well, thank you. I had not thought about that.' So we sat and we colluded, and Brad actually transferred me some of his budget to compensate Alex because he felt that he really had to go a long ways to compensate Eric and Craig, and I didn't have the budget to do something commensurate for Alex. I don't think I was out of dollars. I think I was out of shares. And he transferred me shares from his model so I could give them to Alex and put the guys on an even footing."

Meanwhile, Engstrom had his own issue with compensation—not his own, but that of the team he was building. St. John had agreed to keep people busy internally while Eisler and Engstrom worked on their grand plan. "We absolutely had an agreement," says Engstrom. "I was busy consolidating all of the multimedia technologies under one roof. At the time, everybody thought they should start a little piece of multimedia tech that was half-baked, all across the company. So I would systematically merge them into the DirectX group. And so at one point we had 300 people working for me." The problem was paying all 300 people. At the time, Microsoft paid on a curve, which meant that he wouldn't have the budget to pay some of his best people what they were worth. Engstrom knew his way around Microsoft's rules, however, and he came up with a solution.

"Because Microsoft has this curve, to try to build a superstar team you're going to have problems because a lot of your superstars just ended up being underpaid. So I solved that problem by hiring very highly paid, but useless people who were just worried they'd get fired, because partners contributed 85%... their budget was 85% of that number, and it was a bigger number. Whereas people who weren't partners, it was 65% and of course it was a smaller number. I would tell them, I'm never going to give you any more money, but I will make sure you don't get fired. And you have so many stock options from your original hiring, and that all you really want is to keep getting those.

"And so I collected four or five of those people who were industry pundits, people and had been hired because they talked well or looked good, or whatever. And I would give them the worst mark I could and still keep them employed. That was my deal with them. I was very upfront. And I took the 85% of their larger budget and I spread across all the people who were really making DirectX sing, and that's why we had a better team. We could afford better developers than anybody else in the company. I had a very highly paid—disproportionately well-paid—team at Microsoft as a result of that...

Turns out when I came back to Microsoft after time away, I found that they'd made all kinds of rules to stop people like me from doing things like that. I thought that was a silly thing."

The War is Over

The story of DirectX, from the point of view of Eisler, Engstrom, and St. John, was the story of a war fought in the trenches of Microsoft. As they saw it, they battled their way to success. St. John says, "We had become highly combative, accustomed to having to do everything ourselves, relatively ruthless in dealing with opposition and used to having to shout our message to be heard." Now, riding a wave of success, the three were sought out, invited to senior strategy meetings and actually urged to share their ideas and feedback, which was quite unsettling. St. John even relates how he would become argumentative out of habit, even when everyone in the room was already agreeing with him.

"Now we're big shots and we're famous, and we have lots of allies and lots of enemies and we've been given lots of stock options, so jumping to that point in time, we're now BFDs at Microsoft. Feared and respected, you know? And so Craig and Eric are not guys down in the plumbing. We're all surfaced. We can't do sneaky, unnoticed stuff. Everybody watches everything we say and do now because they realize that we've become very dangerous and powerful… I really liked it much better when I got my way without people knowing what was happening. I didn't like having everybody listen to me and take notes and try to do what I wanted. I didn't enjoy being in charge at all. So I was getting called to these senior meetings… Nobody argued with me. They're 'Oh, what does the genius say? OK, that's our plan then. Let's go do that.' So I weirdly didn't enjoy that. It's funny in retrospect."

In contrast, Engstrom and Eisler were elated about their new positions. They had been promoted and were running teams of their own. They had stock options and respect and notoriety at Microsoft. And they wanted to keep the pressure on as they worked to position IE against Netscape. But St. John didn't share their enthusiasm. He only saw his responsibility to the software developers he had been working for and with. But he did continue to run interference for them. "I'll go interfere with all these guys on Torborg's team that you're going to have to contend with over multimedia. I'll just go make their lives hell until somebody finally gets sick of me and fires me."

The Stress of Success

Almost from the moment he left Alaska, Alex St. John had been pushing envelopes and trampling on sacred cows. None of it really came easy, because easy wasn't his way of doing things. He'd had his victories and his failures. In a risk averse culture, he had thrived on risk, but not without paying a price.

One price he paid was his marriage and family. The long hours and arguably maniacal focus on his professional goals had cost him dearly. And he was tired. "I was burned out. It had succeeded. It worked. And everything is changed, and I didn't care at that point."

And according to many who knew and worked with him, St. John really was waiting for someone to fire him because he couldn't stop on his own. Whatever his unspoken wishes, however, he was not done at Microsoft… not yet.

Chrome

Chrome was to DX Media what the XBOX was to DirectX.

-Alex St. John

Chrome was meant to be the Netscape killer—a super browser that would add speed and functionality that nobody had seen before. The simplest way to describe Chrome is that it put DirectX into the browser with a 3D XML model added, allowing all kinds of multimedia that had previously not been possible in browsers. "The ability to deliver Quake via the browser was the initial vision for Chrome," said St. John.

The idea of the super browser was at the center of a strategy to dominate the browser market and push Netscape out of their top position, if not out of business. Getting DirectX Media approved was a step in that direction, flaws and all. The next step was Chrome, a full-on multimedia enabled browser.

Development of Chrome began in some ways the moment Eisler, Engstrom, and St. John took on the Internet, but it wasn't made public internally until May 14, 1997 when St. John dropped a little hint about it in a long email response to one of Bill Gates' emails about Talisman.

He wrote: "So there is a huge barrier to entry for what I call 'Fat multimedia' adoption by absolutely anybody... let alone a company with no experience in this area what-so-ever like Sun. Set JavaMedia aside for a second, and consider the possibility that the real challenge is not to compete directly with JavaMedia, but to be the first ones to successfully deliver 'Fat multimedia' to the market, particularly the net. Delivering 'Fat Multimedia' is what the Chrome browser project is about. (For Chrome strategy see JohnLu)" Later that morning, John Ludwig (JohnLu) replied saying that Engstrom and Bob Heddle had sent a tape and a memo to Bill Gates about Chrome.

Ultimately, the Chrome project got greenlit with Engstrom leading. For legal reasons, they changed its name to Chromeffects (or ChromeFX), believing that the word Chrome would be hard to trademark (something apparently Google didn't have a problem with).

Chromeffects was previewed on CNET in April, 1998, before the name change, but even if it was still called Chrome, it was no longer the super browser that Engstrom, Eisler, and St. John had envisioned from the start. It was, however, A very powerful technology, far ahead of its time, that allowed developers to use DirectX APIs, including Direct3D, to create 3D images and features in a browser. Project manager Bob Heddle is quoted in the article saying, "It is going to propel the industry. We're moving DirectX from programmers to artists."

Another issue that hadn't been decided as of April was how the technology would be shipped and what the business model would be. St. John says, "Eric had the idea that Chromeffects could be a premium OS up-sell to Windows. His ambitions were boundless and he wanted to create a new profit center." St. John disagreed with this approach, suggesting that if it were to be a Netscape killer, it should be distributed for free, which is more or less what happened. In August 1998, Microsoft offered a free download of an early version of Chromeffects to its developers. Direct3D capabilities were still expected to be added when the product was officially released.

Chromeffects was definitely ahead of its time in many ways, but, like DirectX Media, it was hampered by layers of technology, such as DirectAnimation, which prevented it from fully implementing DirectX APIs in a browser. In its final form, it enabled developers to add full-3D images and features in web pages, but it was still to unable to support browser-based games, which St. John points out was the major reason for having 3D in a browser.

The Ultimate Chrome Strategy

To ensure victory first place yourself beyond defeat.

-Sun Tzu

We had a very unusual mentality trained into us. Plamondon taught that a good plan is one that has many ways to succeed and few to fail. When you embrace that way of thinking, to an external viewer it often appears as though you had a weird way of controlling the future, in practice all you've done is chosen a path that maximizes for positive potential outcomes. It just looks deliberate in retrospect.

-Alex St. John

Although Engstrom had acquiesced to internal pressure in allowing MSR technologies into DirectX Media and into Chromeffects in order to keep the project moving and lead it, St. John states that the prototype Java code written by Wilson and Petchey was secretly added into IE. "Because of the uncertainty and conflict over ownership and control, I recall that shortly after producing this prototype Eric and I sat down with Craig and we said, 'Look. We think we're going to get the charter to build this new super multimedia browser, but given the nature of politics and the battles that will go on here, like the ones we've had with the OpenGL group, we expect to be competed with and subverted at every angle. So, in case we lose… in case we need a way to win out of desperation because we lose the primary battlefront, we need a fallback. Let's secretly ship that prototype David Petchey and Matt Wilson made as part of IE4. We'll just slip it in as it's going out the door. Undocumented, untested, insecure.'"

This secret prototype was just another of perhaps thousands of security holes that Microsoft had left in its software, but it was definitely a bad idea in its way. "The history of Windows XP tells you how little concern Microsoft gave to the scale of the security problems that would end up presenting on the Internet."

Although St. John speaks of their slipping the technology in secretly, Ludwig replies, "They didn't insert anything into IE surreptitiously. There were a lot of excellent developers working on IE. I think we knew exactly what was going on, and we certainly knew they were trying to slip in the underpinnings of this Chrome idea. I don't think that was particularly controversial or mysterious." And as for security holes, he says, "Oh well. We had lots of those. We were running as hard as we could, as fast as we could to beat Netscape."

Ludwig tells a story about one of his early experiences with IE. "I remember—it was probably early '96 or very late in '95—Chris Jones and I had a group of web developers come in and meet with us and we gave them a preview of our next version of IE. And we just got our asses kicked by this group of developers. They basically just told us, 'Nobody gives a shit what you have to say. Nobody cares what Microsoft wants to make. Why don't you just support Java? That's what people are using. Why don't you just support JavaScript?' I mean, we got savaged. And we left the room, both of us, realizing, 'God none of these guys give a shit about us. We are not relevant.'" And so the mandate was to become relevant, and it didn't much matter at the time, how they did it. "We're going to move fast, and maybe everything's not going to be fully buttoned up, but damn it, at the end of the day, we are going to be relevant."

According to St. John, they knew that Chrome had the built-in capability to be the powerhouse Netscape-killing browser that Microsoft really wanted, and they believed that they had options regarding its fate. "At any time that Microsoft's politics obstructed us from shipping that capability, I could simply leak its existence to the press and FORCE it into existence and FORCE Microsoft to support it even if we lost the battle to build it formally." But St. John also knew that his time at Microsoft could end abruptly at any moment, and it's fair to say that he secretly wanted that to happen. He needed time to deal with his personal life and divorce. "Since I was probably going to leave in a ball of fire, the plan was for me to carry away the emergency plan." That "emergency plan" led to another major chapter in St. John's life and a radical technological breakthrough, but that came later. He still had more Microsoft battles ahead.

-22-

Escalating the Graphics Wars

As St. John had suspected, not everybody was happy about the success the DirectX team was having. According to St. John, there were still enemies within Microsoft who would throw roadblocks in the way or try to seize control of their projects. Direct3D was just getting going, and the NT, OpenGL and even the Talisman group were making life a challenge. So it was St. John's role to be the heat shield for Engstrom and Eisler and let them keep working on Chrome without interference from within.

While OpenGL was an established graphics API, Talisman was an internal Microsoft technology that came out of Microsoft Research, which had been started by Nathan Myhrvold in 1991 with the sole purpose of exploring new technologies that would allow Microsoft to stay ahead of its competition and build up a portfolio of patents. Unlike every other division, Microsoft Research, or just Research as people referred to it, had no requirement to develop products or to make money directly. They were pure research. But Myhrvold realized that research without products would not be as effective as it should be, and so Research often worked directly with product groups to implement their technologies into practical implementations.

One of those implementations was Talisman, a clever and somewhat complicated technology designed to speed up 3D animation rendering by only requiring a program to re-render the parts of an image that actually changed, and not the whole image. By doing so, it saved resources and sped up the process, in theory quite dramatically.

Bill Gates was intrigued by Talisman and supported it, but members of the DirectX team, including St. John and evangelist Ty Graham hated it. There are many stories about the internal battles over Talisman, with rationale provided on both sides of the argument, but in the end, Talisman took too long to get to market, and by the time it was ready to be released, the graphics market had passed it by. For that and other reasons, Talisman was ultimately abandoned.

OpenGL, on the other hand, was a different story. The battles between advocates of OpenGL and Direct3D raged for many months, escalating when graphics guru John Carmack wrote what was to become an infamous post on a user group that blasted Direct3D and fully endorsed OpenGL. This came as a shock to the DirectX team because previously Carmack had been very supportive.

The Carmack post ignited some acrimonious argument over emails and raised a lot of questions about which standard Microsoft should adopt.

-23-

The OpenGL Letters—Part 1

Read First:

Some of next few chapters go into considerable detail about Microsoft's efforts to win the 3D API battle, also revealing much of the internal thinking that went into the decisions, complete with original email threads. This level of detail is probably most interesting to technical nerds and people who just find the internal workings of Microsoft interesting. Otherwise, it might be safe to skip or skim those parts. But if you really want to witness the battles that led to the decision to support Direct3D, realize that ***it was that decision that directly enabled Xbox to happen.***

DirectX was like Noah's Ark after Microsoft flooded the world of DOS and they were all refugees trapped with us, having lost the world they were previously free in. It was like building and loading Noah's Ark ahead of a deluge. No time for rehearsals or mistakes. The first boat HAD to float.

-Alex St. John

Toward the end of 1996, Microsoft had adopted a policy of supporting Direct3D (D3D) for Windows as a consumer facing technology and OpenGL for NT as a high-end solution. The two platform groups continued to be adversarial, however, and the NT group was positioning itself to support OGL as a consumer product in competition with the Windows group, essentially thumbing their nose at D3D.

Direct3D was especially in the spotlight for a couple of reasons: One, its launch had been rushed, and two, it had been rushed because of competition, both internally and externally, from supporters of OpenGL. As Servan Keondjian observed, there were still a lot of flaws and unfinished business by the time the first version of D3D was released. And all of this opened the door for a continuation of the battle for 3D API supremacy between OpenGL and Direct3D.

St. John and his fellow evangelists believed that they had largely won the battle, however, with the clear adoption of DirectX. Direct3D was officially supported by Microsoft as the 3D solution for Windows 95, but support for OpenGL still existed inside the computer game industry. Even so, it came as a big surprise when, on December 23, 1996, John Carmack issued what amounted to a public statement in support of OpenGL. Carmack posted his statement on an open forum, causing an immediate storm of commentary within the game development community—mostly in favor of OpenGL.

(Where I have quoted from Carmack's original message, I have done so exactly as it was originally written. This means that there are some typos and misspellings. But Carmack is known for his programming brilliance, not necessarily for his writing.)

In his post, Carmack noted that he had been working with OpenGL for the past six months and that it had impressed him, especially in how easy it was to use. He wrote, "A month ago, I ported quake to OpenGL. It was an extremely pleasant experience. It didn't take long, the code was clean and simple, and it gave me a great testbed to rapidly try out new research ideas."

On the other hand, his experience with Direct3D IM (Immediate Mode) was less satisfying. "I started porting glquake to Direct-3D IM with the intent of learning the api and doing a fair comparison. Well, I have learned enough about it. I'm not going to finish the port. I have better things to do with my time."

He went on to state, "Direct-3D IM is a horribly broken API. It inflicts great pain and suffering on the programmers using it, without returning any significant advantages. I don't think there is ANY market segment that D3D is apropriate for, OpenGL seems to work just fine for everything from quake to softimage. There is no good technical reason for the existance of D3D."

Although he acknowledged that D3D would likely improve with future versions, he advocated for the adoption of OpenGL to save developers from having to go through the evolution of what he called an "ill-birthed API".

Carmack, like most developers, found D3D very difficult to work with, and, like most developers, he disliked the Common Object Model (COM) that Microsoft used. Referring to COM and execute buffers he states, "Some of these choices were made so that the API would be able to gracefully expand in the future, but who cares about having an API that can grow if you have forced it to be painful to use now and forever after? Many things that are a single line of GL code require half a page of D3D code to allocate a structure, set a size, fill something in, call a COM routine, then extract the result."

To Carmack, ease of use was paramount, and between the two APIs, there was no contest.

Carmack's best-case scenario: "Microsoft integrates OpenGL with direct-x (probably calling it Direct-GL or something), ports D3D retained mode on top of GL, and tells everyone to forget they every [sic] heard of D3D immediate mode. Programmers have one good api, vendors have one driver to write, and the world is a better place."

This full-throated endorsement of OpenGL and scathing take-down of Direct3D blindsided people at Microsoft. St. John states, "I just remember the shock my team experienced when Carmack made the post because we had been working with him so long and didn't see it coming."

Internally, the initial responses to Carmack's message disputed his position. One message from Kate Seekings quoted a software engineer named Aaron Peapell, who wrote:

"> Ive seen the complete quake source.

> OpenGL was uses [sic] in the WinQuake src _only_ to blit a buffer to the screen

> thats it. So all the John Carmack on OpenGL vs DX is a load."

Another email sent by Christine McGavran on January 3, provided a breakdown of the relative strengths and weaknesses of some of the existing 3D engines. Calling out four main issues: 1. Usability, 2. Compatibility with 3D hardware, 3. Speed on software only, and 4. Cost, she provided the following information, which summarized the issues and somewhat agreed with what Carmack had written:

"D3d passes 2, semi-passes 3, passes 4, but fails 1. Open GL passes 1 and 4, but currently fails 2 and 3.

Renderware passes 1, semi-passes 2, passes 3, and fails 4. It also has the disadvantage of being doomed to fail eventually through lack of big-company support.

There's also Quickdraw 3d to consider, which I haven't seen much PC enthusiasm for."

St. John's Response

Meanwhile, St. John began an email thread under the subject header "Response to Carmack". Of course, he took Carmack's criticism seriously. In fact, on the subject of Direct3D being hard to use, he wrote, "Yup. He's right."

He pointed out that if a genius like Carmack had a hard time working with it, who wouldn't? He also stated that this was not news, and that they were already producing better documentation and new sample code.

St. John also pointed out that D3D was never meant to be "the ultimate software rendering engine." Its purpose was to provide consumer oriented 3D hardware acceleration. He even stated that Carmack himself made the request, saying, "Get your fat APIs out of my way and let me at the iron." St. John also made it clear that D3D had drivers for every major hardware accelerator, which OGL did not, and that they would evolve D3D faster than OGL. Finally, he revealed that there would be new, primitive APIs like DrawTriangle to make it easier for people to do "quick ports or evaluations to get up and running without the fuss," but with some sacrifice in performance and versatility.

There's much more to St. John's lengthy response, including a comparison of D3D and OGL as being like forks and spoons—designed for different purposes. "Forks and Spoons are both silverware but it hardly makes sense to say that you don't need forks because they're lousy for eating soup, or that spoons suck because you can't eat spaghetti with them. Saying you have to always eat with a spoon, or that you're only going to eat soup because you can't figure out how to use a fork is a fair point, but kind of pitiful and should be fixed."*

**For the record, St. John later said to me, "Must you tell the forks and spoons analogy? That has to be the single dumbest analogy I ever made."* Sorry Alex. I think it's funny.

In his email, he notes that both D3D and OGL are supported by Microsoft. D3D as a real-time consumer multimedia API and OGL as an "industrial strength" 3D API for use in CAD, modeling and scientific visualization. Noting that "it's going to get very weird out there for 3D hardware," he wrote that there was a need for standard driver architecture that is "flexible enough to accommodate innovation, yet rigid enough to actually be a standard that gets used." Not an easy problem to solve, he said, following up with a long list of questions, scenarios and requirements. He closed his post saying, "I dunno, but if you think you've got all the answers then I've got a few questions I'm dying to put to you."

See Carmack's D3D/OGL Post and St. John's Response to Carmack in the Online Appendix.

By early February it became clear that developers were not going to shift *en masse* toward OpenGL and, as Keondjian reported in a February 5 email from a large UK developers conference, there was actually quite a bit of support for D3D, especially for retain mode, as opposed to immediate mode, which is what Carmack had tested. Keondjian also reported, "We had an open discussion about John Carmack's comments and it was surprising to see that not a single developer there seemed to agree with him. Even more so, developers were saying they wanted D3D to become the standard and were keen to push it to be the standard."

Did the 3D Graphics Wars Affect Xbox?

"When DirectDraw was subsumed into Direct3D, it really started to flesh out what DirectX was: a base level high performance API that worked within Windows. This was always the goal/vision of the project as expressed to me by Alex,Eric and Craig, and what I bought into as I knew how bad the rest of Windows was and that it needed a solid path for fixing it. So in a sense, yes, I can agree this created a baseline platform (DirectX) that a console could be made for. And even in those early days we were pretty clear that was something we were enabling by creating it. We just did not think Microsoft would be the ones who went off and built it in the end as 'Microsoft would never make a console, they stay out of hardware' was the common understanding of the company. This is what I believe the Xbox creation was then up against, but that was just after my time there.

"I also believe it was the changes that got pushed out by the rapid development of DirectX that then forced GL to fully mature and become the more workable solution it is today. That was not the case in the early days; it was not a complete enough API to build a whole console with.

"There is a counter argument, that SONY for example with PS2 put together a bunch of libraries with a version of GL for its launch. But this was a very untogether platform, and most developers ended up pretty much re-engineering most or everything from scratch while MS was enabling full easy ports over from DirectX on Windows to the Xbox."

—Servan Keondjian, principal architect of Direct3D

Gates on DreamWorks

A couple of days after Keondjian sent his good news email from the UK, Bill Gates fired off a message about some technology he'd seen while visiting DreamWorks, especially the work around physical modeling, acoustics, and physics. His email asked why they seemed so far ahead of Microsoft's games group.

Gates' email signalled profound consequences for Microsoft because of the person who had most impressed him—Seamus Blackley. More to come...

Gates & St. John

In his email about his visit to DreamWorks, Gate's expressed enthusiasm for what Microsoft could learn from the work he had seen. He recommended that they get their games up to that level of sophistication, and also that they should work on their own technology to incorporate some of the innovative methods that DreamWorks had used. He wrote, "They admitted that others will clone their work so I don't think they would mind the system taking over some of it." Gates was also impressed that the DreamWorks team had incorporated some techniques they had learned from their preview of Talisman.

Within two hours, St. John had sent a reply to Gates' email in which he clarified some of the issues that Gates had brought up. At one point in his email Gates had written, "It seems like these games guys are so far ahead of what we are doing right now that our work is not very leveraged." This comment set St. John off. In his usual colorful way, he refocused the argument toward the need for better, more "robust" multimedia drivers for new and existing hardware and focus on enabling real-time applications like video, games, video conferencing, 3D animation, and interactive web browsing. All of which Gates took well, asking for more of what St. John was proposing.

Of course, St. John—never at a loss for ideas and always prepared—jumped into the opening Gates had left, offering several specific suggestions that would help improve performance, partly by fixing issues in the operating system that sucked up time and memory, such as a CD cache that he claimed could slow input/output by up to 30%. He wrote, "There aren't 10 different processes seeking the drive randomly, so the cache both slows down CD access and eats very valuable RAM thus increasing the amount of disk paging the OS carries out while the multimedia-title/video-player is trying to maintain a steady frame rate."

St. John also suggested that they allow real-time applications (like games) to lock and hold memory and force the OS to stop, or "page out," any unnecessary components before a multimedia application starts. And finally, he suggested that they examine Windows 95 for other areas that tend to suck up time or memory, saying, "Some of this stuff could probably be categorized as just a little bug fixing or architecture tweaking." He makes the point that a lot of the functionality of Windows that is useful for business and productivity applications creates impediments to the best-case scenario for multimedia. He uses an example of web pages vs. real-time games: "One of the reasons that our browser can take over a second to draw a single web page with a little text on it and some tiny bitmaps is that is has to load/call around 21 dll's and go through COM, ActiveX gyrations to get its drawing done. Maybe fine for slow web browsing, but completely ridiculous for applications like Quake."

Gates had also responded to St. John's focus on drivers versus "wizzy" technology, and St. John pointed out that Microsoft's goal was to provide reliability and broad coverages for applications, whereas the hardware companies were much more interested in selling their latest and greatest chip technology… that they were in competition with other chip makers, and so they didn't much care about supporting previous chips. From Microsoft's point of view, this created what he called "a huge driver headache" trying to support all the competing chips and their multiple versions—each with its various tweaks and changes.

Another idea that Gates floated was a certification program for drivers, but St. John countered with a proposal of his own—something he had previously suggested called "Funstones"*. The idea behind Funstones was to create a benchmark suite for multimedia and promote it heavily to the media and marketplace, and also make it available to any consumer. "We'd just tell the press that if an OEM's machine doesn't pass a Funstone test, it's not a working multimedia computer. Instead of running a big certification bureaucracy, we'd just publish the benchmark."

*Funstones was ultimately implemented in the Vista operating system years later.

St. John also wrote about video streaming and synchronization and problems with Windows technology, ending with a note about Java and its similar problems. It was a long, involved email, at the conclusion of which he wrote:

> "-Wow I'm impressed that you read this far. <g>"

(See Online Appendix for the complete email thread.

In retrospect, St. John claims that whenever he wrote a "treatise" to Gates, "it would become gospel to everybody on the thread and everybody he forwarded it to. Windows update, Windows driver WHQL certification all evolved from those dialogs." And St. John worked hard to get Gates' backing and support for better driver quality. "I believed that if Microsoft got religious about the stability of its IHV drivers, Microsoft would rule the consumer market. People always wanted to invent new useless features instead of focusing on very basic stability, speed and robustness, and so I would hammer the point with Gates knowing that a lot of important ears were listening."

Internal OpenGL Squabbles

Life at Microsoft in early 1997 might have been business as usual for many people, but in the aftermath of John Carmack's pro-OpenGL posting, the internal disagreements between the supporters of OpenGL and those who were championing Direct3D were heating up. Long email exchanges debated both technical issues and areas of influence, with Alex St. John once again at the center of the arguments. Only days after Bill Gates' DreamWorks email, St. John was embroiled in a contentious argument with Steve Wright from the OGL team in the NT group. The thread subject line originally read, "Response to Carmack", and later became "Alex St. John on D3D, OGL, and John Carmack".

What follows is a glimpse into some actual email exchanges that occurred during the time in which people were arguing about OpenGL and Direct3D. There is little doubt that contentious emails occurred often at Microsoft in those days, but it's rare to get a ringside seat—so to speak—to an actual exchange.

The argument seems to have begun when Phil Taylor, an evangelist for Direct3D, posted St. John's original response to Carmack's message on a public OpenGL forum. To be blunt, this royally pissed off people on the OpenGL team at Microsoft, notably Steve Wright, who wrote, "These comments include numerous technical errors that I believe can only damage Microsoft's reputation in the 3D technology arena. I don't want to see any further posts on this thread until or unless we have a coordinated and reviewed response to make."

In another email less than an hour later, Wright continued, "…posting Alex's comments without any review to the usegroups was a potentially disastrous piece of bone-headedness." In fact, one of Wright's OGL team, Nicholas Wilt was on the cc list on the original message St. John sent out to seek feedback—before Taylor posted it. Wilt did respond saying, "Looks pretty good," adding some information about Carmack's custom software rasterizer to correct one misconception. St. John had then replied to Wilt and Taylor writing, "Mods made, thanks for the feedback Nick. Ship it Phil."

But Wright had some valid concerns. He and one of his key people, Mark Kenworthy, had not been on the original cc list, for which Taylor later apologized. Wright viewed his team's work to include the management of the OpenGL message as well as relationships with hardware and software companies. In his opinion, posting St. John's response to Carmack was detrimental to their efforts. "The point of this message is to reiterate that we do not continue muddying the waters with more postings like this. This was incredibly inappropriate."

To which St. John replied, "Actually Steve, you're dead wrong, and making these message calls is our job. The only display of ignorance in this regard is yours, and the only damage to our reputation in the industry is the result of you guys bickering foolishly with the D3D guys instead of pulling together. It is our job to communicate Microsoft's strategic messages to the developer community. If you are communicating something contradictory on the usegroups it is you who is 'muddying the waters'." St. John also mentioned that Otto Berkes had visited id sometime before Carmack's post, which he implied might have "stirred the pot" and helped inspire Carmack's posting, an assertion which Wright subsequently denied. St. John ended saying, "DirectX is Microsoft's strategic message to the game development community, it has been for 2 years, nobody involved in our marketing and evangelism efforts has ever been confused about that. Perhaps you should make some time to meet with us so we can sort out our roles and messages a little more clearly."

Wright's response was to attack St. John again, claiming that he could not do his job of messaging without coordinating with his group, also claiming that the original reply to Carmack contained "numerous misstatements about both Direct3D and OpengGL that do nothing but demonstrate that you are out of touch with both the technology as well as our most strategic thinking."

Wright ended his message by claiming to have been "beaten to a bloody pulp" while helping promote Microsoft's 3D strategy, including "pulling together" with Direct3D. "I'd thank you for interposing yourself as a far more vulnerable and incoherent target, but we really need a time to 'repair and nurture' right now, not inflame and antagonize, and that's what you've accomplished."

St. John replied, of course, accusing Wright of doing the evangelists' job where that wasn't his proper role. "Asserting that you have any business doing this while I do not puts you on pretty shaky ground babe. Yup, maybe I inflame, antagonize, misstate etc... it's still my job, and I'm paid to use my judgment about how it's done. Apparently you have a lot of time on your hands from your ordinary responsibilities and feel the urge to dabble in marketing and evangelism a bit... perhaps you'd like an office over here?"

Wright turned down the invitation to join DRG, reiterating that his messaging had always been clear, that OpenGL was for professional 3D applications and Direct3D was for games and entertainment. He asserted that St. John's message was mistaken in its details about the execute buffer / draw triangle issue, adding a personal dig, "…you, or Philip, posted this misinformation to an OpenGL-focused newsgroup where it can only succeed in drawing down a rain of fire, an experience which I understand you personally enjoy, but which is the last thing we need right now."

Another contentious issue involved an apparent visit by OpenGL's Otto Berkes to id, and whether this was appropriate. This also continued in the thread, with St. John claiming that his information had come from id's Jay Wilbur. He then questioned why Berkes was scheduled to conduct a session at the next CGDC about OpenGL for games, pointing out that it was contradictory to the message Wright himself claimed to be promoting.

Wright claimed that Berkes' presentation was originally declined, but that they believed it would be best for someone to represent Microsoft to the game crowd instead of letting SGI control the message, and further, that this decision was sanctioned by Jay Torborg and "management," to which St. John replied, "Bad decision, doesn't have anything to do with Jay's team. Which part of 'multimedia messaging to developers is our job' has been ambiguous in this thread. Apparently we're going to have to burn some exec time having that explained to you at this point."

Wright and Taylor also had a battle of their own, full of accusations and heated rhetoric, the gist of it being about who controls the message and what the message is, ultimately devolving into attacks on and defenses of Direct3D. This goes on for pages of back and forth arguments and rebuttals, with St. John entering the discussion to further emphasize the fact that it was the DRG's job to promote and evangelize technology, not the NT group. The issue of Berkes' visit to id and OpenGL talk at GDC were seen as an attempt by the OpenGL team to encroach on the message that Bill Gates had already settled—that D3D was the API for games, the consumer level API for graphics.

One of the points of contention was that game developers weren't using Direct3D for software rendering, which was true, but finally, after a couple of more exchanges, on February 21, after a star-studded multimedia retreat, St. John wrote "D3D has 5-6 Retain mode games now. But I still agree with you, its primary usage is as a low level API to access consumer 3D HW. Top technology games will never use our software renderers. Bill made his position on OGL pretty clear this week. Let's get on with it."

For the whole long and often technical exchange, see the Online Appendix.

~24~

Multimedia Retreat

In the midst of all the bickering over 3D APIs that centered on OpenGL and Direct3D, as well as Talisman, which Gates still favored, and in the aftermath of Gates' visit to DreamWorks, Gates asked St. John to arrange a multimedia retreat and to invite industry leaders in 3D technology. One specific person he particularly wanted to attend was Seamus Blackley.

Seamus

Seamus Blackley has a background both as a jazz pianist and as a physicist who worked for a time on the Superconducting Supercollider project at the Fermi National Accelerator Lab. He developed a strong interest in video games and ended up working at Blue Sky Productions (later Looking Glass Studios) where he joined some of the most brilliant minds in the game industry, including Doug Church, Paul Neurath and Warren Spector. According to Paul Neurath, Blackley, at the time going by the name "Jon Blackley," was a fan of the Ultima series and came to them looking for a chance to work on games.

"During the interview process I recall that his advisor, who was an eminent physicist, tried to talk him out of it, and later me out of hiring Seamus, as he felt it would be a loss to the world of particle physics."

Even with no game experience, Blackley was hired and learned quickly. His first job was to use his musical skills to write some music for Ultima Underworld II. He then did some programming on System Shock and was lead programmer on Flight Unlimited, where his advanced mathematical skills, along with the fact that he was also a pilot, made him a perfect candidate for the role.

According to Blackley's Wikipedia entry, he was fired from Looking Glass for refusing to work on the Flight Unlimited sequel, instead insisting on working on a combat-based game. Neurath says what Blackley really wanted to do was build a pneumatic-powered motion platform for Flight Unlimited that could be taken to industry shows and even put in arcades. He was even in the process of building a prototype, but LookingGlass declined to greenlight it. Neurath offered some clarification: "Things were going well with Seamus and LookingGlass until after Flight Unlimited was completed. He was the sort of person who was always seeking a new challenge, and I don't think he was all that interested in working on the sequel to Flight Unlimited when it came down to it. The motion platform might have held his interest, but when that did not get the green light Seamus floundered a bit and found himself without a clear next big challenge to tackle." According to Neurath, Blackley's future at LookingGlass was still being determined when he was offered a job at DreamWorks.

At DreamWorks, Blackley was hired as executive producer for Trespasser: Jurassic Park, and even though Trespasser ultimately failed rather spectacularly in the market, the innovative physics work that Blackley had done impressed Bill Gates.

The Retreat and the Decision

St. John was asked to organize a special Multimedia Retreat on February 18, 1997, inviting some of the top people in the field to make presentations. Microsoft was well represented by 3D experts from Research/Advanced Technology Group, the OpenGL team, the current version of the DirectX team (which was now under Jay Torborg and officially part of the Talisman group), and people from the newly re-formed games group under Ed Fries.

Outside experts included Seamus Blackley from DreamWorks and Tim Sweeny, a young genius who had created the Unreal engine for Epic. St. John relates a funny story on his blog. "The first challenge I had with getting Tim out to Microsoft was that he still lived with his parents who were apparently quite protective and suspicious of Microsoft's interest in their son. I had to speak to his mother and reassure her that Tim would be well looked after in Redmond and that he would indeed be meeting with Bill Gates."

Sweeney attended the retreat with Epic's co-founder Mark Rein and remembers being invited into a room "laid out like a classroom" and seeing Bill Gates sitting in front next to Seamus Blackley. "They were chatting like they were old buds," remembers Sweeney. In the audience were many of Microsoft's graphics experts, "a lot of the world's best luminaries in the graphics field."

There aren't many accounts of the Multimedia Retreat, which was coordinated by St. John and Robar, other than what St. John has written about it, and what he has written is typically not very complimentary of his rivals within the company. He recalls that he and Robar had arranged the schedule "to allow all of the ATG and Talisman people to blather on about their work and attempt to impress Gates with their technology achievements."

ATG was represented by Jim Kajiya, who made the case for a real-time NT operating system, ultimately suggesting that to do so would require a special real-time co-processor. According to St. John's account, Kajiya stated that the co-processor was necessary because NT would otherwise be unable to achieve that necessary 1/1000th of a second response times needed for gaming.

Both Gates and St. John simultaneously jumped in at that point, and St. John remembers the exchange as follows:

Bill Gates: "What? That's your solution another CPU!"

Alex: "1/1000th of a second! You don't need that level of responsiveness for a game!"

Jim: "It's the only way to get audio to sync with video reliably"

Bill Gates: "Do you know how much that would add to the cost of a PC?"

Alex: "I'm standing 40ft away from you, that's 36 milliseconds, do my lips look like they're not syncing with my voice?"

According to St. John, Windows 95 had already solved the audio synching problem with DirectSound and DirectVideo—without the need for specialized and expensive new hardware. On the other hand, St. John garnered some disapproving looks. People weren't used to seeing Bill Gates interrupted, particularly during a public event.

Kajiya also remembers the event, although not the specific conversation. He says, "Certainly the claim that syncing had been solved, that's a little disingenuous of him. In fact, there are two kinds of syncing. One where you can essentially sync by delaying everything, so that you don't have any control over latency, but if you delay all your media streams, you can sort of sync them together. So if you're playing back recorded audio or video with an audio stream, you can sync that way, but you'll get horrendous amounts of latency.

"If you're actually generating content immediately, then in fact, you can't afford to do that, and you actually do need to be able to respond very quickly. People are running into that problem right now with VR, that the levels of latency that people tolerate on the desktop versus what you need for VR glasses is much, much different. Essentially, it's a well-known phenomenon, back in the Sixties—it's called simulator sickness. Flight simulators have this issue. If you move the control stick, and things happen like 50 ms or 100ms later, eventually you get sick. And it doesn't really happen when you don't have a wide field of view, so if you restrict everything to a small screen, you can take the latency a lot better. But if you start having anything in your peripheral vision that is delayed by anything from 50 to 100ms... And basically, what they're finding, the less delay there is in your peripheral vision, the longer you can last without getting sick."

Kajiya also said that, although he is not an expert on sim sickness, he thinks that threshold for avoiding the malady may be in the range of 20ms latency. He also says that 1ms latency seems somewhat lower than he would have suggested at the time, but, "people's memories vary."

Next up was the ATG with their demonstration of the state-of-the-art Talisman technology, which St. John derogatorily describes: "By harnessing the full processing power of a dual core Pentium 90 PC they were able to achieve the visually stunning feat of rotating a Phong shaded cube at about 10fps in software!" However, even though St. John was dead set against Talisman as a product, he practically idolized many of the researchers behind the technology. "I had attended their Siggraph sessions on these subjects in the 1980's as a teenager, so I was very conflicted about trying to crush their project. I often found myself in meetings with these guys and Gates or Nathan, telling them what a huge fan I was of their books and work and how much it had influenced me, and then telling Nathan or Gates that they were basically idiots who didn't know what they were talking about when it came to consumer gaming hardware. I hated doing it because I really wanted to hang out with them and pick their brains, but they were also making a mess I had to stop."

The Talisman demo was soon overshadowed—or perhaps I should say clobbered and beaten into the ground—by the demonstrations from Blackley and Sweeney.

Blackley demonstrated the Trespasser engine, which made the Phong shaded cube look dismal by comparison. Blackley's demo was a full 3D, texture mapped world complete with dynamic weather, animated dinosaurs, and real-time physics and impressive audio. Sweeney and Rein then demoed what

St. John described as "the most stunning real-time character animation ever seen on a PC in that era."

Although the event involved graphics demonstrations from various internal and external groups, Sweeney remembers that they weren't allowed to see all of the presentations, but were invited into the room when it was time for them to present the Unreal engine with its real-time software renderer, volumetric lighting and real-time colored lighting, running on a Pentium 90. Speaking about their software rendering technology, Sweeney says, "The GPU revolution had started—the first 3Dfx Voodoo card had come out, and so we were just on the verge of the transition. Everybody realized that the GPU revolution was happening, but there weren't enough of them out there that you could count on in the games. We were showing what we were capable of doing on mainstream computers. And that was really the key point of it. To say, 'Look, we can do 3D graphics, but we can also do it on everybody's machines, not just some crazy high end.'"

Following their demo and a question and answer session with Gates and Microsoft's graphics experts, Sweeney and Rein were about to leave when they were asked to stick around for a while. Eventually they were asked to rejoin the group where they became part of a big debate about Microsoft's future focus on OpenGL or Direct3D—a debate that Sweeney understood was partially in response to Carmack's attack on DirectX. Sweeney also admitted that Carmack was correct. At the time, OpenGL was superior to Direct3D, which was currently in its third iteration. "It was widely derided by developers" according to Sweeney.

Sweeney participated in the discussion, pointing out how poorly thought out and unreliable the early command buffers were. "You loaded a bunch of commands to the buffer and then you told the API go off and do it, but it didn't correspond to actually creating a low-level hardware buffer format. All of the interaction drawbacks of the old approach, with none of the performance benefits of the new approach, and it just made it impossible to debug when something was going wrong. So there was a big push by all the graphics researchers to move to the industry standard OpenGL API, and we're there, suddenly in the middle of this massive debate between the DirectX team defending what they've done and why they want to do it, with the graphics researchers arguing a contrary position, and then Bill Gates kind of mediating and throwing in some strategic insight and asking some smart questions throughout the whole time."

What impressed Sweeney the most was the way the whole debate was run. "It was a total meritocracy." And in the end, the DirectX contingent, whom Sweeney describes as "a bunch of relatively young, new programmers," won the debate against the "who's who of graphics research." The winning argument centered on the issue of control, of course, and the ability to move quickly in a fast-moving technical environment, and according to Sweeney, Gates ended the meeting saying, "OK. We're going to support DirectX. We're going to fix it. We will fix this."

Gates' leadership made a lasting impression on Sweeney who recognized that Gates wanted to do what was right for developers, but to keep control of the software. "Everybody went out of that meeting really understanding it. It was an example of good decision making—meritocracy rather than bureaucracy. I've always remembered it as an example, as Epic has grown, that we need to retain the ability for whoever has the best argument to win, no matter who they are and no matter who offered the idea."

Sweeney also noted that Microsoft did do as Bill Gates had suggested. By the release of DirectX 7 "it had gone way beyond OpenGL in practicality and capabilities. Bill was right. They did fix it."

St. John Gets Fired... or Does He?

St. John recounts an exchange between Gates, Nathan Myhrvold and himself that occurred after the demonstrations from Blackley and Sweeney. In effect, Gates turned to Myhrvold and questioned that he was putting money into graphics research that wasn't at all current or relevant. Myhrvold's response was to pull St. John into it. "I think Alex would have you believe that we shouldn't have a graphics research division," to which St. John replied, "Actually, I'm making the point that we don't have one now."

The banter between Gates and Myhrvold continued for some time until Myrhvold took what St. John refers to as "a friendly jab" at him. At that point, St. John said, "My job is to clean up his messes" and began pretending to be tidying up papers on a desk while brushing lint off Gates' shoulders. "Bill growled, 'Quit touching me St. John. You're fired!'"

Although Gates wasn't serious, there were those in the audience who thought he was... "very alarmed people who apparently saw their Microsoft stock options flashing before their eyes..." As it was with all things St. John, rumors of his firing spread rapidly through Microsoft.

Although St. John had not been fired—yet—the incident triggered an interesting email interchange between him and Gates the next day.

St. John wrote: "I have to admit to some disillusionment with my current position Bill. I'm a little uncomfortable being the face man for multimedia gumbo, and fully endorse the idea of replacing me with somebody who thinks it all makes enough sense to explain it to the developers with a straight face. Personally I think I must be mad if the stuff that seems obvious to me draws such derision from the greatest minds at Microsoft. While I'm cleaning out my desk, I'm going to summarize some of my views for you, just in case they weren't clear at the meeting."

St. John continued by updating Gates on several topics, including problems with NT and latency, a positive meeting with Deborah Black's multimedia team regarding D3D support and the diminished role of OGL and Talisman ("The technology is cool, the strategy has all kinds of problems... Everyone should shut up until there is some HW that does what they claim it will," and so forth—and "I've stuffed MS technology down the throats of these title companies until it is sprayed out of their ears and nostrils. I think I should have a lot of credibility when I tell you what they will and will not adopt.") The email ended with some of St. John's thoughts about multimedia drivers, and a couple of parting shots.

> "It's a pretty weird world in which your lunatic go overboard evangelist is the one advocating a conservative approach here. You should think about that.
>
> <<End Summary>>
>
> I'm thinking I might like a job like Aaron Contorer has working for you. Then you could have the benefit of my enlightened opinion on these things on a daily basis."

Gates responded, "I did not mean to say that you should take a new job. I was joking during the retreat and I hope you understand that." He then simultaneously praised and criticized St. John saying, "You do a lot of things very well in your current job. You have also made some costly mistakes."

Gates also confirmed his agreement with most of what St. John had proposed, except for his teardown of Talisman. Gates wrote, "I forwarded your observations on to others because I agree with everything except your cautionary view of Talisman. In the case of Talisman I think we need to give it some time before we get pessimistic."

See the Online Appendix for the whole exchange.

Epic Offers

Game fans will find this interesting. A few weeks after the Multimedia Retreat, Mark Rein sent an email to Bill Gates which detailed the terms and conditions of Microsoft's offer to distribute the game Unreal and the Unreal Editor as well as details of an offer from they had from GT Interactive, which was the one that Epic ultimately accepted. Rein also listed several other possible games that they wanted Microsoft to consider, including the online version of Unreal, Jazz Jackrabbit 2, and several unnamed projects, also suggesting that Microsoft consider licensing the Unreal technology to create an Internet Explorer 3D saying, "We think we have the 'killer app' for creating, serving and navigating compelling 3D worlds on the internet." This offer, particularly the last item, could have been the killer app that Microsoft needed, in spite of the fact that they had other strategies in the works.

The opportunity to work with Epic—including a proposed online version of Quake—was essentially vetoed by an executive named Bob Herbold because he objected to the idea of Microsoft publishing violent games. In fact, according to St. John, "It took a lot of internal pressure even to make Age of Empires because the catapults left little splotches of blood on the battle field where soldiers got squished."

Rein ended his email by offering thanks and high praise for both Jason Robar and Alex St. John. "You should be very proud of this group knowing that they've had, and continue to have, a huge positive impact on the PC-based entertainment software business."

Signing the Dreamcast Deal

For the DirectX and OpenGL teams, the first few months of 1997 featured the ongoing debates about Microsoft's direction and the technical merits of each API, despite repeated pronouncements from the highest executives that Direct3D would be Microsoft's API for the consumer market while support for OpenGL would continue for high-end business applications. But in the midst of all that, the deal with Sega to provide an operating system for Dreamcast reached a critical milestone with the signing of the contracts at Microsoft's headquarters in Redmond.

Although the DRG team had set up the original deal, all of the actual negotiations with Sega had been conducted by Craig Mundie and Chris Phillips. DRG had been entirely cut out of the process. According to St. John, the decision to pass the project on to the CE division was unfortunate. "The Windows CE guys, with very little input or support from the DirectX team, went off to try to make their own version of DirectX for Sega, and it was kinda fucked up. The thing Microsoft couldn't cope with was that they had something more successful and bigger than anything they had going on, created and run by junior monkeys way down in the trenches of their strategy org. So that weird Sega Dreamcast deal was kind of an example of somebody else, other than us, needing to own that relationship because we couldn't possibly be in charge of it. And of course, that changed very quickly. Over a matter of months it just became clear there was no stopping us, and no controlling us. But it was one of those weird things that happened in that sequence."

Finally, when the day came to ink the deal, several of Sega's Japanese executives were in attendance, including Shoichiro Irimajiri and Yu Suzuki, but nobody from Sega of America was there. St. John writes on his blog that Sega of America president Bernie Stolar was also in attendance, but when I checked with Stolar, he said that nobody from Sega of America attended. In any case, the two principals were Irimajiri and Gates.

St. John was put in charge of keeping the Sega visitors happy. "This however was always a delicate challenge because the Japanese idea of a 'good time' generally involved large amounts of alcohol, Karaoke and hot Australian girls… only one of which could be found in abundance in Redmond Washington." However, there was one thing St. John knew at least one of them would enjoy.

Irimajiri was a fan of motorcycles and had told St. John that he even competed in events in Tokyo in his free time. One time, while visiting Sega in Japan, St. John had talked to Irimajiri about the joys of off-roading in his Hummer and promised to take him for a ride if the opportunity presented itself.

Rampaging through Microsoft's construction sites had become something of a hobby for St. John. At one point, having been reported anonymously for his behavior, he was called into Cameron Myhrvold's office, where he remembers receiving "the stern warning that the next time I got the urge to do something crazy like that I should take him with me so as not to get in trouble...."

On this occasion, however, St. John figured that he was covered. From St. John's blog:

"Immediately after the signing event with Gates, I drove my plum purple H-1 through Microsoft's central courtyard and picked up the SEGA executive team. Microsoft was undergoing a massive expansion at the time so much of the campus was a giant construction site pocked with dirt mounds and giant new garage pits. Naturally I calculated that my odds of getting fired for tearing up the new campus constructions site in my H-1 full of senior SEGA executives including Irimajiri, Bernie Stoller [sic] and Yu Suzuki immediately after signing a major Microsoft OS deal with Bill Gates in the name of entertaining our VIP guests was relatively slim. We had a blast! The nice thing about doing crazy things with Japanese guests is that they are always good about politely appearing to have a good time even when they are scared s**tless. Naturally since the existing campus buildings overlooked this spectacle there were hundreds of witnesses and inquiries to which I enjoyed responding; 'Top secret, I don't have to explain myself to you... ask Bill.' Of course when I got the executive; 'Was that REALLY necessary email?' I got to respond; 'Would you prefer to sign a massive strip club expense report?' Of course after several years of entertaining visits from id Software to Microsoft, Jason Robar and I had become proficient at inventing new and creative ways to avoid getting stuck with a strip club tab."

-25-

The End of Talisman

Even though there were good reasons to believe that the Talisman project would come to market too late to be competitive by it's projected launch in May 1997, Bill Gates was still considering its viability, just as he had back in his previous email exchanges with St. John in February. On May 13, 1997, after reading a summary document about Talisman from Jim Allchin, he wrote a long email in which he states "I understand Talisman better today than before. I still believe it is a very important technology."

The email was sent to Jay Torborg, but cc'd to a long list of highly placed individuals within Microsoft who might have some interest in the subject matter: Deborah Black, Moshe Dunie, Jim Allchin, Paul Maritz, Jim Veres, Nathan Myhrvold, Aaron Contorer, Mike Abrash, Carl Stork, Ed Fries, Robbie Bach, Alex St. John, John Ludwig, Todd Nielsen, Craig Mundie, Moshe Lichtman, Jim Kajiya, and Alvy Ray Smith.

However, Gates also expressed some concern, saying that there was "more uncertainty about Talisman's role than ever before" because of what was going on in the industry with initiatives by Intel and the growth of PC graphics hardware. He continued, discussing the probability that SGI would soon introduce Intel based workstations. He saw this as a good thing because they would then endorse Windows NT, but also stated that Microsoft would offer them any of the extensions that Microsoft makes to their graphics APIs, "but we don't want to give them away to Nintendo." He also observed that SGI could ultimately be an ally or an enemy with regards to graphics APIs. Gates ended his email with a list of questions, some of them quite technical, and another list of action items, beginning with what amounted to an invitation for St. John to jump into the conversation:

"a. Make sure we are making the right choice by starting with the OGL code. We need to listen carefully to what Alex and the game developers are saying to make sure we can succeed with this approach."

Talisman

GRAPHICS & MULTIMEDIA SYSTEM
PROJECT OVERVIEW · OCTOBER, 1995

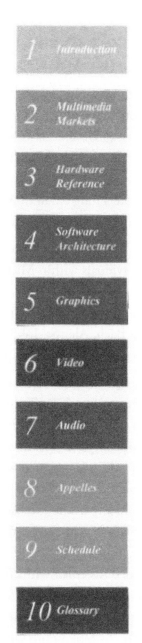

Microsoft
CONSUMER SYSTEMS DIVISION

Confidential and Proprietary

Talisman

GRAPHICS & MULTIMEDIA SYSTEM

Microsoft

Table of Contents

Gates expressed several concerns, including the report's recommendation that they use OpenGL.

"It's very disappointing to me to have to start with the OGL code since its based on a standard we do not control but I do understand why this is the recommended choice and that we can move it in that direction."

And that's where St. John jumped in, and his reply the next day at 6:44am was typically blunt.

"This is kind of screwy stuff you guys. I understand that you have a lot invested in this Talisman thing, but the strategy is bad. You're going to get that special Microsoft Sound System kind of win out of this with a touch of At-Work and a dash of NT MIPS platform for all this effort. I'd really like to be able to help you here, but everybody seems to have a bad case of cotton ears. You don't need to make a chip, or change the entire industries 3D paradigm to get the results you want."

He then recommended four goals:

"1.) Make the PC the most advanced multimedia platform on the market

2.) Make sure we control it through some kind of leverage and/or IP

3.) Ensure that the PC multimedia market is the biggest and fastest growing one

4.) Make evil competitors in this space go away."

St. John then pointed out that support for D3D was growing, with six chips in development "specifically designed to accelerate our internal D3D data structures," referring to both Intel and NVidia and pointing out that there's no need for a "monolithic chip." He writes, "We're already on a winning course if we just recognize it."

In the email, St. John suggested that Microsoft's winning strategy is not in high level APIs or 3D hardware, but in the driver, "because the driver is the lowest level at which we can have control while staying cleanly and snuggly in the OS business."

Having delivered that message, St. John continued, tackling the OpenGL vs. Direct3D issue and pointing out that "when it comes to multimedia 3D applications precious few of them will ever use OUR software rendering code base for anything." Differentiating D3D from OGL, he says that he sees the former as a driver architecture for consumer hardware and the latter as an API that doesn't come with a driver model, writing:

"I don't care what code base the VESTIGIAL software emulation layer that no real-time application is likely to use comes from. It doesn't matter, it's not going to be used. I care that the driver architecture which is hugely problematic even after 2 years of work, evangelism, developer support, meltdowns, may get discarded casually in favor of a new one (MCD), and we'll have to start all over again with a brand new 3D driver mess, because nobody understood that the issue had nothing to do with the high level API, or software rendering code, and therefore can't be solved by changing it."

He recommended that Direct3D Immediate Mode should be the consumer 3D driver model with OpenGL mounted on top of it, ending with,

"If you want to chuck D3D's API look, and rendering code yeeehaw! Just don't chuck the investment and leverage you've acquired with the driver architecture. Extend it, mutate it, but don't lose it. You've already won if you just stick with it."

Shifting focus, St. John addressed on the next "big fat hairy scary multimedia" issue, JavaMedia. He wrote,

"Trying to get anybody outside the game/multimedia community to add multimedia functionality to their serious productivity applications is like trying to lift a bowling ball with tweezers,"

and supports his assertions with a long list of reasons why JavaMedia was nothing to be concerned with.

At this point, St. John used the idea of "fat multimedia" to mention the secret project that Engstrom and Eisler were working on. He wrote, "Delivering "Fat Multimedia" is what the Chrome browser project is about."

Finally, St. John summarized his email:

"• Kill Talisman asap, it's a really bad idea, or have another strategy fast.

• You can have the 3d control you want without the risk or the dramatic change in course.

• It doesn't matter what our software API for 3D is going to be, nobody that matters in consumer MM is going to use it. Just don't screw up the drivers any more than they already are.

• Don't attack JavaMedia directly, it just lends them credibility.

Let's make them follow us somewhere for a change by having our own ideas about bringing interactive content to the net.

- Focus on your MM drivers, and driver architectures, they are the way to success.
- I'm a major reason you have any multimedia ISV's to mess with. I hope you're listening.

Last comment:

All of this is kind of moot if our next 'Consumer OS' is a great walrus of a beast that can't guarantee ~20ms latencies to 1 real-time application in the foreground, and cough over control of memory resources. This functionality should be a 'Feature'."

Back to OGL—Torborg's Reply

Even though the initial thread that Gates had started was somewhat focused on Talisman, he was laying out some of Microsoft's strategy in the 3D arena, which included considerations of using OpenGL as a base for a standard API. In response, John Ludwig wrote to Torborg asking for details about the OGL discussion that Gates' referenced.

In his reply to Ludiwg, Torborg also attached two memos, one written by him and another written by Mike Abrash. (Abrash's memo was written on April 4, 1997, which prompted St. John to call it a "smoking gun" that showed Abrash's involvement in the OpenGL vs. Direct3D battles even while he was still at id, despite his assertions that he was not in any way concerned with the issue during his time there.)

In his email, Torborg wrote

"D3D is missing some key features which are necessary to replace OGL in the broader market—specifically printing and metafile support, and software fail-over.

"We evaluated the possibility of enhancing the D3D code base to add these features, as well as starting with the OGL code base and modifying to support better DirectX integration and D3D features. Frankly, D3D has no significant technical advantages over OGL, and OGL is more robust, better documented, and has the broad market features we need. The key D3D strength is driver support and our market momentum."

Abrash's Memo

Reading Abrash's memo, it seems likely that it was the source of Torborg's conclusions, or at least that he and Abrash had been communicating given that their assessments of OpenGL's strengths and advantages and Direct3D's weaknesses and deficiencies were identical. Abrash further states his belief that there should be one API to support games and consumer products, and high-end workstations, and he asserts that none of the software developers for the high end would be likely to switch to D3D, even if it were brought up to the same standards as OGL. He acknowledges that Microsoft is better off with a proprietary technology that they own and control over one that is an open standard that might not improve or innovate as quickly. "To put it bluntly, D3D has no compelling technical advantages and many disadvantages relative to OpenGL. If the both APIs were Microsoft-proprietary and a choice had to be made between the two, it would be no contest."

He summarizes by writing, "…we have an API that does what we need but isn't proprietary, and one that doesn't do what we need but is proprietary. We can either spend a modest amount of time and resources making OpenGL proprietary, or a huge amount of time and resources making D3D adequate. Either way, we get a single proprietary API, but at very different costs."

Torborg's message prompted Ludwig to write privately to Brad Silverberg and Eric Engstrom the following:

"per your questions, yes they are dumping d3d, driver model, and api. I assume you knew all this eric."

The Case for Putting Talisman Out of its Misery

Meanwhile, the Talisman issue remained front and center for Alex St. John. On May 18th, St. John wrote and shared a document entitled, "The case for putting Talisman out of its misery." Responding directly to Torborg's "DirectX and Talisman Update" and attached documents, St. John spent 16 pages taking Talisman apart. At the top of the document, he summarizes some of his main considerations:

1. "The Talisman strategy takes very poor consideration of how consumer multimedia HW is made, adopted, or used by real titles. The entire strategy is painfully naïve about what it's really like out there.

2. Talisman may be a very powerful cure for the disease that ails the industry, but the delivery mechanism is a coconut sized pill studded with razor blades. It will do more damage than it will cure.

3. Stable robust driver technology is the basis for all multimedia HW technology adoption and innovation. Talisman distracts our focus away from our most critical leverage point.

4. We've already blown our image and momentum to the market, tipped our hand to competitors, and positioned ourselves to disappointingly under deliver without having even shipped a beta technology.

5. Mutant Talisman designs made by the worst 3D chip makers in the industry will fundamentally damage our developer community and platform, not help it."

Never known for an abundance of tact, St. John still could be relied upon to introduce some creative bon mots into his messages. Here are a couple of examples from his Talisman takedown:

"Let's start with an explanation of the game business written by somebody who probably actually knows very little about it."

"There's a lot in these documents that suggests that the people who wrote them don't actually have a much better idea of how games really work than the Talisman people do. When I see statements like the following in these reports it makes me feel like I might be witnessing a bunch of baboons speculating about how a toaster might work…" (The statement in question ignorantly seemed to presume that developers didn't know how to make 3D applications, and that they would have to learn how if they were to adopt Talisman technology—and, in addition, presumed that the Talisman SDK would somehow fix the issue.)

Engstrom Closes the Show

On May 19th, Eric Engstrom also replied to Gates' email with a very lengthy and detailed message, starting off by saying,

"Executive Summary: Adopt Mike Abrash's proposal with the following caveat, kill MCD and use Direct3D IM as the blessed MCD (mini client driver) model for Direct3D Pro and OpenGL."

Even though the email continued for several pages worth of explanation and detail, there was one statement, almost buried among the other statements, that changed the game.

"IE4 uses D3DRM and IM so legacy applications no longer mean just games."

While St. John had been fighting the internal battles, Eisler and Engstrom had been secretly working to hook D3D into Internet Explorer, just as they had previously hooked DirectX into Windows 95.

John Ludwig put the the pieces together in his reply.

"i'll stress one thing eric said

"IE4 uses D3DRM and IM so legacy applications no longer mean just games."

IE4 is now dependent upon D3D, and it is our plan that in the IE5 timeframe we incorporate even more mm functionality into IE -- that is build a greater dependency on D3D and its successors. the IE code-base is a longlived codebase unlike some games. a decision to change at a fundamental level our 3d api will have important engineering implications for IE."

St. John simply replied to Ludwing,

"BLAM!"

Engstrom did suggest a compromise plan that adopts much of what Abrash had proposed and supports that plan in considerable detail. He then ended his message commenting on John Carmack's decision to back other software over DirectX saying,

"Should we listen to John's complaints and try to address them, absolutely. Should we let him guide our multimedia strategy? I don't think so."

The significance of this email was huge for St. John in particular. It meant that he and his partners in disruption had won the battle for D3D dominance. OpenGL would continue to exist, but the only remnants of Talisman would soon be technical elements that ultimately got incorporated into D3D. Once again, the trio of Engstrom, Eisler, and St. John had outmaneuvered their internal rivals and prevailed.

"Even the compromise was engineered," says St. John. "Like the Bunny-Gate maneuver, my job was to completely polarize the issue so Eric would sound reasonable and balanced proposing a compromise approach that I could then stun everybody by "grudgingly" approving of. In truth, getting the OGL guys to support D3D drivers with the OGL API is all we wanted all along. I just had to get them way out over their skis in order for Eric to tip them over."

The Death of Talisman

The irony about Talisman was that it never existed as anything more than a hardware specification that was NEVER BUILT. There was nothing to defeat other than the claims of Microsoft's famous researchers about its theoretical performance if anybody ever built hardware that did it. We didn't know about it when D3D was started and it defeated itself by never existing.

-Alex St. John

There were some test prototypes of the Talisman hardware, which, according to St. John, consisted of 5 custom ASICS (Application-Specific Integrated Circuits). Microsoft engineer Mikey Wetzel remembers his first and only look at Talisman in operation. "A handful of us, maybe three or four of us were in a room and the hardware guys brought it in and, 'Well, before we officially kill it, thought you might want to see it.'"

The writing was on the wall, as one-by-one the outside partners who had signed up to implement Talisman dropped out. It had become clear that advances in what Wetzel called "brute force method, just raw polygons and things like that," and the fact that many of the graphics card manufacturers were developing their own patented technologies, spelled the end for Talisman. However clever Talisman technology had been in 1994, it was not competitive in 1997. On the hardware side, it was already obsolete, while on the software side, the Microsoft evangelists, led by St. John, had found nobody in the game industry interested in developing for Talisman.

Even though the Talisman project ultimately died out, many of its engineers continued to work on 3D technology at Microsoft. St. John says, "Some of the engineers who came with the Talisman group like Chaz Boyd were really brilliant. They were a little caught in the middle over the Talisman nonsense but once it died they went on to do some great stuff for Direct3D and became very responsive to the developer community." However, he does clarify that DirectX and Direct3D were successful before the Talisman developers came on. "Historically because it was such a battle and Talisman lost, I think they have tried to write themselves into the DirectX history book by pretending that it wasn't really successful until they came along. That story is a HUGE stretch, but I can confirm that they and the former OpenGL guys like Otto Berkes who came to work on Direct3D did great stuff with it in their time."

Colin McCartney, one of the original Rendermorphics engineers who would eventually play an important role in the early adoption stage of Xbox, was aware of Talisman and its battles with DirectX. At the time, he completely backed the direction taken by DirectX, and believed that Talisman was not the most practical solution at the time it was first promoted publicly. However today, he sees the project somewhat differently. "Talisman was being sold because they thought traditional approaches to 3D graphics were going to hit a wall, and couldn't go further than that. They needed something better. From the D3D people, there was quite a bit of skepticism that wall was going to show up any time soon, and to be honest, I think that's proved accurate. My opinion on the Talisman stuff has softened over the years, though. Microsoft Research continues to do interesting work on image-based rendering, and now I think one of the pieces of the Talisman stuff might have been just ahead of its time."

Talisman was only one of many battles being waged in the halls of Microsoft in the late 1990s. "The real battles were not about 3D API's," says St. John, "they were about power and who controlled the API's AFTER DirectX had succeeded! I was battling for control and to force these Microsoft platform groups to be accountable to developers... all the rest was just the shrapnel in the air from all the fighting. I was making it impossible for Microsoft platform groups to hide in their safe offices, vest their stock options and play all day at making technology with zero accountability to the thousands of external developers who were depending on us for their livelihoods, which these guys really hated. Actually making commercially usable technology is much harder, boring and thankless than making 'cool' technology with your friends and getting rich while Microsoft's stock soars."

On the next page is a Talisman postmortem by Jim Kajiya from Microsoft Research.

Jim Kajiya on Why Talisman Failed as a Product

"The main reason that the Talisman project failed is one of execution. First of all, Talisman was not intended to be a competitor with anybody's graphics cards. It was intended to be a way of pushing the state of the art that anybody could use. They'd have to pay some nominal license to Microsoft, but Microsoft didn't want get into graphics cards. They really wanted to make a technology demonstrator of the ideas, because obviously, if you just talk about ideas but don't actually implement them, then you're nowhere. So the idea was to implement something to have impressive graphics performance, but not to actually create a product that would compete with 3Dfx and all those other guys at the time.

"We picked a vendor to do the card because we wanted something real that people could see that these ideas actually worked. That was the whole point of that card. The problem with it is that we picked Cypress Semiconductor, which, unbeknownst to us, was going through some severe financial difficulties at the time. And so Cypress, they spun up a team to work on it, and I actually met some of the team members years later, and to this day they're still believers, but apparently they were always budget limited because the company was not financially sound at the time. And eventually the project just got cancelled because the company decided it didn't want to go in the graphics card direction. What they wanted to do was serve the telcom market. And so they cancelled the project. And our error was to give Cypress a one year exclusive access to the technology before we gave it to anybody else. And because they couldn't spend enough money on it, it took them a long time to develop, and when they finally came out with it, it was just too late. The graphics card business is extremely competitive, and if you make one error in execution, you're dead. And that's what happened.

"It would have come out a year earlier if we had made the right decisions and had executed properly. Two years earlier it couldn't have come out. We were still doing the basic designs and stuff."

-26-

Hecker Shakes Things Up

The Windows 95 org was at the Windows NT team's throats; they were very competitive groups. The NT guys refusing to share their OGL license with the Win95 team and then freaking out when the Win95 guys launch their own 3D API that becomes a hit, thus REQUIRING them to support it, really heated it up. I think it had more to do with Microsoft's internal competition between OS groups.

From a story point of view I think the point of the arguments was to win a power battle. Their substance was irrelevant.

-Alex St. John

The whole Direct3D vs OpenGL debate was more political than technical. I think OpenGL could have easily satisfied the needs of game developers on the PC platform, particularly once decent 3D hardware was available, but the culture at MSFT in those days was very much about owning the APIs.

-Jay Torborg

As Talisman was on the verge of its demise, the battle for supremacy between OpenGL and D3D seemed to be settled internally at Microsoft, but some game industry developers were still on the warpath—most notably Chris Hecker.

Hecker's Letter

Hecker hit Microsoft from two fronts almost simultaneously. In the April/May 1997 issue of *Game Developer*, he wrote a long article entitled, *An Open Letter to Microsoft: Do the Right Thing for the 3D Game Industry*. In his opening statement, Hecker states, "A debate is raging in the game development community on an incredibly important topic: 3D APIs for the PC, and specifically, Direct3D versus OpenGL. This debate has its share of contentless flames, but at its core is an issue that will affect the daily lives of 3D game developers for years to come."

Hecker's article, which was written for developers, made a strong case in favor of OpenGL, offering many technical comparisons between the two APIs, which he claimed to substantiate with anonymous agreement from various Microsoft engineers and sources from various 3D hardware vendors. His main message was that a) OpenGL was superior in just about every way to Direct3D and b) Microsoft should give full support to OpenGL and allow developers a choice as to which 3D API they wanted to use.

Hecker's *Game Developer* article did not create a noticeable level of concern at Microsoft, but a real shitstorm was yet to come. On June 12, 1997, Hecker sent the following email. Note the recipient list, which included Paul Maritz, Deborah Black, OpenGL team members Berkes, Wright and Hock San Lee, as well as Mike Abrash. Notably, none of the Direct3D team was included in this email.

From: Chris Hecker [SMTP:checker@netcom.com]

Sent: Thursday, June 12, 1997 4:40 PM

To: Paul Maritz; Deborah Black; Otto Berkes; Steve Wright; Hock San Lee (NT); Mike Abrash

Subject: Top Game Developers Call on Microsoft to Actively Support OpenGL

The following press release went out at 4pm today. It's very important to me that you guys not think this is an attack or anything like that. I've tried to write the release as inclusively as possible, and we really do want to work with Microsoft on this.
Chris

(Hecker's press release text us reproduced in sidebar on next page.)

What made Hecker's press release most significant was the who's who of game developers who signed onto it. Although not all of them were household names to most of the world, many of the 56 people who signed Hecker's letter were highly influential in the game industry, such as John Carmack, Tim Sweeney, Chris Taylor, Matt Toschlog, Jay Patel, Greg Zeschuk, and John Romero. Some of the signatories were people who had worked with and/or supported DirectX efforts in the past, such as Zachary Simpson, Seamus Blackley, John Miles, and of course John Carmack and Tim Sweeney.

Why did people sign the letter? Certainly everyone had their reasons. One of those who signed the letter was Chris Taylor, who had made a name for

Top Game Developers Call on Microsoft to Actively Support OpenGL

We, the undersigned professional game developers, call on Microsoft to continue its active OpenGL development, to ship its DirectDraw bindings for OpenGL and the Windows95 MCD driver-enabled OpenGL, and to continue to improve its implementation of the OpenGL API and its driver models by aggressively supporting common extensions and future ARB-approved standard features. As developers, we believe the choice of which 3D API to support for our games should be ours alone.

We want any 3D API competition to happen on an open technical playing field, with us, the people who actually write the games, deciding which APIs we should and should not use. This open technical competition is healthy for the industry and will result in better games and 3D technology. We recognize Microsoft must take part in creating this technically competitive environment because of their control over the operating system, and we urge the company to be a positive force in doing so by actively supporting OpenGL. The entire PC game industry will benefit as a result.

Signed,

Bill Baldwin	Brian Hook	William Scarboro
Sean Barrett	Andrew Howe	Jason Shankel
Ken Birdwell	Brent Iverson	Zachary Simpson
Seamus Blackley	Rick Johnson	David Stafford
Stefan Boberg	Dave Kaemmer	Tim Sweeney
John Carmack	Donavon Keithley	Chris Taylor
Glenn Corpes	Jason Leighton	Dave Taylor
Steve Crane	John Lemberger	Trey Taylor
Mark Dochterman	Peter Lincroft	Cameron Tofer
Jim Dose	Mike Linkovich	Matt Toschlog
James Fleming	Jonathan Mavor	Neall Verheyde
Rick Genter	Stan Melax	Charlie Wallace
Ed Goldman	John Miles	Kevin Wasserman
Chris Green	Doug Muir	Patrick Wilkinson
Robin Green	Casey Muratori	David Wu
Mike Harrington	John Nagle	Pat Wyatt
Ryan Haveson	Mike Newhall	Billy Zelsnack
Chris Hecker	Jay Patel	Greg Zeschuk
Lawrence Holland	John Romero	

Time will tell if Microsoft listens to the development community.

himself as the designer of the hit game Total Annihilation for Electronic Arts and subsequently founded Gas Powered Games. Taylor had issues over Microsoft being monopolistic and forcing people to use their technology instead of having choice—like most developers at the time. But he also puts the whole thing into perspective, pointing to Hecker's passion on the subject saying, "In a lot of ways, we sort of said, 'Look. It's a god damn API. Are we going to impale ourselves on the sword over an API?' But Chris Hecker probably felt a little different. He probably felt that it was worth impaling on the sword. It was worth dying… well not dying for, but it was worth going to all the trouble of writing a letter and getting… What do you call it when you're ostracized… you're identified as a guy in the industry who's against a giant company and what they want to do, and so on. And we respected him for leading a charge with the open letter, and I signed it because it was like, in principle, he's right. Is it something that keeps me up at night? Do I give a shit to the point where I'm willing to maybe even give a whole Saturday in a youth rally or something? No. No, I'll sign a letter, now… fuck, what's for lunch? There's way bigger issues. There's clean drinking water for people, a billion people on the planet apparently don't have clean drinking water."

The Advisory Board

Hecker's open letter press release was effective enough to get coverage on some gaming websites, such as *Next Generation Magazine Online* and C/Net's *gamecenter.com*, as well as a release in the *Seattle Times*. There was also an article in *Wired* about Hecker's letter that referred to a roundtable summit that Microsoft was planning and quoting several people, including Jay Torborg, although I've found no details about the roundtable, if it occurred at all.

Hecker's letter and the publicity it received would have profound consequences at Microsoft—far more profound that anyone, including Hecker, had probably anticipated. One of the postive results was that, partially in response to Hecker's letter, Direct3D evangelist Andrew Walker set up an industry advisory board to allow frank and open discussions over the issues of 3D graphics.

Walker sent out invitations to leading developers like Tim Sweeney, John Carmack, Michael Bryan of Blizzard, and Seamus Blackley. Although Carmack declined the invitation, most developers joined the advisory board, which, according to Walker, "gave them a forum for those guys to rag at the Direct3D team and air their grievances, and for the Direct3D team to listen and to ask questions." The advisory board met regularly, sometimes once every quarter, and provided the necessary feedback in both directions to further the development of Direct3D, which continued to improve at a pace much faster than OpenGL at the time. Not only did the meetings allow the sharing of technical information, but it also gave the Microsoft engineers and program managers a chance to explain their rationale for the decisions they made and the directions they were taking. "You could really tell that they were buying it. The questions became less about, 'Why are you doing it this way,' and they'd actually start coming in with proposals. 'I think this is better. What do you think?' And there'd be more going back and forth. So I ran that for as long as I was part of the DRG team."

Tim Sweeney remembers the advisory board meetings as being very productive. "The Microsoft guys would have no problem saying, 'This is our current plan. We know it sucks, but we have to do this because this hardware is coming in this timeframe and that vendor's doing that thing, and we have to find some way to reconcile it. And then developers would be completely open in criticizing and praising Microsoft for different initiatives. It was not in any way committee-like or political. It was completely a bunch of programmers sitting around talking."

Sweeney also mentions how real innovation came out of the meetings. "They took an older system and replaced it with a completely new programmable assembly language shader language running on GPUs in real time, which completely upended the entire graphics pipeline. Really great thinking emerged from that. It's hard to tell where each idea originated. Some came from developers. Some came from hardware makers, things came from Microsoft, but the rate of progress back then was so fast."

http://chrishecker.com/OpenGL#Blasts_From_the_Past

http://web.archive.org/web/19990127171343/http://gamecenter.com/News/Item/0,3,929,00.html

http://archive.wired.com/science/discoveries/news/1997/07/4952

At some point, probably years later, Hecker did indicate some acceptance of the 3D API situation. While he still supported (and was using) OpenGL, Hecker acknowledged that Direct3D had "won the war." He wrote in an undated post on his blog, "SGI is basically dead, the OpenGL Architecture Review Board is mostly reactive instead of proactive, and Direct3D is the stable and mature platform that drives the features for each generation." Later, he added that "…if you want a better chance of getting your code to work using 'mainstream cutting edge features' (say, lots of render-to-texture, deep render target pixel formats, etc.), and you don't want to fight a battle with your publisher, you're probably better off using Direct3D. If you only need to use a safe subset of features that lags the cutting edge by a year or so, and you want the nicer programming experience, or if you want to use the most bleeding edge stuff that's only available in vendor extensions, then you should use OpenGL."

http://chrishecker.com/OpenGL

Chris Taylor offers another, even more up to date opinion from a 2013 interview saying, "It's interesting. What I was thinking is that maybe Chris was right, but for the wrong reasons. But then the wrong reasons became the right reasons in history, because right now, OpenGL is winning. It's winning and it will completely win. The only thing that's hanging on to DirectX in a very serious way, and you're probably going to disagree until I tell you the whole thing, is Xbox One. Because PC, you have a choice. It's whatever you want to do. And the Chronos Group, which controls OpenGL, is a consortium of representatives from Apple, Google, IBM… even Microsoft. Xbox One and maybe a phone or something are the last castles they're defending. OpenGL is used on everything else, whether it's your car navigation system… I mean if your microwave oven ever gets a touch panel display put on it, which it might, or your refrigerator—there might already be millionaire guys that have these incredible refrigerators that talk to them what time it is and where their stock is at—I guarantee you that it's running OpenGL."

Microsoft Internal Responses

Walker's advisory board was a positive outcome of the situation, but that was not the immediate response. At the time it first appeared, people at Microsoft immediately started alerting upper management about Hecker's open letter, including Jim Kajiya and Kevin Bachus. And things soon went from bad to worse.

Within hours, Deborah Black sent an email to Morris Beton (St. John's boss), presumably after consulting with Paul Maritz and possibly other executives. Beton responded quickly (at 3:02 am Saturday morning).

From: Deborah Black
Sent: Thursday, June 12, 1997 8:27 PM
To: Morris Beton
Subject: FW: Top Game Developers Call on Microsoft to Actively Support OpenGL

Heads up. Chris Hecker has published the following letter today.
I've discussed with PaulMa. Our response should be something like:
"Our current position is that D3D is the primary games API, there are xxx games, drivers, etc. in development/market. We see OGL as being extremely important API for professional market. We will obviously take the opinions expressed into account".

Debbie

....

From: Morris Beton
Sent: Saturday, June 14, 1997 3:02 AM
To: Morris Beton MM - Games
Subject: FW: Top Game Developers Call on Microsoft to Actively Support OpenGL

Importance: High

OK - now that PBS has made the D3D decision let's try to offer our support. Phil is heading up an effort to validate the number of D3D games/apps under construction. it would be really good to drive this effort to closure and be able to definitively say that 300+ D3D apps are under construction. it would also be good to find out how many companies are represented in the developer list below."

Meanwhile, not included in any of these email exchanges, St. John went off:

Sent: Friday, June 13, 1997 12:08 PM

To: Bill Gates; Paul Maritz; Eric Engstrom; Deborah Black; Jay Torborg; Kevin Dallas

Subject:

FW: Developers Petition for Open GL

Boom! Well this has clearly gotten out of hand. This took the concerted effort of a lot of groups to achieve. Some really poor evangelism and account management, a little bad media handling, a really screwed up 3D strategy for too long, and a proactive effort on the part of some current and former Microsoft employees to push this through. Chris Hecker was kind of enough to orchestrate the authoring and signing of this petition for us.

I've asked some of the folks I know on this petition to send some email to me explaining WHY they feel OGL should be our 3D API. They say perfectly reasonable things like;

1. It's easier to program to and better documented

2. I don't get enough support from Microsoft

3. I just care about 3DFX HW this Xmas, and they have an OGL driver for it that supports functionality on their card, their D3D driver doesn't. (3Dfx is tanking on supporting D3D features now, because they perceive themselves as being in competition with Talisman)

4. I don't get support for the 3D functionality I want/need from Microsoft fast enough so, I'm hoping SGI, and open support for extensions will do a better job.

5. I associate all the broken driver problems I'm having with Microsoft and D3D. I think having OGL (== API support from SGI) will mean having fast working drivers.

Our 3D strategy and messaging is an ongoing fiasco. I got back from Europe this week to learn that there had been a Paulma meeting where this was all resolved. "Resolved" to me would mean that we have 1 3D driver model for consumer HW on top of which all of our 3D API's sit, that our effort to make a "Talisman chip" is kept well clear of association with that driver model, and that we make it a major priority to rapidly innovate that driver architecture, and religiously ensure broad, fast, robust support for 3D HW. Until something like this is done, there will be no "resolution" for this, just slow painful decline of our leverage and credibility in this space. Would somebody please make my day and tell me this was "resolved". Because if it was we really need to get some clear messaging out there fast."

There is some irony in the fact that St. John's email was written on Friday the Thirteenth, and, as we will see, it ultimately spelled some significant luck for him—good or bad, depending on how you look at it.

Also on June 13, an article appeared on Cnet's *gamecenter.com* that published the open letter and included some comments attributed to Hecker. One such comment read, "Hecker says Deb Black, a director in the systems division at Microsoft, asked him what the demand was for OpenGL and wanted him to reconcile that with the fact that so many developers are currently using Direct3D." Hecker is then quoted as saying, "Some of the developers on the list are using Direct3D right now, but it's not like they have much of a choice. That's what the letter is all about: We want to be able to choose OpenGL, and we'd like Microsoft's support in this decision."

On June 14, Maritz responded to St. John's email, and in doing so he revealed several parts of Microsoft's ongoing strategy. He began by acknowledging Direct3D.

"This has been decided. Or strategic direction is D3D."

Maritz continued by indicating that they would continue efforts to evangelize Talisman's "approach and design," stating that they had met with Intel's graphic architects who validated the key ideas behind Talisman—specifically chunking and anisotropic texturing—as going in the right direction.

Maritz then turned to OpenGL, stating:

"…we have to ensure that we have good OGL support for NT in workstation market. We would like to cut our effort in this however, and let SGI pick up the work." Maritz also revealed some of SGI's future plans and their decision to build "no-compromise NT machines. In mid'98, they plan to introduce a $3.5K NT based machine that will have same performance as the mid range of their current Octane line ($35K machine today)."

As for OpenGL, there was some talk about some deeper level of connection between it and Direct3D. "We will have follow-up mtg to discuss: (a) them picking up support for OGL on NT, and (b) to understand how they think D3D and OGL can share more (apparently they have ideas on this, but paranoia has prevented them from sharing this to date). Obviously given the position on D3D above, we do not want to compromise our progress on D3D, but we should listen with open mind."

St. John replied with a positive email, commenting

"Working with SGI on common API that isn't OGL and WE OWN sounds like a positive direction. We need one 3D driver model that we stand behind religiously very badly."

St. John also commented again on Talisman, stating that many of its best ideas were already being implemented in the market, and that it wasn't the quality of the ideas, but the implementation plan and strategy was flawed. He ended his message stating,

"I'd like our message to be clear, and unmuddied by internal laundry leaking into public forums in the future. I'm very glad to hear you saying some concrete things about our direction on this. I'm looking forward to talking to the world instead of you guys for a change. :)"

It's quite possible that the ideas Maritz mentioned—the ideas that SGI was reluctant to share—were connected with what became the Fahrenheit (see also *Game of X v.1* page 22) co-venture between SGI and Microsoft, which was made public for the first time in December 1997.

All Hell Breaks Loose

By June 16, an even bigger shitstorm began, set off in part by the *gamecenter.com* article, but mainly because of the Direct3D team's suspicions that somebody connected with OpenGL had been actively sabotaging their efforts, possibly working with Abrash, and now, Hecker.

It was this comment from the *gamecenter.com* article: "Hecker says Deb Black, a director in the systems division at Microsoft, asked him what the demand was for OpenGL and wanted him to reconcile that with the fact that so many developers are currently using Direct3D." The mention of Deborah Black and Chris Hecker in the same sentence seemed to connect some of the dots for D3D evangelist Phil Taylor, and for Alex St. John.

At 11:13am Taylor wrote a long and angry email that started,

"I have sent several messages about the OGL team leaking data. Now I find its their manager. No wonder I get no answer to the question of 'how come all this information is coming out on OGL' from Deb Black.

"Its not her team thats leaking. Its her."

Taylor continued by accusing Black of releasing private correspondence to Hecker and actively working against the D3D evangelism team. He went so far as to call for her termination.

"There is no way evangelism can overcome a hostile manager with a private agenda. Either that, or she is so incredibly naive she let herself get used and is a complete danger to our multimedia strategy.

Either way, this leads to consideration of removal from the post. I repeat - she is dangerous."

Taylor ended his email by quoting sections of the *gamecenter.com* article.

Fortunately, Taylor did not send this angry diatribe to upper management or directly to Black, but to a more select group, mostly of people involved in the DirectX team, including Torborg, Engstrom, and St. John. He did, however, include some people higher up the chain, including Tod Nielsen and Morris Beton.

Several hours later, Taylor issued a retraction saying:

"After looking at the gamecenter article again - my conclusion in this email is unsupportable from the data at hand and just plain wrong.

I apologize to Deb for casting her in such a light, I can only say again how wrong I am.

Apologies after the fact seldom repair the damage done, I can only hope this one does.

Phil"

St. John Burns His Bridges

Minutes after Taylor's first email and before his retraction, St. John had already taken up the torch:

"You know, I find this pretty stunning Deborah. I thought the foolishness of spewing this kind of stuff to Chris Hecker and external people happened beneath you. I guess I understand now why you've never bothered to discuss any of these issues with me, but seem to have plenty of time to talk about it with Hecker, a guy who has never written a game. I can't work against this kind of BS, apparently you feel I'm full of shit, or deliberately lying to you and are going to pursue a course of action without my input, and you're actively going to subvert my evangelism work, by directly leaking your own message out there. You've made it clear that my effort here is unwanted, and unrespected… they're all yours now. I'm fed up with trying to help you here."

Maritz responded to St. John at 12:08pm in an attempt to clarify the situation, and in doing so, escalated the thread to the highest levels:

"From: Paul Maritz

Sent: Monday, June 16, 1997 12:08 PM

To: Alex St. John; Deborah Black

Cc: Bill Gates; Brad Silverberg; Morris Beton; Moshe Dunie

Subject: RE: GAMECENTER.COM–game news–Developers demand support for OpenGL

Alex–this is completely uncalled for.

Deborah "does not have plenty of time to talk to Hecker". Hecker sent me a piece of mail some weeks ago asking to meet with me. That mail sat in my mail box, I ignored it, until he sent it again. This was after we had made decision to focus our energies on D3D—a decision that was made with input from DRG. One of the key reasons for decision NOT to focus on OGL was because Deb & co. explicitly asked DRG to give them numbers of people doing D3D development.

At any rate, I then fwd'd the Hecker mail to Deb and asked to meet with him (he was asking to meet with me) to see if there was any way to get him to calm down.

We may very well have had other folks leaking stuff outside of MS during this process, but it is not Deb, and you owe Deb an apology."

At 2:36pm St. John sent a completely unrelated email to Bill Gates and other executives, including Paul Maritz and Deborah Black, suggesting the need for compliance and performance testing of drivers. He wrote,

"The unfortunate thing about drivers is that they are not glamorous or exciting technology, and they exist at the junction between us, an OEM, and an IHV. When they blow up, everybody points at each other, and the media assumes Microsoft is the cause. They are also some of our most powerful platform IP. If we are serious about being the leading consumer platform, we need to get serious about being a stable platform."

St. John made a compelling case for creating standards and testing so that Microsoft should know about problems and have solutions available. "I believe a proper driver conformance/performance suite would be a powerful tool for improving stability, by making the standard crystal clear for everyone, and by focusing attention on the transgressors who ship busted or uncertified drivers."

According to St. John, this email led to the adoption of WHQL driver certification and also to the Windows Update service, which was originally created to deliver DirectX driver updates. If so, it was his last productive act at Microsoft, but one that had profound impact on the company. It was also the last email he sent to Bill Gates. Four minutes later, he committed career suicide.

Crash & Burn

Responding to the email from Maritz, St. John sent the following email (unedited and reprinted in full below):

"From: Alex St. John

Sent: Monday, June 16, 1997 2:40 PM

To: Deborah Black; Paul Maritz

Cc: Bill Gates; Brad Silverberg; Morris Beton; Moshe Dunie

Subject: RE: GAMECENTER.COM–game news–Developers demand support for OpenGL

I have expressly warned you and Deborah about this guy in email Paul. I have absolutely zero feedback from you or Deborah that anything I've said has ever sunken in. I have never been invited to any meetings where any of these decisions have been discussed or made, so how am I supposed to have any idea what is transpiring. The mail from Hecker to Deborah threatening to ship the press release was viewed by you and Deborah four days before he shipped it, forwarded to me only after it was released. HOW DO YOU EXPECT ME TO MANAGE THESE ISV's or manage the media on something like this when nobody is communicating with me, or DirectX marketing?

I can't think of a better vote of no confidence from you guys then to be bypassing us to handle disgruntled ISV issues directly. Isn't "developer relations" my job? Not that Hecker is actually a developer, he just writes articles on it, in which case he needs to be handled like press. I knew this guy would backstab anybody at MS who tried to work with him, I'm still pulling knives out from WinG. It would have been your name in that press interview if you'd met with him Paul.

I have tremendous knowledge and experience in this space that nobody is using, and while I'm shouting "LOOK OUT FOR THE ROCKS!" at the top of my lungs and being ignored, you're telling me to apologize for getting angry and frustrated with Deborah for running the ship aground. I told you and Deborah that the guy was on an angry vendetta and heard no response. What am I supposed to think when I know the guy is having regular meetings with people in her group, spraying that internal information into public forums, and nobody does anything about it?

You know, I sent a piece of mail to Bill asking him if he wanted me to continue this debate or just move on to something else quietly. He forwarded that mail to you, and asked you to deal with me on it. I still haven't gotten a response. I'd really, really like to be done with this, and all you have to do is relieve me of this lingering sense of responsibility to all those companies who listened to me, and I'll be happy to move on with fresh air in my lungs. Somebody please just tell me it's not my job to worry about them anymore, and I'll instantly stop being a headache.

I actually have soooo many things to apologize for, I'd just like to vet them here if I may;

I'm sorry I personally promised so much technology and support to so many ISV's and IHV's and lived to see them burned so badly by our blundering and lack of focus.

I'm sorry that I've been so ineffective in getting our multimedia strategy on an even keel when the course has always seemed so clear to me.

I'm sorry I falsely accused Deborah of maliciously leaking internal information to Chris Hecker. It's clear to me now that it was just a foolish mistake that she made despite being warned. My humble apologies.

Deborah is really just one of dozens of probably well intentioned people that have contributed so much to this well oiled machine that is Multimedia at Microsoft that I've maligned unfairly over the years. I'd like to apologize to them as well;

In no particular order, I'd like to apologize to;

Tony Garcia, Bruce Jacobson, and Patti Stonsifer. I see now that they weren't making dull, uninspired multimedia titles just to annoy me and deliberately loose money. They just couldn't help themselves. It's too bad about their DreamWorks legacy.

Paul Osborne. I realize that he's just a nice well intentioned guy who did his best to beat QuickTime by rotely pursuing the uninspired strategy of doing whatever Apple did, a year or two after them, without ever dreaming that "multimedia" could mean so much more.

Joel Spiegel, and Dick Neese. A couple nice guys from Apple who showed us how great multimedia technology could be made through compromise and cooperation.

Jay Torborg, Mark Kenworthy, Jim Veres. Three great worker bees who did their level best to satisfy their management, and justify the massive R&D investment of our brilliant 3D luminaries. (who I also must apologize to, that progressive mesh thing is actually useful for something) I also grudgingly acknowledge that that "Scrunch" compression thing they came up with is actually a pretty good idea to.

Colin Campbell; Salim AbiEzzi. I'm sorry I gave ActiveAnimation such a hard time for being useless and having no identifiable customers. I realize now that it's just the kind of API morass I can use to tangle lots of web page designers with if only I had a tool that sprayed the stuff out like a PostScript driver.

Alistair Banks I'm sorry I stepped all over you trying to stop you from announcing "Quartz", and promising Adobe and Macromedia it would deliver them from QuickTime, two years before the entire development team in England was finally disbanded, and you had moved on to another project leaving me with the angry press and developers to answer to. I see now that my effort was futile, and challenging your video architecture just made its inevitable failure more stressful for everybody without actually solving anything.

Mike Van Flandern I apologize for the run in we had over the "Raptor" joystick API that you still haven't shipped. In retrospect I think Consumer might have sold just as many newfangled digital joysticks without Direct-Input driver support, because your group still can't seem to make a simple joystick driver work, let alone the vastly complex one you envisioned delivering one day, told all of the game developers about, and never wrote a line of code for.

Mike Abrash, On-Lee, Otto Berkes, Steve Wright, Hock San Lee, And all the other folks at Microsoft who aspired to deliver a real-time 3D API before and after the acquisition of RenderMorphics. With so many people working on so many different API's and drivers how could we help but stumble onto a solution one day.

Finally I'd like to apologize to Chris Hecker, who taught me that the only way to get WinG to ship after promising it to 300 developers and not finishing it was to have Craig Eisler sit on him to get it done.. and really.. really piss him off.

I'm sure there are other things that I should apologize for, and I invite everyone here to submit them for my consideration. I'll do my best to get to everyone. I'm sorry."

This email was St. John's swan song—a major thrusting of the middle finger at Microsoft, a release of the tensions that had been building up… and ultimately, his way out.

If St. John's "apology" email was an act of career suicide, it came as no surprise to some of his closest associates. James Plamondon knew what was going on in St. John's private life as well as his struggles at Microsoft. "There were nights—dozens of times—where I would come into the office and he'd be sleeping on my couch. But my couch was just a love seat, and he's a big guy, and this was before he lost weight. He was a really big guy, and so for him to be sleeping on this little tiny loveseat… his head was tilted up too far. The loveseat just barely held his body. It didn't hold his legs at all, so they were propped up against the wall. You could only sleep like that if you were absolutely fucking exhausted. And you wouldn't sleep well. And he was doing that night after night after night because he couldn't go home because he was getting divorced, and that was such a mess."

Plamondon had no doubts. "I have every confidence that it was intentional. Absolutely. He knew exactly what he was doing. You criticize in private and you praise in public. He knows all that. He had not only known it, but practiced it. I know that he just wanted to get fired. He couldn't bring himself to quit, and he knew he had to leave… he was so drained."

Self-Destruction

Some people thought it was because of the Judgment Day II spaceship debacle that St. John was ultimately fired. Even Brad Silverberg, his former boss, who had initially resisted and ultimately supported St. John's efforts and over-the-top methods, believed that the spaceship was his ultimate undoing, but Morris Beton knows what really happened, because he was the one who fired Alex St. John.

"My boss was Todd Nielson. My boss's boss was Brad Chase. I fired him without them even knowing. I fired him without HR knowing. I only told my HR person the day it was going to happen, literally a couple of hours before it happened."

St. John still believes that Beton was following orders from Maritz, possibly with approval from Bill Gates, but Beton insists that it was his decision alone. Clearly, it was the exchange with Deborah Black that tipped the scales, because up until that time Beton had not intervened, despite the fact that St. John had a history of distributing what Beton describes as "rude and abusive" emails. "He would in public forum disparage people right and left, insult people, to the extent that it was incredibly inappropriate for anybody to behave that way in any business or social setting."

Even to this day, people remember the firing of Alex St. John and can't believe that Beton did it on his own. But he told me, "Alex tells the story that it was kind of my boss's boss's bosses made the decision to have him fired, but the fact was that my boss didn't know, his boss didn't know. It's actually funny. Several months ago I had lunch with Brad Chase and he brought this up. He said, 'I always think about this. I couldn't believe you didn't tell me.'"

On June 17th, presumably in response to St. John's "apology" email, Beton sent him a message saying, "I want you in my office at 9am tomorrow morning, and if you're not there, consider that to be your resignation." Early the next morning, Beton informed the HR representative Larry Dart to wait in the office next door, saying that he was going to talk with St. John. "I'll let you know when I need you."

Meanwhile, at 6:32am that day, St. John sent his last official Microsoft email in response to a query from Kevin Dallas:

From: Kevin Dallas

Sent: Tuesday, June 17, 1997 11:17 AM

To: Alex St. John

Subject: email to the press

Importance: High

Do I have the green light on July 18? Who will be driving the roundtable?

From: Alex St. John

Sent: Wednesday, June 18, 1997 6:32 AM

To: Kevin Dallas

Subject: RE: email to the press

Hang on for an hour, let's see if I still have a job.

(St. John believes he was fired on June 17th, but the email of the 18th suggests that it was a day later. As Beton confirmed in an email, "This happened so long ago that I just don't know the details and timing. I would say however that if Alex sent mail to Kevin on the 18th from his Microsoft email then he was still employed. Access to corp email is shut down immediately upon termination.")

St. John arrived at 9am, carrying a shiny, fresh red apple. St. John's explanation for the apple? "I brought him an apple the day he fired me, trying to make him feel better. I go, 'You know, Morris, you're going to be famous for having to do this. I'm sorry I made you do this. I want you to have a good story to tell, because you're never going to hear the end of this.'"

The end came without fanfare or histrionics. Beton remembers telling St. John to sit down saying, "You've done about as much as you're going to do. You are fired effective immediately. Walk with me. I've got Larry Dart next door, and he'll escort you out. You're done." It was unceremonious and perfunctory. Unlike most of St. John's history, there was no drama. At least not with St. John.

On the other hand, as Beton remembers it, "Within an hour of that there was a swarm of activity and my boss, who was on vacation, Todd Nielson, calls up and says, 'What did you do?' And I said, 'I fired Alex.' And he says, 'Oh my god. You didn't tell anybody.' I said, 'That's right.' And he was kind of laughing, but he was in shock and surprise, and he said, 'You know he's really close with Bill,' and I said, 'I don't care if he's close with the President of the United States.'"

Then somebody called Brad Chase and said, "Well Morris fired him and didn't even give him a performance improvement program, you know a PIP," to which Beton replied "You must be kidding. I don't give PIPs to people at that level. I don't. I just refuse. I didn't really care what HR policy there was. I just refused to do it.

"So that was what happened, but it had nothing to do with building the spaceship, and it had nothing to do with what I admired about him, which was his brilliance and his rogueness, and his going outside the box, and all of these things that made him what he is. It was, I don't care how good you are, there is a level of decency and respect that you have when you work with other people, that you have if you work for me. And if you go beyond that, I'll tell you a couple of times, but I'm not going to tell you too many times. So that's what happened. And it was unfortunate because I really, really admired him."

"Later Eric wanted to talk to me about it, and we had lunch, and we had a good discussion, and then after that we had a lot of mutual respect for each other and got to be kind of distant friends. I think part of it was he just wanted to understand more because when something like that happens, there are a lot of versions to the story. And depending on who's telling the history, you're going to get a lot of variations on the theme."

St. John recently told me a story that puts a little belated humor into the situation. "My brother has joined Intel as an 'Evangelist for the Internet of everything' and works with Morris Beton. I had him bring Morris an apple, there's a picture in the blog post of Morris receiving it."

"IBM's initial motto was 'THINK!' Think. Innovate. Do new things. Listen to the customer," says Plamondon. "And they just drifted away from that once they got to be a certain size. The bureaucrats take over. Watson called them the 'wild duck who refuses to fall in formation with everyone else.' The guys like Alex. The fact that Microsoft couldn't retain Alex's services over the long haul shows that they just had become too corporate. I mean, he did intentionally self-destruct. He knew exactly what he was doing. He knew by calling what's-her-name what he called her, that it was just completely over the top."

Alex St. John Post Mortem

People know that having a disruptive idea isn't good enough. You need to be a disruptive person to get that disruptive idea through.
-Brett Schnepf, Product manager & hardware evangelist

Alex St. John: Never one to underdo anything.
-Colin McCartney

Alex St. John made quite an impression, to put it mildly. For years he had rampaged through Microsoft like a force of nature. He made friends and enemies, had admirers and detractors. And there's no question that he had an immense impact on the course of games for the Windows platform, and that what he did led directly to the Xbox. Here's what a few people had to say about him:

We never saw eye-to-eye on a lot of stuff, but I did have a lot of respect for him. He's a very strong personality, which I think helped in getting DirectX to market and getting game developers to support Windows and stuff like that. But he and Eric both tended to have somewhat abrasive personalities, and that made it harder for people at Microsoft to see eye-to-eye with what they were trying to accomplish and support them. But they did great work. Without those guys, efforts toward games on PCs would have been nowhere near as effective as they have been.

"I didn't fire Alex. Fortunately he pissed off someone more senior than me. I think he said some things that were way beyond appropriate to more senior people than me, and I think that's what ultimately got him fired, but with me he just pretty much argued his point. He sometimes would do it very bombastically, but as long as you were willing to look over his remarks, he had a lot of good points to make. I could appreciate where he was coming from, even though I didn't necessarily always agree with him.

-Jay Torborg

Alex would get into these enormous fights internally. Enormous. Because Alex, fundamentally, is an entrepreneur, and he was in a giant corporate structure. And what he was doing… what he knew to be true could not be proven on paper, could not be quantified in a way that a corporation liked to quantify it. It's only after the fact that you can say, oh it was worth it. So basically, you had a series of events where Alex was told no. And he just does it anyway.

-Jace Hall

When asked if St. John was like Don Quixote, tilting at windmills, Brad Silverberg said, "When you said Don Quixote, the thing that came to mind was Genghis Khan. They acted like Genghis Khan. Absolutely. There was a negative side, but the absolute value of their behavior was extremely high, so there's a lot of collateral damage, but they also did an incredible amount of great work in building trusting relationships with gamers who were predisposed to dislike and not trust Microsoft, and they created an industry. They really turned the world from console-based into a PC-based world. Xbox notwithstanding, they changed the world. They created a market that hadn't existed before, and made the PC the premier gaming machine. And a whole class of PCs. Now there are gamer PCs. There are $4000 machines, overclocked PCs and big fans and water cooling, push the state of the art in terms of graphics and displays and CPU technology and design, all to run PC games. And it was all enabled by the work that those guys did. They did incredible work. They created an industry.

-Brad Silverberg

Silverberg also said, "I think it was a game to Alex… like how far could he go before he'd get fired?"

Alex was one small piece of what I had in DRG. I inherited Alex. He's a brilliant guy, and he did a ton of great stuff, and would be one of those people who I would really call one of the major influencers of Xbox.

I didn't really see Alex as Don Quixote. I really saw him more as an Attila. Attila the Hun.

-Morris Beton

St. John provided his own post mortem in a recent interview. "The funny thing is that Gates was trying huge initiatives… billions of dollars being spent on trying to have a consumer strategy that would stick, and Apple was constantly winning. And suddenly, somewhere out of his organization something completely different takes over, and I perceive that he and Ballmer sat back and go, 'You know, we just gotta let this happen. We didn't plan it. We don't understand it. But this is a good thing.' And they let us go wild for a long time. And added to all of these failures in trying to make a consumer platform, we have something that's got a life of its own, and we couldn't possibly have designed this. We could never have recruited these crazy people, and no company would ever tell them to go do this and wreak havoc, and yet that's exactly what we needed to become a successful consumer platform. And so if I were to track the history back to DirectX and the Xbox, I'd say that it was that moment… it was that force of trying to become a consumer platform and something finally working that caused all the rest. The Xbox and the consumer media division suddenly making something other than Julia Child's Wine Guide, and god-help-us McZee, I think without that force of gaming sweeping the company, you never would have seen that happen there.

"If I'm not trying to tell amusing stories, I think that's the deep insight that I think is so fascinating about it. Even though I know I was instigating it, I feel fortunate to have been swept along by it as well because 90% of it I didn't plan or anticipate. It's nice to have people calling you brilliant in retrospect, but at the time I had no idea what I was doing."

WildTangent

Although St. John's personal life was falling apart, his "vacation" from work didn't last long. While he was trying to figure out what to do next, St. John initially began using office space provided by Monolith—Jace Hall's company that had spun off after making the DirectX sampler to make massive multiplayer games and their own DirectEngine for making games. He started writing for *Boot Magazine* (which later became *MaximumPC*) and working on early development for the web service, IGN. While doing so, he met or became aware of the investors in Silicon Valley who were funding the dotcom boom, and it dawned on him that he was in a perfect position to capitalize on the growing interest in games and web technologies. He had the contacts and the experience… and great name recognition.

St. John called in Jeremy Kenyon (Jez) to come partner with him in his new endeavor. Kenyon was the brilliant engineer that St. John had worked with so long ago at Harlequin in England.

"We used to argue incessantly," Kenyon, remembering the early days at Harlequin. "People used to refer to us as an old married couple. Alex often used to say that he learned everything he knew about arguing from those days arguing with me. Microsoft was a walk in the park after that, because there was just about nobody who could hold an argument with him. The exception was probably Eric. Of course, while that was an effective way to get things done, it probably didn't make him many friends, which brought his MS days to a rather premature end—not that he was bothered—I think he was done with MS, for then, and wanted more freedom, hence starting WildTangent."

When St. John started the business plan for the company, he called it Pandora until Kenyon pointed out the potentially negative associations that could be drawn from the Pandora's Box story. And so the name was changed, and WildTangent, Inc. was born. They incorporated in 1997, and St. John writes on his blog, with obvious amusement, "WildTangent's first customer was… wait for it… Microsoft."

In fact, Engstrom had tried to get St. John hired back into Microsoft right after he was fired, but to no avail. Instead, he hired St. John and WildTangent, Inc. to come in and continue much of the strategic work he had been doing on Chromeffects previously, but now as an outside contractor. But while Microsoft was helping pay the rent, St. John was pushing forward with his own vision—to create the technology that Chrome could have been.

The initial concept for the new company, according Kenyon, was to do something with threaded email, but then they got involved working for Microsoft on ChromeEffects. One of the engineers they hired, Radu Margarint, thought they could improve on the concept. "He persuaded us he could make a better engine, built on DirectX Retained mode, and create an Active-X plugin and interface to Java. So we ended up with the webdriver."

St. John sold some of his Microsoft stock, bought a house with a big basement where he figured to start his company. In addition to Kenyon, he also hired several web designers, including Daevid Vincent from Boot and Travis Baldree, who later co-founded Runic Games. At the time, Baldree was running the Seattle Seahawks' web site, which he described as a weird organization. "I sat on the floor for a portion of it, and for a while I had a piece of particle board set across two filing cabinets as a desk while they were putting in a multi-million dollar locker room on the floor below me. It was a weird organization."

WildTangent's first demo was a technology called Mapstream which they patented and later sold to Google to become part of Google Maps. According to Kenyon, St. John's penchant for the dramatic remained with WildTangent, "It was much more bonkers. Whether it was the chrome Harley we took to Seattle recruitment fairs, or the dressing up as a priest, complete with choir, to present at GDC, we did things for impact, but low cost."

Meanwhile, back at Microsoft, there were another storm was brewing, and this time St. John was not involved.

-27-

Facing The Man

The departure of Alex St. John did not stop the wheels of Microsoft from turning, but there was definitely something more ominous looming ahead. Before the hammer came down, however, Bill Gates did something that, to some, was a surprising move. In retrospect, it was not.

Saving Apple

On August 6, 1997, Steve Jobs got up in front of an audience at MacWorld in Boston and gave a speech about "Meaningful Partners". In that speech he announced that one of Apple's new meaningful partners was Microsoft. It as a masterful speech that made it sound as if both Microsoft and Apple had finally learned to get along. The deal was that Microsoft would invest $150 million in non-voting stock and agree to keep Office on the Mac for the next five years, while Apple would drop its trademark infringement lawsuit over the Windows UI and the embedding of Internet Explorer as the default browser. The agreement also stipulated that Microsoft would continue to develop and ship for the Mac, not only Office, but future versions of Internet Explorer and other Microsoft tools.

On the surface this investment seemed to benefit Apple the most, because Apple was in financial trouble at the time, but Bill Gates was looking down the barrel of a Department of Justice action against Microsoft. As James Plamondon puts it, "Microsoft needed Apple for a couple of reasons. It needed Apple to defend itself against anti-trust suits. The existence of Apple proved that Microsoft didn't have 100% of the market." Apple was arguably only months from bankruptcy when Steve Jobs was brought back as CEO, and according to Plamondon, "First thing Steve Jobs did was hop on a plane, come talk to Bill Gates, Bill Gates invested $150 million in Apple, got them through the bad rent period."

To some people, it looked like a philanthropic move by Gates, but in reality it was consistent with Microsoft's long-term strategy, and in any case, $150 million was chump change to Microsoft at the time. And it didn't mean that Microsoft intended to cede any market control to Apple or "play nice" when it came to platform dominance.

If helping Apple was a strategic move, it probably was no accident that it occurred while the wolves were circling, and Gates certainly knew that Microsoft was their target.

The Cost of Winning at Any Cost

DOJ announcement http://www.justice.gov/atr/public/press_releases/1998/1764.htm

On May 18, 1998 the Department of Justice issued a press release entitled:

JUSTICE DEPARTMENT FILES ANTITRUST SUIT AGAINST MICROSOFT FOR UNLAWFULLY MONOPOLIZING COMPUTER SOFTWARE MARKETS

In a way, it all started with Bill Gates' 1995 long and detailed "Internet Tidalwave" memo. Toward the beginning of the memo, he wrote:

> "The Internet is at the forefront of all of this and developments on the Internet over the next several years will set the course of our industry for a long time to come. Perhaps you have already seen memos from me or others here about the importance of the Internet. I have gone through several stages of increasing my views of its importance. Now I assign the Internet the highest level of importance. In this memo I want to make clear that our focus on the Internet is crucial to every part of our business. The Internet is the most important single development to come along since the IBM PC was introduced in 1981."

This was a call to arms for the entire company, and he outlined a strategy for going forward in the rest of the memo. (*The whole memo is available. Just search "Internet Tidalwave*). Once Microsoft realized the importance of the Internet, they were no longer competing solely with giant competitors like IBM, Apple, and Sun Microsystems. They were just a little late getting started, and Netscape had grabbed pole position, showing no indication that it would slow down.

Knowing Bill Gates

Cameron Myhrvold offers some insight into Bill Gates' decision to help Apple. "This goes all the way back to the original story of Bill meeting IBM, and Bill saying, 'Oh, you need an operating system. You should go talk to my friend at Digital Research.' And then IBM goes down there and the guy had just bought an airplane and decided to blow the meeting off and fly his airplane. And then, they went back to Bill and said, 'Well, we don't want to work with those guys, so will you do it for us?' And this is a story that nobody tells. And I've got to tell you that it predates me, so I don't know if it's true. It may not be true, but what I have heard is that, in discussions afterwards, somebody had said, 'Oh did you know there's a rumor that Digital Research is working on a BASIC compiler, and when Bill heard that, he said, 'If they're going to build a BASIC compiler, then we shouldn't feel bad about getting into the operating system business.' And that is what flipped the bit. Now again, I don't know if that's true. It could be that it never happened, but I'll certainly tell you, knowing the personality of Bill, it's a highly believable story. So then you fast forward to decisions like giving Apple the loan. What would the world be like if we hadn't loaned them the money to keep them in business? What if we had canceled Office for the Mac? Pretty interesting."

Any number of projects sprung up at Microsoft after Gates opened the door. Under Nathan Myrhvold and Rick Rashid, MSR was fully engaged in researching set-top boxes with the goal of delivering broadband connectivity into everyone's living room. A content authoring system code-named "Blackbird" was in development to compete with HTML. However, the primary—and among the early projects, the only successful one—was Internet Explorer.

Microsoft was no stranger to lawsuits. Apple had previously filed a "look and feel" lawsuit against Microsoft that ultimately failed. As Plamondon observes, "We had a license to the user interface. We had a written license on paper, and then they tried to claim that the license didn't really matter, and it totally got thrown out of court. It was absolutely without merit, but nonetheless, they rode that PR pony, and for two years they were able to beat us over the head with what an evil, nasty bastards we were."

Microsoft had also been sued for dumping products on the market with unfairly low prices, and they were also sued for setting prices too high, prompting Plamondon to ask, "How can anyone choose the sweet spot in between those two … the Scylla and Charybdis there?"

It's likely that none of the previous lawsuits caused as much consternation at Microsoft as the one that the DOJ filed in 1998. As previously described, DRG had done its best to drive the industry leader Netscape off a cliff using the marketing strategy of distributing IE for free, but that alone was not enough. Microsoft had also tried to make a deal with Netscape that would leave them free to make their Navigator browser for all platforms except Windows, leaving IE without any significant competition on its own platform. However, Netscape refused the deal, and Microsoft was faced with the real problem of getting people to leave a successful browser for one that was unproven and not yet up to the same standard.

Although Internet Explorer improved with each release, and began to gain 20-30% market share by late 1997, it was still way behind. The solution seemed to be to bundle IE with the upcoming Windows 98 and make sure it was the default browser for that operating system, and they tried to enforce contracts that would prevent hardware manufacturers from bundling any other browser. In essence, they tried their best to make the most of their clear operating system advantage to gain the upper hand on Netscape.

John Ludwig thinks that Microsoft's strategy regarding IE was a mistake. "You just didn't need to make it so blatantly obvious." He was an advocate of including all available browsers, suggesting that they were going to end up on the machines anyway. To illustrate his point, he once went out and purchased 10 machines at retail and invited Paul Maritz to observe that every one of them already had a bunch of competitive browsers on it, even though Microsoft was insisting that IE be the default, and in some cases, the only browser to be sold with the machines. "And my point was, look, this horse is out of this barn. They're already shipping other browsers. Don't kid yourself that we have any control over that anymore… I think Microsoft made some decisions that needlessly inflamed the situation."

St. John has suggested that the most damning part of the anti-trust suit was that Microsoft had used its muscle to try to force a smaller company out of business through its control of the operating system and financial advantages. But at Microsoft, the idea that Netscape was somehow a poor and defenseless adversary didn't fly, in part because of statements by Netscape's CEO, Mark Andreessen, who liked to say that Netscape would render Windows into "a poorly debugged set of device drivers." This statement and others were broadcast through email to the engineers at Microsoft and sufficiently motivated them to banish any thought of Netscape being a weak adversary who would be easily vanquished. (In an interview with *Wired* years later, Andreessen admits that the quote was not his originally, but that he had gotten it from 3Com founder Bob Metcalfe.)

Because we can watch DVD movies on PCs, Eric Engstrom became a witness in the trials. "I was the person that put DVD playback on Windows, which seems ridiculous now, that that was even a fight, but it was a fight. Why wouldn't a PC be able to watch movies? That was after Alex left the company, and that resulted in me ending up in the anti-trust trial. Media players and all that stuff, trying to fix it so people could watch a video on the internet without installing software. If you think about it today, it all just seems ridiculous."

St. John disputed Engstroms account, saying, "Playing DVDs was NOT the reason Eric was a DOJ witness. He was in charge of killing Netscape, Real Networks and Apple at that point. Ballmer had basically said to him at that point, 'Stop killing your managers and use that energy to take out these guys for me. You're in charge already!'"

Reading the DOJ's documents, however, it's clear that the "browser wars" and Microsoft's tactics against Netscape were at the crux of the matter.

St. John on DOJ

"The DOJ trial had a huge impact because it distracted all the senior management team for a long time, and crippled the company because of its outcome. Really crippled it culturally. So my view was, when I look back, of course the culture was always evolving, but the things I remember vividly was a malaise after shipping Windows 95 and wave after wave of reorgs, followed by a kind of crippling DOJ trial. And I don't think Microsoft was ever the same after that."

-Alex St. John

By the time the DOJ announced its suit against Microsoft, St. John was already out of the picture, but that doesn't mean he was ignorant of what was going on. "There's no doubt that from '92 to at least '96-'97 Microsoft was conquering the world, killing Apple, capturing everything it saw, its stock was splitting over and over again," says St. John. "I definitely saw that going on. And Bill Gates wasn't used to losing up to that point. Losing was not something that had ever happened to Microsoft.* And I think that had a big impact. What I've heard a lot from people was that the company was really dominated by adhering to the punitive restrictions of the DOJ settlement, and so there was a lot of fear of enforcement and paranoia that dominated the organization. So the first time you really saw Microsoft, instead of focusing on conquering the universe and feeling good about that, literally obsessed with reigning itself in in all the ways that it had been required to."

**Plamondon adds this comment: "Yes, it had, actually -- a lot. It's just that Microsoft was relentless, and kept picking itself up, dusting itself off, and re-joining the fray...until it won. That's not the same as 'never losing.' Alex knows this; he simplified for effect."*

-28-

Chrome—Plan B

By November 1998, Microsoft had shelved Chromeffects indefinitely, moving Engstrom over to MSN as a general manager for Web product development while Deborah Black took over as general manager of Windows presentation technologies. There were several "official" reasons for the failure of Chromeffects, mostly having to do with lack of developer support, complaints that Microsoft was ignoring web standards as provided by the World Wide Web Consortium, and the negative view around the industry that Microsoft was trying to take over web standards and make them proprietary.

Ludwig saw Chromeffects as a missed opportunity for Microsoft. "I was excited about the Chrome project, and it's too bad that it didn't happen at that time, because it took many years to reintroduce some of those ideas on the Web. And that's unfortunate because I think Microsoft could have led the way there years ago."

By the time Chromeffects development was halted, Ludwig had moved over to work in the MSN division and David Cole had taken over his previous position. He believes that the project was halted because there was just too much work left to do for it to become viable. "It was a lot of work back in those days to ship a full product. These days you can send out a beta forever and live with it, but back then that was not the case, and I think the judgment was that there was way too much work left to finish this thing." On the other hand, he concedes that if he had still been managing the project, "I probably would have figured out a way to do something."

According to St. John, none of that tells the real story. He contends that the DirectAnimation approach that Chromeffects used just wasn't suitable for the market, but that was only one reason for its apparent failure… and not the one that mattered. He says, "Note that if lack of developer support or web standards was a reason for Microsoft to cancel anything, IE and Silverlight and C# would have been abandoned years ago as well. None of those are a MICROSOFT reason for failure."

The real reason for cancelling Chromeffects, St. John states categorically, was the imminent threat from the DOJ. "Eric finished the 1.0 Chrome on schedule. It was done… not fast, but it worked. Nobody had the power to stop Eric at that point except Ballmer himself. Eric had to walk away from it because he knew that he was going to be pegged hard in the DOJ trial and was going to end up testifying. The DOJ trial was not a distant possibility at the time Chrome was canceled; it was an absolutely real threat to the company's existence, and Bill and Steve knew it. The jets were scrambling to deal with it, and Eric had a bull's-eye on him because he as the most prominent Apple, Netscape and RealNetworks assassin left standing at MSFT."

From the perspective of WildTangent's offices on the Microsoft campus at the time, St. John was able to observe what was going on first hand. "Eric was in constant DOJ trial prep meetings in the weeks before Chrome was canceled. It was all super-secret. Eric knew it had to be canceled. He didn't stop it, and it was his baby." St. John characterizes the MSN general manager position Engstrom was moved into as a "retirement job" that was given to him directly by Steve Ballmer.

In retrospect, St. John describes the pros and cons of the Chromeffects technology. "Chrome was utterly revolutionary, more powerful than even HTML5 today nearly 20 years later. But there's a reason it's taken 20 years for anybody to 'want' HTML5... it's not clearly useful for much. Suffice it to say that the idea of human web monkeys authoring this stuff manually was the dream of smart people who don't understand that 'enabling' monkeys with powerful tools won't turn them into Thomas Edisons. They'll just be monkeys banging around with expensive tools. HTML 5 and Chrome suffered from that condition. You can't expect junior engineers with simplified tools to actually build extremely rich interactive web experiences just because it's now possible for a genius to do it. It was the wrong 'formula' for media on the web. It either needed to be done with tools OR as the early DX prototype embraced, you just had to enable the full power of DirectX and let the people smart enough to use it make the products for everybody else."

Accomplishments and Security Holes

St. John recounts the contributions of the DirectX team to online media. "Our contributions to online media after DirectX included naming the ActiveX API, doing the deal with Macromedia to ship the Flash plugin with IE, building the Windows media player and server, shipping the VRML 3D plugin for IE, and starting development on the technology that would ultimately become Windows Update… however our most exciting and significant contribution may have been a technology that never shipped… Chrome."

St. John offers some interesting personal perspective on the DirectX team, and a shocking admission: "I worked with some amazing people and they're maybe humble, and they're also quiet. History should remember some of the things they did and that went on because there were some amazing achievements and some amazing risks taken that people at the time would never have thought were a good idea.

"Some amazing mistakes were also made that had consequences through the ages that I really hate confessing to. ActiveX. Don't get me started. They wanted to call it Direct Internet or something because Direct was such a cool API, and this was when Microsoft was transitioning to the internet revolution and we were going, oh god, don't screw up our branding. We don't want whatever your plugin nonsense for allowing media apps to run on the browser to be called a Direct API because you have no idea what it means. So I was sent with the job of convincing them to call it something else. And everybody liked the "X" name, so I gave them a list of other blah blah blah X names and they picked ActiveX for it. And it was originally engineered to allow Flash to run on the browser, but it was also the pathway for enabling media apps, which I became in charge of. A lot of people don't know that. And so the ActiveX was the single, biggest, most destructive security hole ever created in the Internet that caused viruses and spyware problems in Windows XP down through the years. I eternally sit in my basement and go, 'God, I hope when history books written, nobody associates me with being responsible for helping create that API.' Oops. I opened my mouth."

WildTangent Implements Plan B

Fully incorporating in August 1998, WildTangent successfully implemented the features Engstrom had hidden in IE4 to realize St. John's vision of what Chromeffects could have been. The result was that the first time, full real-time 3D games were playable inside a browser, resulting in a great deal of press coverage and providing St. John with a lot of personal publicity. Today, playing full 3D games on a browser may seem mundane, but when WildTangent first released their technology, it was a huge step forward.

Over time WildTangent's website became host to numerous games and more than a million subscribers. St. John ran the company from 1997 to late in 2008. In addition to the success of the WildTangent services and technology, St. John developed multiple patents, including the patent for asynchronous updates on computers and a patent, which he sold for $500k to Google, for streaming real-time maps, which he had first prototyped while at Microsoft and rewrote at WildTangent.

According to Travis Baldree, senior engineer at WildTangent, St. John had intended to create a Web3D platform that would become universally adopted, and that at one time the company had about 200 people, many of whom were trying to pitch the technology to various different business and military operations. He also recounts the many experimental projects they engaged in, which he found often useless, such as a 3D stock ticker. But Baldree's real interest was in making games, and after Chromeffects was canceled, much of the company's non-investment revenues came from making games for various companies, such as Toyota.

WildTangent also ported mainstream games to work in browsers, including Need for Speed and Tony Hawk 2. Baldree says he had only two months to port Tony Hawk 2 and that he was not allowed to even look at the source code because they wanted to develop their own code which could be reused in future projects.

"So what I had to do was sit with two computers. I had one next me running actual Tony Hawk 2, and then I had mine, and I would count under my breath to see how long it would take for me to get from one location to another or how high I could jump. And just tried to gauge it and screenshot it so I could figure out these distances and times, which is really difficult for games like Tony Hawk 2 that are trick based, and where you have to very precisely jump from here to here." He was also prevented from using quaternions* for his camera work, because the original game used them, and so he had to use matrix math instead.

* *quaternions: a complex number of the form* $w + xi + yj + zk$, *where* w, x, y, z *are real numbers and* i, j, k *are imaginary units that satisfy certain conditions.*

Eventually, Baldree believed that he had enough tenure at the company to do a project of his own—an action role-playing game that he called Fate. He was given two months to do his project, but it took six. He says that some people at WildTangent had tried to discourage him from attempting the game, thinking it not casual enough to have broad appeal. However, Fate—an action RPG in the same genre as the mega-successful Diablo series from Blizzard—found a large and enthusiastic audience and helped WildTangent make a transition to games and away from the idea of a universal platform. Baldree eventually left WildTangent, and, after a brief stint at Flagship Software, he started Runic Games with Blizzard veterans, Max Schaefer, Eric Schaefer and Peter Hu where they expanded on Baldree's success with action RPGs by creating the very popular Torchlight and Torchlight 2.

Sony and WildTangent

Among WildTangent's investors was Sony, who invested $1 million in 2001. St. John relates how he received a visit from Shinichi Okimoto, chief technology officer at Sony Computer Entertainment, before Xbox was announced. Okimoto-san was asking about the possibility of Microsoft releasing a game console, and if they did, what direction would the likely take. St. John told Okimoto-san what he thought and advised that Sony should take its PS2 architecture, add memory, more graphics options and faster clock speed and call it a PS3, thus leveraging their PS2 developers and existing tools—advice that Sony clearly did not take.

After the Sony investment in WildTangent, Okimoto-san flew to Redmond again, and this time St. John decided to have some fun with him. "I couldn't resist." Because he was still doing contract work at Microsoft, St. John had a key card, and so he took Okimoto-san to visit the cafeteria in the Xbox building, which was only blocks from the WildTangent offices. "Nothing like that would ever happen in Japan, right? He came to do spying and intel, and I walked him right into Microsoft lunch campus and pointed out Stuart Moulder and all the executives, and so forth. I think he was mortified that I might introduce him to somebody. I had a real thrill doing that."

St. John relates a very interesting conversation he had with Okimoto-san regarding the advanced cell architecture that Ken Kutaragi had planned for the PlayStation 3. Okimoto-san was not happy about it, calling it a "crazy cell architecture," and noting that it would cost Sony billions of dollars. St. John adds that the Japanese have "a very nuanced way of criticizing their bosses," so it's probable that Okimoto-san said something far less blunt. But the gist of it was that not everybody at Sony was crazy about the direction Kutaragi had taken.

About Microsoft's possible entry into the console business Okimoto reputedly said, "You don't know how these crazy Americans are going to make consoles." St. John predicted a strategy that had not yet been determined, suggesting that Microsoft would "run you to death on the software side," but Microsoft could leverage its PC development base, make software as a service and add multi-player, communities and online gaming. "Whether or not you have the best graphics and hardware capabilities, Microsoft's going to define the competition for you based on online services. I said I could predict that with almost certainty because I shaped that strategy a lot. How they execute it, who knows?

"Okimoto-san said that they were basing their system on Linux. I said, 'You know it's really going to come down to, can you guys build operating platform software APIs, online services and online communities, online commerce… can you build that stuff? Because that's where Microsoft's going to drag you.'" According to St. John, Okimoto-san left Sony three months later—whether he quit or was fired was unclear, but it was clear, according to St. John's conversations with him, that he was not completely onboard with Kutaragi's strategy.

Ultimately, Sony put Phil Harrison and the U.S. based teams in charge of building much of the software and services, and at one point St. John received a phone call from Sony of America's vice president of engineering asking for some advice.

WildTangent had a lot of experience in building online publishing and services, and when Sony's VP of engineering asked, "What do I do?" St. John replied, "Here's how you've gotta do it. Here's what you've got to build. Here the way you've got to think about it. Here's how you handle your developers… and this and that."

St. John says the man was extremely grateful and said, "Thank you. You've been incredibly open. Aren't you worried that I'm a competitor?"

"No, absolutely not."

"Why is that?"

"Because if you do absolutely everything I just told you to do, you'll go out of business."

St. John says the man paused, stunned. "What do you mean?"

"Don't you get it? Microsoft doesn't care about consoles. They care about the Windows operating system. If they can drive the game business into an online business model where the hardware's irrelevant, then you're dead. And that's what it means to do this. The minute the device is just an API and platform, and games can work everywhere, and the service is portable, and so forth, the console's just another commodity box. And so, you'll be gone as a competitor if you succeed at this. Microsoft doesn't care because they'd be happy to see consoles be gone and go to the PC or laptops."

Today, after a stint as CEO of High5, at the time of this writing St. John is CTO of Nyriad: *http://www.nyriad.com/company/*

~29~

Culture Changes

Did the competitive, dynamic culture of the early to mid-1990s slowly give way to something different? According to some observers it went from feisty to something more conventional as it approached the Millennium. If this is true, what happened?

It's entirely conceivable that, while success at a young age at Microsoft in the 1990s conferred obvious benefits, it may also have had unintended consequences. There is no doubt that Microsoft treated its employees well, especially in terms of generous stock options, and so as the stock continued to rise in value, many of those who had been at Microsoft for years were now worth small—or not so small—fortunes. They were Microsoft millionaires. Ferraris became the vehicle of choice. Driving onto the Microsoft campus in a spanking new Ferrari showed your co-workers that you had "made it."

According to several Microsoft veterans, too much success had adverse effects on the culture of the company. As a young, brash new employee, Alex St. John recognized the intelligence of his new co-workers. He realized quickly that he was in the company of people with really high IQs. "And these people knew it and thought very highly of themselves. You couldn't tell them anything. They couldn't hear anything. To change their point of view took astronomical arguing and convincing. And so I found when I arrived there that the company was very arrogant, that people there were just very self-assured."

In retrospect, St. John has refined his opinion. "Microsoft was so concentrated in intelligence, and so competitive, even with itself, that people felt like they couldn't own their job or identity without always appearing flawless and failure-less and infallible. And that emphasis meant that every decision had to be right, completely analyzed, completely logically supported by facts, because if you shoot from the hip and get caught doing it, three other guys around you will bust you and humiliate you for it."

The conclusion St. John came to is that risk averse people who couldn't ever admit to being wrong also couldn't innovate. To innovate implies taking risks, and risks imply the possibility of failure. "The people who really were tremendously successful, who were tremendously innovative or doing something out of the box, not only had they taken great risks, but they'd often failed catastrophically many times. I was very comfortable with falling off the bike as many times as it took to learn to ride it."

Microsofties

Rob Wyatt, a deep-level programmer who came over from DreamWorks with Seamus Blackley, saw a distinction between those who came to Microsoft to pursue a passion or to achieve a more personal objective, and those who were what he called, "entrenched Microsofties."

"We're probably going to leave when we've done it and go our own way. Ultimately all the guys who had the passion did that. We did our thing. We left when the time was right. For whatever reason we left and we all went back to doing what we did before. Went on to new endeavors. The people who were against that passion were the people who were the entrenched Microsofties who had been there for years. Their stocks had grown, their grants had grown. They were very much invested financially and career-wise in the Microsoft way. A lot of these guys couldn't have got a job anywhere else because things were becoming open source, things were becoming standards and Microsoft to this day is still doing its own thing. So if you've been there long enough, you'll have no use outside of that company. Which is one of the reasons I wanted to get out. It's like I just don't like the way this is. It's like you're kind of brainwashed into seeing it the Microsoft way."

What's Your Number?

People who came later to Microsoft had a different perspective from those who had been there for years. What newer employees observed was a privileged group who had lost whatever had inspired them in the first place. From the perspective of Mikey Wetzel, who joined Microsoft too late to participate in the stock boom that made so many wealthy, the company had gone from "the haves and the will haves" to "the haves and the never will haves."

Wetzel didn't necessarily resent people for having money, but for their focus on the money more than the work. In the days when the stock was rising, people would ask, "What's your number?" because everybody had a number: the amount of money they would be worth when they decided to retire. Wetzel states that, where most people were busting their asses at work, arriving on time, staying late, some of those who had made their number would do what he called, "calling in rich…" "Instead of calling in sick, they'd call in rich." Another symptom of change was called "resting and vesting," where people who had little left to do in the company, but whose stock options hadn't vested yet, were given middle manager jobs so they could stay in the company until completely vested.

Greg Meredith calls it "fuck you money." Meridith, who joined Microsoft in 1998 after working with Oxford University's renowned computer scientist, Samson Abramsky, saw Microsoft as a means to an end. "I went to Microsoft specifically to do business process orchestration. They didn't know that. I really gave Microsoft essentially an incubation platform." Using his background in mathematics, Meredith developed the highly successful BizTalk program as its principal architect. Like many before him, he faced obstacles, challenges from other groups, and even resistance from his own managers. At one point, when Microsoft was considering purchasing a company for $2 billion to do essentially what he was planning on doing, he told them, "Look, you give me $2 million and I can build what you want to build."

Meredith witnessed first-hand the changes in Microsoft culture, from yelling in the hallways to get things done, to what he calls "the culture of civility," but, he says, "They couldn't pull it off because it wasn't genuine." To Meredith, the new culture felt more evasive than genuinely civil, and it didn't work at all for him. "It wasn't that I missed the yelling, I just missed the honesty."

Meredith left Microsoft in 2004 to start his own company, his mission accomplished. One of the reasons he left was that Microsoft had forgotten the idea that to make good products, you had to listen to your customers. But, like Alex St. John, Meredith wanted to make products that would succeed, not just because the people around him thought they were doing something cool. To be truly successful, he needed to be in contact with the customers, and his bosses just didn't get it.

Meredith worked with a lot of people during his time at Microsoft, and shared some observations. In particular, he talks about interacting with Bill Gates. "I remember the first face-to-face meeting I had with Bill. There was a room full of 12 people. We're all sitting around, and I'm watching Bill very intently, and I'm observing a man who can listen, and can listen with a quality that was unparalleled in my experience. He could listen to a room of 12 people with a concentration that allowed him to be present for 45 minutes, and at the end of 45 minutes say, 'OK. This is where we agree. This is where we disagree. This is the data I need to resolve the disagreement.' I was like, Whoa. I'm in the presence of someone who is a completely different order of human being.'"

James Plamondon is another veteran who eulogized the impending death of the old Microsoft. "Old age had started to creep in. The company had become very set in its ways, and the idea that you would get ahead by out-yelling your competitor in the hallway—which was the old Microsoft approach—now the company had become much more Japanese. We have to work very hard not to offend our peers and compromise in ways that are disadvantageous to everyone in the company and all of our customers, except us."

Plamondon saw "all of these Ivy League guys making their striped-tied decisions, which were not in the benefit of the platform, of the company, of the customer, but it was to the advantage of their little clique." More than one Microsoft veteran referred to evolving internal culture as the "Microsoft Army," a culture that assimilated you, made you into what it needed to succeed. In contrast, Plamondon liked to think of himself and his peers as "kamikaze nerds, damn it." (Adding "damn it" was a necessary part of the description, apparently.) They were the guys whom Cameron Myhrvold referred to as having "great grenade jumping skills... willing to lie down on the railroad tracks, jump the grenade... whatever." The question was, did any of those people still exist?

See *Game of X v1: Xbox* for the answer.

~Epilogue~

The Prequel

The stories and events recounted in this book focus primarily on the late 1980s through the late 1990s—a period of approximately 10 years. While interesting in their own right, these stories would be far less noteworthy if they hadn't ultimately led to Microsoft's much more notable entry into the world of video games: Xbox.

The early games and the pioneers who created and promoted them may not have led directly to Xbox, but they did establish, over time, a growing game division, particularly after Ed Fries took over the Game Group. But perhaps even more directly, the development of DirectX and the battles to make Windows a gaming platform, along with the struggles over 3D graphic APIs, did set the stage for Microsoft's eventual entry into the video game console business.

The culmination of these events is the entire subject of Game of X, volume 1, and I intentionally led off with that volume. If you have already read it, you know how the story of Xbox began and how it turned out. If you have not yet read it, you can continue the story initiated in this book almost seamlessly.

To produce this book, as with any history, I relied on research and the cooperation and contributions of a great number of people, including:

Grant Fjermedal
Ed Fries
Robert Donner
Kathie Flood
Russ Glaezer
Kiki McMillan
Tony Garcia
Alex St. John
Craig Eiseler *(not interviewed)*
Eric Engstrom
James Plamondon
Jason Robar
Cameron Myhrvold
Brad Silverberg
Robbie Bach
Morris Beton
John Ludwig
Rick Segal

Andrew Walker
Jay Torborg
Rick Rashid
Nathan Myhrvold
Jim Kajiya
Phil Taylor
Mike Abrash
Chris Hecker
Jace Hall
Chris Phillips
James Spahn
Zach Simpson
Tim Sweeney
Mark Rein
Jay Wilbur
Mike Wilson
Chris Taylor
Greg Meredith
Mikey Wetzel
Richard Garriott
Otto Berkes
Paul Neurath
Kevin Bachus,
Seamus Blackley
Tavis Baldree
Mike Calligaro
Jon Solon
Joel Berez
William Volk

DRG and everyone who helped developed DirectX.

And, of course, Bill Gates, who was central to the story, but did not participate directly.

And, finally, gratitude to the many engineers, evangelists, designers, and business people, and all the people who contributed without getting any specific credit. It was a large effort, and there's plenty of credit to go around.

Author's Postscript

So this is the prequel to *Game of X v.1*, which is focused entirely on Xbox and Xbox Live. Believing that more people would be interested in the Xbox story, I made that the first of two volumes; however, I also believe in the power and entertainment value of the stories in this book, *Game of X v. 2*. I hope you have enjoyed it as much as I enjoyed researching and writing it.

- I chose to focus on Microsoft as a game company, but also, to some degree, remained focused on how the events depicted in this volume led to Xbox.
- I chose to speak to as many people as I could find who would talk to me, to tell the many stories that made up the whole; many stories with many actors instead of singular story with fewer actors. Clearly, one person—Alex St. John—has an enormous presence in this book. He spent many hours working with me, reading manuscripts, and providing additional insight. In hindsight, I think Alex was able to see his history anew and provide perspective, not only on his adventures and antics, his successes and catastrophes, but also on the often chaotic and always evolving organism he infected for so many years with his disruptive, driven, and ultimately highly impactful career at Microsoft.
- As much as possible, I used people's own words, their language, their expressions because I enjoy language and the way individuals express themselves. I wanted not only to tell stories, but to reveal something about culture and life at Microsoft over the years. Something about the strategies of massive companies doing business and competing against other massive companies—and against just about everyone, including their own internal groups.
- As much as possible, I used original source documents and included many of them in the chapters or the Appendix.

I hope you enjoyed the book, the stories, the people. I thoroughly enjoyed researching and writing it.

-Rusel DeMaria